Domestic Constraints and the Breakdown of International Agreements

DOMESTIC CONSTRAINTS AND THE BREAKDOWN OF INTERNATIONAL AGREEMENTS

JEFFREY S. LANTIS

PRAEGER

Westport, Connecticut
London

Library of Congress Cataloging-in-Publication Data

Lantis, Jeffrey S., 1966–
Domestic constraints and the breakdown of international agreements / Jeffrey S. Lantis.
p. cm.
Includes bibliographical references and index.
ISBN 0-275-95948-1 (alk. paper)
1. International relations. 2. Treaties—Ratification.
3. International and municipal law. I. Title.
JX1391.L335 1997
327—dc21 97-11074

British Library Cataloguing in Publication Data is available.

Library of Congress Catalog Card Number: 97-11074
ISBN: 0-275-95948-1

First published in 1997

Praeger Publishers, 88 Post Road West, Westport, CT 06881
An imprint of Greenwood Publishing Group, Inc.

Printed in the United States of America

The paper used in this book complies with the Permanent Paper Standard issued by the National Information Standards Organization (Z39.481984).

10 9 8 7 6 5 4 3 2 1

For My Family

CONTENTS

FIGURES

PREFACE AND ACKNOWLEDGMENTS

In 1988, Robert Putnam published an article featuring a new model to explain linkages between domestic politics and international relations. His "two-level game theory" of international negotiations drew a considerable amount of scholarly attention and quickly emerged as the archetype for contemporary thinking about domestic-international linkages. This book revisits two-level game theory, and a second generation of work on double-edged diplomacy by Putnam and others, by examining the domestic political conditions that foster defections from international commitments that often materialize in the "post-commitment politics phase." This is the period when domestic conditions and actors align relative to an international agreement—*after* a leader makes a commitment to cooperate with other members of an international organization, but *before* the final foreign policy decision to allocate government resources to sustain the commitment.

A breakdown of the ratification process into sequential stages allows scholars to shift focus to the consensus-building process among specific domestic political actors in the post-commitment phase. For this study, I posit that five key conditions in this process can influence the durability of a leader's promise to cooperate with other countries. They are major party unity, ruling coalition consensus, issue area, election performance, and public support. I test hypotheses about the role of these conditions in eight case studies of German foreign policy behavior toward NATO and European Community agreements during the 1970s and 1980s in order to explore the dynamics of post-commitment politics. A comparison of the cases shows the sequential, complex, and time-consuming nature of the ratification process and the fact that international commitments can awaken dormant domestic constituencies along the road to ratification.

A great many individuals contributed to the development of this book. I would especially like to thank Charles F. Hermann, Director of the Bush School of Government and Public Service, for his guidance and insight throughout this effort. Chadwick Alger, Kimberly Marten Zisk, Joseph Kruzel, and Alan Beyerchen also spent many hours reviewing and commenting on the project over the years. In addition, I received valuable advice from Michael Young, Bill Swinford, Juliet Kaarbo, Marijke Breuning, Michael Snarr, Ryan Beasley, and many others. Research support was provided by the Mershon Center and the Department of Political Science at The Ohio State University.

At The College of Wooster, my colleagues in the Department of Political Science have offered their encouragement and advice on this project, and I benefited from the assistance of several excellent student researchers. I gratefully acknowledge research support provided by the Isabel and Elizabeth Ralston Presidential Endowment Grant and the Faculty Development Grant program at The College of Wooster.

I would also like to express my gratitude to the many scholars and experts who took an interest in this project and supported my work in the Federal Republic of Germany. Helga Haftendorn at the Frei Universität Berlin provided valuable insight and suggestions. Karl Kaiser and his colleagues at the Deutsche Gesellschaft für Auswärtige Politik generously provided research support during my time in Bonn. Regina Mehl provided friendly advice and valuable assistance at the Arbeitstelle Friedenforschung in Bad Godesberg. Ilke Meijer, Wolfgang Rüb, and Herbert Kossmann offered valuable research assistance and access to the archival collection at the Bundesregierung Presse- und Informationsamt in Bonn. Archivists at the Auswärtiges Amt, Verteidigungsministerium, Friedrich Ebert Stiftung, Konrad Adenauer Stiftung, and the Friedrich Naumann Stiftung all provided assistance for this project.

Thanks are also due to my editor at the Greenwood Publishing Group, James Sabin, who has supported the refinement of this manuscript, and to the excellent production staff who saw the project through to conclusion.

Finally, I owe a great debt to my family for their love and support for my work, and to my extended family in Germany for their inspiration over the years. I especially wish to thank and acknowledge my most consistent supporter in this endeavor and closest associate, Holly Lantis.

The final version of the book—and responsibility for its contents—of course remain my own.

1 INTRODUCTION

On December 10, 1991, European leaders unanimously agreed to an outline of the Maastricht Treaty and proclaimed it a "major step forward for the European Community." Among other provisions, the treaty called for the establishment of common foreign and defense policies and included a set of preconditions for recognizing new states. Only five days later, however, German leaders announced that they would unilaterally recognize the breakaway Yugoslav republics of Croatia and Slovenia *without any preconditions*.[1] German leaders reneged on the promises they had made at Maastricht and resisted subsequent international pressure to change their foreign policy course.

Such defections from international commitments are not uncommon, and they raise important questions about international cooperation. The central research puzzle for this book is: Why do leaders sometimes decide not to sustain international commitments even though they believe cooperation to be in the state's best interest? Defections from international organization programs are sometimes quite surprising—occurring where structural conditions would predict cooperation (i.e., where there is serious international pressure for cooperation). And defections are sometimes "involuntary"—occurring even though the leader believes cooperation to be in the state's best interest. This book explores the origins of several surprising and involuntary German foreign policy defections from international commitments in the last 20 years, such as the 1985 German veto of Common Agricultural Program reforms and the 1989 rejection of a NATO plan for modernization of short-range nuclear forces.

Robert Putnam presented the most popular explanation of such defections in a 1988 work, where he argued that they result from the simultaneous effects of international and domestic factors on leaders playing "two-level games." However, this study shows that the two-level game construct pays too little attention to the longitudinal nature of the foreign policy process behind cooperation and the implications of time for the ratification of international agreements. This project extends Putnam's work by interpreting international defections as the product of domestic constraints on foreign policy making that materialize in the "post-commitment politics" phase as a direct result of leaders' efforts to place an issue on the public agenda. This post-commitment phase is the period when domestic conditions and actors align relative to an international agreement. This occurs *after* a leader makes a commitment to cooperate with other states in the context of an international organization, but *before* the final foreign policy decision to allocate government resources to sustain the commitment.

Eight case studies of German foreign policy decision making relative to commitments in the European Community (EC) and the North Atlantic Treaty Organization (NATO) are developed. They all explore the role of domestic political conditions in the post-commitment phase. The comparative case study method is employed to draw valuable lessons about the dynamics of international cooperation.

TWO-LEVEL GAMES AND DOUBLE-EDGED DIPLOMACY

In 1988, Putnam presented the two-level games framework to explain the interaction between international and domestic politics.[2] His work has drawn a great deal of scholarly attention and has served as the archetype for contemporary thinking about domestic-international linkages.[3] Putnam drew on ideas from the game theory literature originally presented by scholars like Robert Axelrod, Paul Snyder, and Glenn Diesing who suggested that "cooperation under anarchy" was possible in certain circumstances.[4] Axelrod concluded that strategies for playing Prisoner's Dilemma changed for iterated games and that Rapaport's tit-for-tat strategy of playing "nice, forgiving, and retaliatory" was the best overall way to engender cooperation among players.[5] Axelrod also recognized that factors like the "shadow of the future" and "third party threats and inducements" could promote international cooperation.

In his development of the two-level game, Putnam recognized Axelrod's contribution that "the temptation for negotiators to defect [from an international commitment] can be dramatically reduced among players who expect to meet again."[6] But Putnam departed from the traditional game theory by adding a new, domestic politics dimension to the negotiating framework. In so doing, he presented a challenge to what he saw as unidimensional models of state behavior. He criticized structuralist approaches because they interpreted cooperation as a function of systemic forces and ignored domestic dynamics. At the same time, he charged that institutionalists had let any role for domestic factors slip more and more out of focus in their theoretical constructs over time.[7]

As an alternative, Putnam created a two-dimensional framework to illustrate how "Janus-faced" national political leaders simultaneously work solutions to international (Level I) and domestic (Level II) games to bring about international cooperation. While maintaining that the two-level game construct was a metaphor, he suggested that a more formal exploration of leaders' techniques for the *simultaneous management* of dual political environments might be in order. Putnam said that political leaders face "distinctive strategic opportunities and strategic dilemmas" related to building support for cooperation. Solutions to these situations, he argued, could be found in negotiated "win-sets"—policies around which a winning domestic coalition could be built.[8] Recognizing domestic-level influences on international negotiations produced what Putnam termed "general equilibrium theories that account simultaneously for the interaction of domestic and international factors." Finally, he closed his article by inviting others to explore domestic-international linkages, saying, "We need to move beyond the mere observation that domestic factors influence international affairs and vice versa. What we need now are concepts and theories that will help us to organize and extend our empirical observations."[9]

In fact, a number of scholars have answered Putnam's call. Perhaps the most important extension of his work was a collaborative project directed by Evans, Jacobson, and Putnam himself that produced an edited volume entitled *Double-Edged Diplomacy: International Bargaining and Domestic Politics* (1993). Many well-known foreign policy scholars were involved in this project including Janice Stein, Richard Eichenberg, and Jack Snyder, and each authored new case studies of cooperation applying the two-level game framework.

This project reinforced many of Putnam's original arguments. Contributors found the general framework quite useful, although they changed the focus to a "double-edged diplomacy" model to move away from the formal connotations of two-level games construct. Editors underscored Putnam's original argument about the "simultaneous and mutual" effects of international and domestic factors on international cooperation.[10] Contributors also drew some interesting insights from a focus on leaders' strategies for influencing their political latitude measured through negotiated "win-sets." Finally, they identified strategies such as "tying hands," "cutting slack," "reverberation," and "targeting" that could have a direct impact on international negotiations.[11]

Overall, this work generated some important new ideas about cooperation, but it also underscored several weaknesses in Putnam's construct and clearly left room for further theoretical development and modification.[12] These weaknesses are examined here and a modified, post-commitment politics conceptual framework of cooperation is proposed as an alternative.

PUTNAM REVISITED: THE PROCESS OF COOPERATION

The two-level game approach can be modified to examine the foreign policy process behind international cooperation and to recognize the ways that domestic political conditions can intervene in this process. In practice, Putnam and his supporters have focused more on leaders' strategies at the international negotiating table, and they have left at least two important aspects of the process question open. First, they have not systematically explored how international agreements are ratified. Second, Putnam and his supporters have not identified the important domestic political actors in the ratification process, or the ways in which they might influence foreign policy decisions about cooperation.

Putnam's original presentation of the two-level game construct placed the leader in a situation where domestic political alignments were given, and expectational effects about domestic political support ruled his or her final decision on support for an international agreement. While Putnam defined ratification as "a formal voting procedure at Level II . . . [or] any decision process at Level II required to endorse or implement a Level I agreement," he chose not to explore the politics or process behind such decisions.[13] He believed that any "sequential decomposition into a negotiation phase and a ratification phase was not descriptively accurate." Editors of the 1993 volume also supported this interpretation.

I contend, however, that a breakdown of the ratification process into sequential phases is quite useful and more descriptively accurate than the alternative. This allows the examination of how domestic factors can unravel previously reached agreements in the post-commitment phase. Case studies in *Double-Edged Diplomacy* supported this argument by demonstrating that ratification of international agreements involved a longitudinal process. Authors referred to strategies for ratification of international agreements in changing circumstances. For example, Eichenberg argued that in the German intermediate-range nuclear forces (INF) debate, "The mobilization of public sentiment . . . was itself sufficient cause for parties and governments to reexamine their negotiating positions over time."[14]

Arguments in *Double-Edged Diplomacy* about the need for information certainty and techniques for the manipulation of public support for international agreements also underscore the need for a study of the sequence of events leading to ratification. Evans argued that the "manipulation of foreign perceptions of ratifiability is not an effective strategy, even for those who head authoritarian regimes" and that leaders were "surprisingly likely to misjudge what was ratifiable in their own polities."[15] Both statements imply that international agreements really just mark the beginning of a post-commitment politics ratification phase.

Another limitation of the two-level game construct is that while Putnam and his supporters have suggested that domestic political factors are important for international cooperation, they have not systematically identified the important domestic political actors in the ratification process; nor have they assessed their relative influence on foreign policy decisions about cooperation. In his 1988 work, Putnam only generally referred to domestic political pressure and coalitions that could constrain a national political leader's latitude at the international negotiating table.[16] But contributors to the 1993 volume found this to be a much more important issue. They argued that when leaders put an issue on the international agenda, they could not help "but awaken and mobilize constituencies with the potential of undercutting the attempted agreement." Evans summarized the results of the case studies in his argument: "The more clearly international options become defined, the more leaders are constrained by mobilized interest groups and trapped by personal investment in the on-going negotiations."[17] Recognition of the need for "synergistic issue linkages" and the growing proliferation of transnational alliances also suggested the importance of multiple actors.[18]

Editors of the 1993 volume concluded that a more adequate account of domestic determinants of foreign policy and international relations must stress *politics*, but they provided no standard for the identification of those domestic political conditions that could affect ratification. Instead, different contributors to the volume identified different domestic political actors that played a role in the ratification process. For example, Stein suggested that the political maneuvering in the Israeli cabinet drove Israel's peace negotiations with Egypt; Eichenberg argued that public opinion and factions in political parties were the most important influences on decisions about INF modernization in Germany; and Milner focused on interest group opposition to the Anglo-American oil agreement of 1944.[19] Unfortunately, the net result of these efforts was to produce the kind of ad hoc list of domestic factors that Putnam originally sought to avoid—leaving room for development of this aspect of the process question.

In sum, Putnam and his supporters have not given enough attention to the process behind cooperation and the possibility that domestic political factors could derail leaders' plans to sustain major international commitments to cooperate. To address these weaknesses in the two-level game construct, I propose a post-commitment politics framework founded on three arguments:

1. International cooperation is the product of a sequential process—not just a simultaneous alignment of domestic and international conditions. A leader's initial commitment to cooperate with other states in the context of an international organization (regardless of issue area) mobilizes domestic political actors and conditions and demarcates the beginning of the post-commitment phase
2. In the post-commitment phase, leaders must build consensus in support for international cooperation. At least five domestic

political conditions can influence the durability of a leader's prior international agreement to cooperate, including: major party unity, ruling coalition consensus, the symmetry of effects of foreign policy decisions, election performance, and public support.

3. The proximity of these domestic political conditions to the ruling elite determines their relative impact on foreign policy decisions about cooperation.

Each of these arguments is developed and supported in the following sections.

International Cooperation as Sequential

It is important to recognize that international cooperation is a product of at least four sequential stages:

1. The leader seeks international cooperation and calculates domestic support.
2. The leader makes an initial commitment to cooperate with other member states within the context of an international organization by setting the agenda.
3. There are subsequent elite efforts to confirm (or ratify) the commitment.
4. There is a final foreign policy decision to sustain or defect from the commitment.

The first stage examined in this study is when the leader sets the agenda by seeking cooperation and makes assumptions about domestic support for cooperation. As illustrated in Figure 1.1, the leader must calculate expected domestic political support for, and opposition to, international agreements before making promises of support to

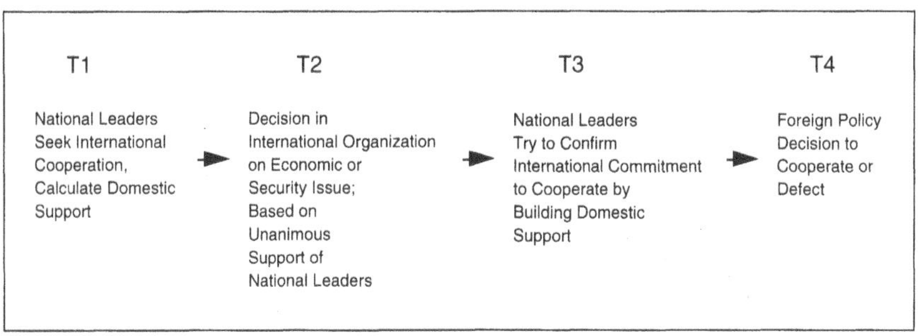

Figure 1.1 Cooperation as sequential.

other leaders. Putnam suggested that this was accomplished through "prior consultations and bargaining at Level II," before any commitment was made. I submit, however, that leaders of parliamentary democracies actually travel to the international negotiating table with either limited information about domestic support for an agreement or with no information at all. Leaders' assessments of domestic political support for cooperation are limited because most domestic political actors simply do not become sufficiently engaged on an issue until after a leader makes an initial commitment to cooperate, placing the issue on the public agenda. Instead, leaders must make gut-level calculations (at T1) about the likelihood that international agreements can gain confirmation in the post-commitment phase.

The initial elite commitment to cooperate (T2) starts a post-commitment chain of events in the domestic arena.[20] A leader must return home to build consensus in support of a foreign policy decision to authorize the allocation of state resources to cooperate with others (T3). In part, this is a function of institutional arrangements in parliamentary democracies. Leaders gain confirmation for international commitments through formal voting procedures, such as a *Bundestag* vote, or through a set decision process required to legitimate and implement the commitment.

Developing a clearly defined position on complex international programs requires time and resources—both of which are limited commodities for individuals and groups in the domestic political arena. Studies of interest group behavior have shown that there is often a lag between the time that an issue is placed on the agenda and when groups mobilize.[21] Because domestic actors are familiar with the policy process and are often preoccupied with the crisis of the moment, the most efficient use of their collective energy is in lobbying the government only when an issue has mobilized government, private, individual, and media resources. Evans described this phenomenon as an "awakening," whereby the mobilization of constituencies could eventually have the potential of undercutting the attempted agreement.[22]

When leaders approach the final foreign policy decision about cooperation or defection (T4), they again must make calculations about domestic support for such a move. Domestic constraints may emerge in the post-commitment phase that change leaders' assessments of the political risks in cooperation or defection—and reduce their decision-making latitude. In this way, conditions at the time of the final foreign policy decision can override the leader's intentions to cooperate.

In sum, leaders of parliamentary democracies often make initial commitments to cooperate without clear information about domestic political support for a program or decision. Case studies from *Double-Edged Diplomacy* supported this claim, and the editors even argued that it was "hard to find a clear constituency-driven logic at the stage when negotiations were initiated." The sequential (and time-consuming) process behind international cooperation, the lack of information certainty, and the fact that international commitments can indeed awaken dormant domestic constituencies make upholding international commitments quite difficult. Therein lies one of the keys to understanding subsequent, involuntary defections.

Key Domestic Political Conditions

During the post-commitment phase, leaders of parliamentary democracies must try to build consensus in support of international cooperation among specific domestic political actors and conditions.[23] Putnam recognized that international and domestic pressures are rarely in alignment and implied that consensus building was an important step toward the consolidation of a negotiated win-set, but surprisingly, no model of the process was ever developed.[24]

As illustrated in Figure 1.2, I contend that leaders of parliamentary democracies must consider five specific domestic political conditions to gain confirmation for an international agreement: major party unity, ruling coalition consensus, symmetry of effects, election performance, and public support. These conditions are identified for two reasons. First, they are derived from (and relate to) ongoing theoretical debates about their importance in the foreign policy process. Hypotheses formulated later in this chapter relate directly to comparative foreign policy arguments. Second, these specific conditions were identified from a survey of comparative studies of parliamentary democracies.[25] Many such studies have demonstrated the importance of party politics; for example, as the nexus between the public and government.[26]

Major party unity and ruling coalition consensus can affect foreign policy cooperation because party leaders seek to shore up their political power base at all times. Conditions technically outside the government—the symmetry of effects of cooperation, election performance, and public support—can also unravel international

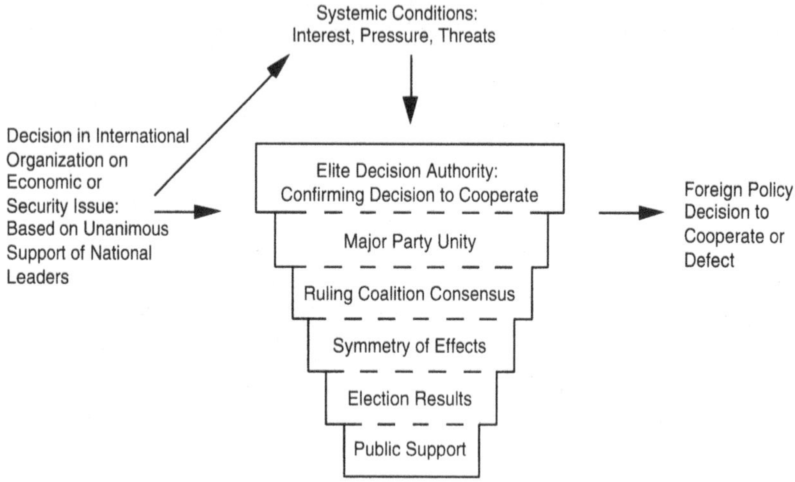

Figure 1.2 Conceptual framework.

commitments over time. German Finance Minister Stoltenberg once illustrated the importance of these conditions in an admission that "the limit of . . . cooperation lies in the fact that we are democracies, and we need to secure electoral majorities at home."[27]

For each factor identified in Figure 1.2, hypothesis statements are set out for confirmation or disconfirmation. These hypotheses, and the theoretical foundations from which they are derived, are discussed as follows:

Major Party Unity

Consensus in the major party in government is essential for leaders to implement foreign policy programs in parliamentary democracies. Factionalism in the major party can be a primary constraint on the leader's ability to implement a preferred foreign policy toward international organizations because it can, in fact, endanger the predominant leader's own position. But major party dissensus is also a condition of the domestic political arena that is often masked or hidden from public view and overlooked by many scholars. An hypothesis about the impact of dissensus in the major party on foreign policy that can be drawn out for exploration is

> Hypothesis 1: An initial commitment to cooperate with other states in the context of an international organization is less likely to be sustained in the post-commitment phase, *ceteris paribus*, when the leaders of the major party in government are divided over the issue.

This hypothesis is based on arguments derived largely from comparative political studies.[28] Important debates about the role of party leaders and organizations were originally presented in comparative studies by scholars such as Duverger, Rose, DeSwaan, and King.[29] These authors argued that elites can have direct and personal impact on policy decisions and that control of the policy process is a function of elite political maneuvering.[30]

A second subset of the comparative politics literature focuses directly on the relationship between factionalism in party organizations and policy making. For this book, factionalism can be defined as formal or informal divisions among elites within a party organization based on different beliefs about the proper conduct of policy.[31] Hofferbert and Klingemann have argued that factionalism can hinder consensus building in support of a policy initiative; it can hinder coalition-maintenance efforts; it can shorten the political tenure of party leaders; and it can broaden the spectrum of ideas in a party platform.[32] Works by scholars like Tanaka, Brass, and Eusebio have directly argued that factionalism can seriously constrain the power of the party leaders on foreign policy questions by threatening their power base.[33] Finally, Clemens applied this level of analysis to German politics in the 1970s and concluded that factionalism affects the ability of the party to formulate, legitimate, and implement foreign policy.[34]

In sum, this literature provides compelling evidence to support the argument that factions inside party organizations can intervene in policy making. Alderman and Cross have shown that a key indicator of dissensus inside the major party in government can be changes in cabinet ministers (or "cabinet reshuffles"), which dilute the authority of certain leaders or serve to change policy direction. They argued that reshuffles are generally taken at a "time when the leader considers them most appropriate," based on considerations of ministerial performance, personnel management concerns, policy considerations, or electoral cycles.[35] Focusing on these and other indicators of major party unity/disunity suggest interesting avenues for studying the effects of factionalism on foreign policy over time.

Ruling Coalition Consensus

Maintenance of consensus among party elites in coalition governments is also a critical concern for leaders in many parliamentary democracies. The relationship between the major party in government and those parties needed to assure a majority in control of parliament (junior parties) represents the foundation of government stability in many such systems. In the Federal Republic of Germany, for example, leaders have formed coalition governments with two or more parties since the first federal elections. But as with factionalism, this critical relationship is often overlooked by scholars and is only beginning to get more attention. To date, there is a relative dearth of material focusing on the relationship between interparty coalition relations and foreign policy decision making.

Because leaders from all parties in government make up the elite decision authority, leaders of the major party must attend to the interests of junior parties in government. Junior parties, in turn, may gain influence over foreign policy decisions by using the leverage of their continued participation in the coalition. Therefore, interparty politics can have a profound effect on the ability of the leadership to uphold earlier commitments to international organizations.[36] The following hypothesis will be explored in case studies for this book.

> Hypothesis 2: An initial commitment to cooperate with other states in the context of an international organization is less likely to be sustained in the post-commitment phase, *ceteris paribus*, when leaders of different parties in the coalition government are divided over the issue.

This approach is derived from comparative politics literature on the relationship between major and minor parties in coalition governments.[37] In this literature, one basic assumption is that junior parties play an important role in coalition governments and that their impact on policy choices provides a real key to understanding policy. Recently, scholars have begun to build on these frameworks to review the complex ties between coalition politics and foreign policy behavior. Lothar Wilker, a German scholar, argued that foreign policy questions are the main purview of interparty politics and that understanding the interrelations between party leaders may provide a great deal of insight about the causes of certain foreign policies.[38] Wilker then proposed a research program that looks for correlations between interparty rifts and foreign policy behavior, but the results are less interesting than the basic insights. Blondel and Thiebault took this theme a step further by looking at the relationship between individuals, ministerial roles, and policy domains in Great Britain.[39]

The value of this scholarship is twofold. First, significant progress has been made in the past ten years toward understanding the important, yet subtle, influence of interparty coalition politics on foreign policy making. Scholars like Haftendorn, Dodd, Boutwell, and others have called attention to the power of junior parties in policy formulation and implementation. Second, this scholarship has advanced to the state where foreign policy making is seen as a series of bargains and trade-offs between individual leaders in key ministries. This foundation is extremely relevant for an in-depth exploration of conditions that intervene in foreign policy decision making over time.

Symmetry of Domestic Effects

Decision makers must also consider the satisfaction of domestic interest groups when approaching decisions about foreign policy, which is directly related to the relative symmetry of effects from international cooperation. Here, I integrate the arguments from the corporatist literature about the connection between the number of competing interests and policy stability, works on issue area and symmetry, with studies of foreign policy decision making:

> Hypothesis 3: An initial commitment to cooperate with other states in the context of an international organization is less likely to be sustained in the post-commitment phase, *ceteris paribus*, when it involves economic/developmental issues rather than military/security issues.

The scholarship on foreign policy analysis suggests that economic/developmental issues often involve tangible potential costs or benefits, and the struggle of many different groups for influence over policy makes stable cooperation with international organizations less likely.[40] Domestic interest coalitions will line up on many sides of the issue and will have to be taken into account by the leader managing the situation. Karns and Mingst, for example, argued that "the larger the number of competing groups, the more likely it is that the policy making process with entail bargaining and coalition-building and that the policy outcome will reflect the least common denominator among the policy options favored by the different groups." Often, that least common denominator is a decision not to cooperate with controversial programs or decisions of international organizations. On the other hand, military/security issues have more of a symmetrical potential impact on the populace, some scholars argue, and will therefore have less of a tendency to attract a divisive debate about potential policy resource distribution.

In comparative foreign policy studies, Katzenstein and Gourevitch have examined the links between interest groups and economic policy choice in relation to foreign economic policy. These works on domestic structure argue that foreign economic policy should be seen as a product of the relative centralization of power in the state or in the society. For example, Katzenstein argued that changes in policy can derive from social movements inside states like Germany, that are in turn influenced by production technologies and political change.[41] Recently, Snyder drew a causal connection between domestic interests in the polity, their ability to form coalitions, and the foreign policy of state overexpansion.[42]

Some key arguments from the corporatist and neocorporatist literature are related to the domestic structural literature—demonstrating how domestic interests can have a marked impact on policy across issue areas. Wilson argued that corporatism is likely only where political system is highly centralized, permitting development of hierarchy of interest groups.[43] Lembruch and Schmitter both recognized that there are different types of corporatist arrangements, and they argued that relative centralization of decision-making authority in a state will affect how decision makers regard a single organized interest with access to the government or a "plurality of organizations usually representing antagonistic interests."[44] Regarding Germany, Risse-Kappen has argued that it comes "closest to the corporatist type of domestic structure, in which the policy networks with strong intermediate organizations linking state and society play a significant role in the decision-making process."[45]

Finally, the corporatist argument is relevant to this book given its linkage to a related approach from the comparative foreign policy literature. Zimmerman proposed a model that specified the types of domestic political actors that mattered most in different issues of domestic and foreign policy. The fundamental questions posed by Zimmerman's model were: 1) Is the decision perceived to be symmetrical in its impact on politically relevant domestic political actors? and 2) Are the political goods at issue exclusively tangible? Zimmerman said that the relative symmetry of costs and benefits of a foreign policy issue will affect foreign policy decisions and that this could account for differences in foreign policy across issue areas. In fact, his work was built on the foundation of Lowi's early arguments about issue areas. Lowi argued that where distributive (economic) issues arise, one expects more logrolling, compromise, and a decentralization of the decision process that then affects policy choices.[46] In sum, these works support the hypothesis that cases of cooperation with external actors in the distributive (economic) arena are less likely. The power of symmetry as an intervening condition will be examined through the structured, focused comparison of cases.

Election Performance

Another domestic political condition recognized in the conceptual framework is party performance in national and regional elections. The argument that popular support in democratic systems can affect foreign policy behavior dates back to the work of Kant and Bentham, who implied that democratic elections serve as the key, mediating institution linking popular opinion and policy choice. For the purposes of this book, it is suggested that both the timing of elections and their results can have an impact on the leaders' ability to uphold controversial commitments to international organizations.[47]

> Hypothesis 4: An initial commitment to cooperate with other states in the context of an international organization is less likely to be sustained in the post-commitment phase, *ceteris paribus*, when the major party loses support in national or regional elections.

This hypothesis is actually derived from recent comparative foreign policy studies that have employed popular support as a variable to explain the foreign policy behavior of democratic states. The base of this argument is a challenge to the "Almond–Lippmann consensus" that public opinion does not have a significant impact on foreign policy. In contrast, scholars like Mueller and Graham have demonstrated that public support can be related to specific types of foreign policy outputs.[48]

Comparative politics scholars have begun to explore specific vehicles by which public mood affects foreign policy behavior, and some comparativists have begun to focus on the role of elections as a mediating factor.[49] For example, Morgan and Campbell have looked directly at the specific mechanisms by which the decisions of leaders are constrained in a democracy. Gaubatz also took up this argument, suggesting that election timing can have an influence on foreign policy behavior.

Finally, this hypothesis is also based on relatively recent work on the impact of elections on foreign policy behavior. Based on the literature, foreign policy decision makers who are concerned about their party's performance in upcoming elections may track popular support through public opinion polls. For example, Gaubatz argued that elections and election timing represent a strong, intervening institution between public mood and war proneness. His working hypothesis serves as a basis for this aspect of the conceptual framework: "The closer the society is to an impending election, the greater will be the societal restrictions on the courses of action the state can follow."[50] Further, Quandt has argued in a piece on the American system that the electoral cycle represents a de facto limit on presidential power and latitude on foreign policy issues. He argued that the result is a foreign policy that is excessively geared to short-term calculations, "narrow domestic political considerations," and a loss of consistency and coherency as a result of a high turnover rate of leaders.[51]

Overall, this work supports the idea that election timing and election outcomes can serve as key intervening factors between public opinion and policy outputs. By focusing on the ties between elections and foreign economic and security policy making, this book widens scholarly perspective on these relationships.

Public Support

A final domestic political condition examined in the conceptual framework is public support; specifically, the change in public opinion toward ruling parties in the period leading up to a final decision. This is an important intervening factor in parliamentary systems with rotational regional election schedules (Germany, France, Denmark, and others), where leaders must always be concerned about their party's performance in upcoming elections. Thus, a leader's ability to uphold an international commitment may be seriously affected by perceived declines in public support (that reflect the shadow of upcoming regional and national elections). The following hypothesis is presented for exploration:

> Hypothesis 5: An initial commitment to cooperate with other states in the context of an international organization is less likely to be sustained in the post-commitment phase, *ceteris paribus*, when the major party loses support in public opinion polls.

Comparative foreign policy scholars like Page and Shapiro have argued that public opinion can have an impact on the foreign policy decision-making process. In the 1980s, a series of surveys by Holsti and Rosenau also noted that public opinion could be viewed as a solid and consistent construct.[52] Recent studies by Eichenberg, Jentleson, Hermann, and Risse-Kappen undergird the argument that public opinion can be refined and can have a marked impact on the foreign policy process.[53]

Scholars have also begun to relate public support to specific types of foreign policy outputs, in particular, war making and war proneness. Mueller pursued the question of whether democracies may be less war prone than other types of political systems. He called attention to the fact that American presidents saw an increase in public support when they engaged in any short form of foreign policy crisis. Recently, scholars including Layne and Russett, have revisited the "democratic peace" thesis and developed detailed arguments on both sides of the debate.[54] The popular consensus in this debate is that in the face of upcoming elections in parliamentary democracies, leaders are concerned about popular support for their government, party, and policies.

Figure 1.3 summarizes the hypotheses set forth for explanation.

POLITICAL PROXIMITY

Finally, a major assumption in this book is that the proximity of the domestic political condition to the power center is important. As illustrated in Figure 1.4, this can be interpreted as a framework composed of concentric circles around the decision-making authority, where major party unity may have a much higher degree of impact on a leader's decisions about cooperation than, say, election performance.

This assumption is derived from comparative foreign policy studies and represents another extension of the post-commitment politics conceptual framework. The focus on the relative impact of

1. *Major Party Unity*

   An initial commitment to cooperate with other states in the context of an international organization is less likely to be sustained in the post-commitment phase, *ceteris paribus*, when the leaders of the major party in government are divided over the issue.

2. *Ruling Coalition Consensus*

   An initial commitment to cooperate with other states in the context of an international organization is less likely to be sustained in the post-commitment phase, *ceteris paribus*, when leaders of different parties in the coalition government are divided over the issue.

3. *Symmetry of Domestic Effects*

   An initial commitment to cooperate with other states in the context of an international organization is less likely to be sustained in the post-commitment phase, *ceteris paribus*, when it involves economic/developmental issues rather than military/security issues.

4. *Election Results*

   An initial commitment to cooperate with other states in the context of an international organization is less likely to be sustained in the post-commitment phase, *ceteris paribus*, when the major party loses support in national or regional elections.

5. *Public Support*

   An initial commitment to cooperate with other states in the context of an international organization is less likely to be sustained in the post-commitment phase, *ceteris paribus*, when the major party loses support in public opinion polls.

Figure 1.3 Summary of hypotheses for exploration.

domestic conditions on behavior integrates important arguments from two fields about proximity and intensity: public policy and comparative foreign policy studies. Kingdon developed the concept of proximity and intensity in his 1981 study of congressional voting decisions. Meanwhile, comparative foreign policy scholars like Hermann and McGowan and Shapiro have argued that the more proximate the domestic political condition is to the "ultimate decision unit," the more influence it will have on foreign policy behavior.[55] Hagan also supported this argument in a recent study of domestic oppositions and foreign policy making.[56] In sum, the

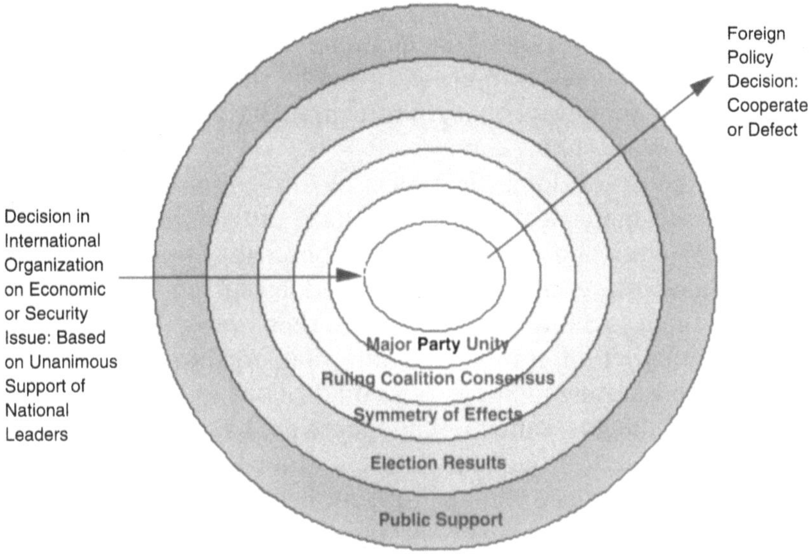

Figure 1.4 Role of political proximity.

political proximity assumption represents an integrative next-step approach to studying the effect of domestic political conditions on decisions about international cooperation.

Specifically, major party unity is assumed to be a more important intervening condition for the cadre of party elite than are ruling coalition consensus, the symmetry of effects of foreign policy cooperation, election performance, or public support, for several reasons. Major party unity represents a variable that is inside the system. Intraparty political maneuvering occurs daily within parliamentary democracies, and it represents a challenge to the power base of key actors. And in some cases, it represents a very personal challenge to their positions of authority.

Accordingly, I assume that ruling coalition consensus matters less than major party unity, but more than the symmetry of effects from foreign policy cooperation, election performance, and public support. Like intraparty politics, interparty politics is a concern that develops from inside the government and is a factor that has a direct and personal impact on the decision-making structure and process. Further, interparty politics in the form of coalition politics can have a direct impact on foreign policy behavior in parliamentary democracies because key ministerial posts can be split across parties and because a combination of party organizations implies an ideological difference between the organizations. This condition is expected to be more important than domestic interests or public support because it can approach (but not always change) foreign policy in a way that actors outside the system simply cannot.

The symmetry of domestic effects of foreign policy cooperation matters more than election performance, but relatively less than major party unity and ruling coalition consensus. Domestic interest group support represents a condition of domestic politics that must work to gain access into the system. In other words, this group represents a number of formal and informal organizations that are focused on promoting their positions on the issue to the government, not as part of the government. While there are overlapping memberships among elites, in general, interest groups must work to gain access to leaders, must attempt to form coalitions to persuade the government, and must actively promote their own interests within the larger dynamic of government operations. But domestic interest groups are relatively more effective than public support because they represent well-organized, goal-driven, well-funded, and often narrow interests that can affect the foreign policy decision-making process.

Election performance matters less for the foreign policy decision-making process, relative to major party and coalition consensus and the symmetry of domestic effects of foreign policy cooperation. Election performance as a measure of public support is included in this domestic politics model because there is increasing evidence of a linkage between electoral cycles, public attitudes, and foreign policy decisions. Relative to other dimensions of domestic politics, election performance is not as significant because it is cyclical and can only have an indirect impact on the behavior of political leaders.

Finally, I assume that public support matters least as an intervening condition in the foreign policy decision-making process, relative to major party and coalition consensus, the symmetry of domestic effects of foreign policy cooperation, and election performance. However, the role of public opinion in the larger domestic politics model is assumed to be limited because public interests are diffuse, non–goal-directed, and are outside the political system. Therefore, public support can only indirectly affect foreign policy decision making.

The political proximity argument is presented as a foundation for the book and as impetus for a systematic review of the way that different conditions of domestic politics can affect foreign policy behavior. There may be circumstances, however, in which this metahypothesis should be modified. For example, intensity may influence the relative significance of these actors and forces on foreign policy decisions. This is defined as the salience with which a foreign policy decision is viewed by actors in a dimension of domestic politics, including the significance of the issue, its relation to the interests of different actors, and its value in relation to related goals of the actors in the framework. The intensity corollary could confound the political proximity assumption when the more-proximate condition is marked by dissensus on the issue. Thus, the less consensus in support of foreign policy cooperation demonstrated in the upper levels of domestic politics, the more likely would intense consensus for or against cooperation at lower levels be to have an impact on foreign policy behavior.

RESEARCH DESIGN

Recognizing the significance of post-commitment politics, I present a research design for exploration of the ways that domestic politics can supplant international agreements. Four variable sets are employed to analyze case studies of the foreign policy decision-making process for this study. The dependent variable is a foreign policy decision to sustain, or defect from, a leader's initial commitment to cooperate with other member states within the context of an international organization. The independent variable in the project is the elite commitment to cooperate with an international organization program or decision. Three control variables are the character of the decision unit, time, and issue area. Finally, domestic political conditions that may have an impact on foreign policy behavior toward international organizations represent intervening variables: major party unity; ruling coalition consensus; symmetry of domestic effects; election performance; and public support. These conditions are scaled relative to the intensity of the issue for actors in the foreign policy decision-making process.

Dependent Variable

The dependent variable for this study is the foreign policy decision to sustain or defect from an international agreement originally supported by unanimous consent. It may be argued that cooperation is the result of "conscious policy coordination." Therefore, cooperation occurs when state leaders decide to meet all the requirements of a decision or program in an international organization that was formulated by unanimous consent at some earlier meeting. Defection, or a failure to cooperate, occurs when state leaders fail to uphold the tenets of a decision or program. For the purposes of this research, cases of cooperation (as expected) and involuntary defection are identified based on the modified structuralist literature. States are expected to cooperate when future transaction costs will be lowered and where information certainty will be enhanced.[57] Structuralists argue that there is often strong pressure in the international system from allies to cooperate (by balancing or bandwagoning). Therefore, this measure of political pressure incorporates the role that political threats from allies and real structural conditions can play on elite perceptions and foreign policy decisions.

Independent Variable

The independent variable for this study is the initial elite commitment to cooperate with an international organization program. This commitment is shaped by a leader's sense of responsibility to the international community and by direct agreements at the international negotiating table. Generally, leaders would not be expected to renege on commitments when they perceive that such a move would bring (broadly defined) harm to their own states. To establish that leaders were committed to cooperation in all cases, the following questions are posed:

1. Did the elite leadership express its support for cooperation within the context of an international organization?
2. Did the elite leadership perceive strong pressure from other member states in the organization to cooperate before a final decision was reached?
3. Did these threats take the form of challenges to future certainty about bilateral and multilateral relations—or threats regarding cuts in economic or military ties?

Control Variables

Nature of the Decision Unit

A small number of party elites can truly influence foreign policy decisions in parliamentary democracies. In other words, the real significant actors in the foreign policy process are the cadre of party elite in parliamentary democracies that play in and out of the process at all stages of formulation and implementation.

The elite decision authority in parliamentary democracies is a single group of elites from the political parties in coalition government who have the authority to allocate state resources. This elite decision authority is composed of all politicians with seats in the cabinet, combined with the primary political leaders of factions of the major party in government. The authority is vested in officials like the German chancellor, the minister of defense, the foreign minister, the minister of finance, agriculture, economics, and the like. The leadership of the major party in government—including the party general secretary and the leader of the *Bundestag* party *Fraktion*—also have a great deal of decision-making authority in parliamentary systems.

As representatives of the people and of the government, party leaders serve as a vital nexus between government and public responsibility. In proportional representation systems, these leaders often interact with at least one other party to form a coalition government. Therefore, foreign policy must be viewed as the sum total of the alternative positions advanced by members of this cadre, where logrolling and negotiation can yield some large degree of explanation. Finally, examining the different personalities involved in the decision units during both recent eras of coalition government in Germany (i.e., the Social–Liberal government from 1969–1982, and the Conservative-Liberal government from 1982 to the present) also builds variance into the research design.

Issue Area

Categorizing different issue areas of foreign policy provides further boundaries for this book, and such efforts are built on the tradition of works of Brecher et al. and Baldwin.[58] They argue that there are at least two different types of issues in foreign policy behavior—military/security issues and economic/developmental issues. This typology allows for comparisons to be made across issue area:

1. Military/security issues—Brecher et al. argued that military/security issues are those "which focus on questions pertaining to violence, including alliances and weaponry, and those which are perceived by the foreign policy elite as constituting a security threat." For this project, military/security issues can be classified as those best associated with allocations from the defense budget and integrally related to the physical security of the population.

2. Economic/developmental issues—Brecher et al. defined economic/developmental issues as those that involve the "acquisition and allocation of resources, such as trade, aid and foreign investment." Economic/developmental issues are best associated with trade, finance, or international economic ties; those seen as integrally related to the fiscal security of the population, economic sectoral interests, or general state prosperity.[59]

Time

Particular care is taken here to identify cases of foreign policy decision making that have the same configuration of elites and major-minor party relations over time.

Intervening Variables

The conceptual framework presented here is based on the assumption that key leaders of a parliamentary democracy must manage domestic political pressures that are exerted in relation to foreign policy commitments. For each of the five key domestic political conditions, three, equally weighted questions for exploration have been developed. Where at least two of the three questions in each category produce a similar response, that category can be coded accordingly. Equal weighting and careful question formulation allow readers to look at different qualitative aspects of the same foreign policy decision-making environment. Further, the framework provides a series of scaled coding categories based on the intensity of the particular domestic political condition. Each of the measures applied is designed to capture some facet of these domestic political conditions, thus providing structure (a combination of richness and rigor) for this history-based analysis.

Major Party Unity

Major party unity is presented in this book as the most powerful dimension of domestic politics. Factionalism in the governing party can be a strong, but often hidden determinant of foreign policy behavior. In order to evaluate politics at this level, three sets of coding questions and categories are posed:

A. Policy statements—*How often have leaders in the major party in government publicly expressed different positions on the issue at hand?* Coding categories are as follows:

1. Repeated different statements
2. Few different statements
3. No differences
4. No differences, repeated similar statements
5. No information.

B. Policy preferences—*How much substantive difference was expressed by leaders of the governing party on the issue at hand?* Coding categories are as follows:
1. Many different positions
2. Few different positions
3. No differences
4. No differences, repeated similar statements
5. No information

C. Elite dispute—*Is there any public record of dispute among elites within the major governing party on the issue, and how serious was this dispute?* Coding categories are as follows:
1. Very serious disputes
2. Serious disputes
3. No disputes
4. No disputes, strong consensus
5. No information

Ruling Coalition Consensus

Coalition maintenance is the second-most-powerful dimension of domestic politics recognized in this framework. The following coding questions and categories are posed:

A. Policy statements—*How often have party leaders from different parties in government publicly expressed different positions on the issue at hand?* Coding categories are as follows:
1. Repeated different statements
2. Few different statements
3. No differences
4. No differences, repeated similar statements
5. No information

B. Policy preferences—*How much substantive difference was expressed between major governing and junior parties on this issue of cooperation in international organizations?* Coding categories are as follows:

1. Many different positions
2. Few different positions
3. No differences
4. No differences, repeated similar statements
5. No information

C. Interparty elite dispute—*Is there any public record of dispute among elites in the governing coalition on the issue at hand, and how serious was this dispute?* Coding categories are as follows:
1. Very serious disputes
2. Serious disputes
3. No disputes
4. No disputes, strong consensus
5. No information

Symmetry of Effects of Cooperation

Another factor that can have a significant impact on the foreign policy decision-making process is the symmetry of effects of cooperation on the polity. Arguments from the corporatist literature about the connection between the number of competing interests and policy stability, comparative works on issue area and symmetry, and related works on interest groups in the foreign policy process are integrated in this section.

A. Symmetry—*Was the foreign policy decision perceived to have a potentially symmetrical or asymmetrical impact on the general public?* Coding categories are as follows:
1. Intensely asymmetrical
2. Asymmetrical
3. Symmetrical
4. Intensely symmetrical
5. No information

B. Public benefit—*To what degree will the general public be affected by a decision about cooperation with an international organization?* Coding categories are as follows:
1. No public impact
2. Indirect public impact
3. Some public impact
4. Direct public impact
5. No information

C. Economic sectors—*How many sectors of the economy will be affected by a decision about cooperation with an international organization?* Coding categories are as follows:
   1. One sector
   2. Few sectors
   3. Some sectors
   4. Many sectors
   5. Symmetrical, no information

Election Performance

A fourth important domestic political condition that can influence foreign policy cooperation in an international organization is the role of popular support, filtered through the institution of elections. This is based on the expectation that elections can have an influence on decisions about policy in the domestic arena. The following coding questions and categories are posed.

A. Propensity of election to influence foreign policy—*Were national or regional elections held in the year leading up to the decision on foreign policy?* Coding categories are as follows:
   1. Highly influenced
   2. Influenced
   3. Uninfluenced

B. Election outcome—*If there were recent national or regional elections, what was the outcome and how serious were the results for the parties in coalition government?* Coding categories are as follows:
   1. Very negative
   2. Negative
   3. Positive
   4. Very positive
   5. No information

C. Interpretation of election results—*How were the results of national or regional elections interpreted in the period leading up to this foreign policy decision?* Coding categories are as follows:
   1. Intense support
   2. Support
   3. Little support
   4. No support
   5. No information

Popular Support

Finally, I posit that public opinion can affect decisions about foreign policy cooperation with international organizations. Assuming that election performance and timing can have an influence on decisions about policy in the domestic arena, leaders may track popular support for their party through public opinion polls in the period leading up to a final decision about an international commitment. Three questions and coding categories are offered at this level.

A. Propensity of election to influence foreign policy—*Are there upcoming national or regional elections that might be affected by this foreign policy decision?* Coding categories are as follows:
   1. Cooperation is less likely
   2. Cooperation is more likely

B. Public opinion survey results—*What was the net change in popular support for major party in government in the year leading up to the final decision about cooperation?* Coding categories are as follows:
   1. Very negative
   2. Very positive
   3. No information

C. Interpretation of public opinion polls—*How were public opinion polls interpreted in the period leading up to this foreign policy decision?* Coding categories are as follows:
   1. Intense support
   2. Support
   3. Little support
   4. No support
   5. No information.

METHODOLOGY: STRUCTURED, FOCUSED CASE COMPARISON

The comparative case studies method is employed to assess the effects of domestic political conditions on a state's propensity to cooperate in international organizations. Structured, focused comparison of cases (working from a set list of theoretically relevant, general questions) represents an excellent method for exploring and explaining the conditions that affect the foreign policy decision-making process.[60] This method is both powerful and unique in the way that it allows for a mixture of "richness and rigor" in a comprehensive study of political behavior.[61]

The case method is extremely useful for getting at the richness of the foreign policy decision-making process. The method involves a process tracing of the factors behind foreign policy decisions, enabling the close examination of the domestic political conditions prevalent across the time span from an initial international commitment to the time of a final decision to cooperate or defect. In fact, this is one of the few methodological approaches in the social sciences that give the observer a real feeling for the political context of decisions.

The method also offers some degree of rigor in the process tracing of foreign policy decisions. Lijphart argued that the comparative method provides some structure in that "cases are selected in such a way as to maximize the variance of the independent variables and to minimize the variance of the control variables."[62] Lijphart also noted that "generally, the problems of reliability and validity are smaller for the researcher who uses the comparative method." The researcher can "analyze his smaller number of cases more thoroughly and is less dependent on data that he cannot properly evaluate."[63] Accordingly, a uniform set of questions and a coding scheme are employed for the analysis of the impacts of the variables in this study.[64]

Finally, Mill's Method of Difference will be employed in the analysis of case study results in chapter 6. The method allows readers to compare and contrast the conditions associated with cases of cooperation against those in cases of defection. This comparison will provide the foundation for further arguments about the post-commitment politics conceptual framework and key lessons for policy makers.

Case Selection

Eight case studies of the foreign policy decision-making process in the Federal Republic of Germany from the 1970s and 1980s are developed in this book. The cases were chosen based on their fit to the variables in this study. In order to control for the structural effects on state foreign policy behavior, four cases where external pressures appear to predict cooperation were selected along with four cases where such factors do not explain surprising defections from international agreements. These cases were also selected in accordance with Lijphart's arguments that case selection should maximize the variance in all variables. Variance in issue area, the role of interest groups, intra- and interparty relations, and public impact through elections are incorporated in this project. Finally, cases were selected from the 1970s and 1980s to encompass differences across two types of coalitions: the Social-Liberal coalition of the 1970s and the Conservative-Liberal coalition of the 1980s. Figure 1.5 presents a summary of the cases to be examined.

The Federal Republic of Germany is assumed to be representative of other parliamentary democracies in the case selection process. Indeed, Germany shares a number of common characteristics with other parliamentary democracies including the importance of political parties and the responsibility of the government and elected officials to the citizens. Like many other democracies, Germany has a federal system of government that allows a distribution of power at the federal, state, and local levels, and votes are distributed in accordance with a modified proportional representation electoral system. As in many democracies, political parties play an important role in the political process, and party leaders can serve in the cabinet as authoritative decision makers.

	Military-Security Issues NATO	Economic-Development Issues EC
Cooperation	1983 Decision for INF Modernization 1979 Decision for Dual Track Plan	1985 Decision for Single European Act 1978 Decision for Common Monetary System
Defection	1989 Decision against Lance Modernization 1982 Decision to Build Siberian Gas Pipeline	1985 Decision against Cereals Price Cut 1975 Decision against Regional Development Fund

Figure 1.5 Case studies.

But while the Federal Republic shares political, cultural, and social traditions with many of its European neighbors, Germany is in some ways distinctive because of its history. German foreign policy behavior in the 1970s and 1980s was clearly influenced by its historical experience—particularly its involvement in two world wars—which has been manifested in the political system in several ways. First, as a divided state from 1945–1990, German leaders experienced limited sovereignty and allied occupation. Second, Germany became an integral member of the NATO alliance and served as the peacetime base of operations for combined military forces from 14 other countries. Third, German political leaders maintained strong civilian control over the military, and the German Defense Ministry has been driven by partisan concerns since the founding of the Federal Republic. Finally, German foreign policy behavior in the 1970s and 1980s was also clearly influenced by economic achievements. Germany experienced tremendous economic growth after World War II, and had one of the strongest economies in Europe by the mid-1970s. The relative size of its economy gave leaders more latitude and influence in regional economic and political initiatives.

These same conditions that make Germany distinctive, however, also deepen the irony of German foreign policy defections from international commitments in the 1970s and 1980s. German leaders were deeply committed to the NATO alliance and to economic cooperation in Europe through the EC in this period. Therefore, a study of the origins of German defections from the EC and NATO programs should provide very valuable insight into the domestic political dynamics of international cooperation.

CONCLUSION

The work of Putnam and his supporters on the two-level game construct has highlighted the importance of domestic-international linkages. This chapter has demonstrated, however, that important questions about actors, process, and timing have been left open for further development. The post-commitment politics conceptual framework is put to the test in the following case studies of German foreign policy decision-making from the 1970s and 1980s in chapters 2–5. Finally, chapter 6 presents a structured, comparative analysis of the case study results and draws important conclusions from the study for contemporary international relations.

NOTES

1. "Bonn wird Kroatien und Slowenien am 15, Januar anerkennen," *Frankfurter Allgemeine Zeitung*, December 18, 1991, p. 2.
2. Robert D. Putnam, "Diplomacy and Domestic Politics: The Logic of Two-Level Games," *International Organization*, Summer 1988, vol. 42, p. 438.
3. Other works in this genre include: Dan Caldwell, *The Dynamics of Domestic Politics and Arms Control*, 1991; George Tsebelis, *Nested Games: Rational Choice in Comparative Politics*, 1990; Duncan Snidal, "The Game Theory of International Politics," *World Politics*, 1985, vol. 38; Stephan Haggard and Beth Simmons, "Regime Theory: Conceptualization and Progress," *International Organization*, Fall 1987, vol. 73; Joseph Grieco, "Anarchy and the Limits of Cooperation: A Realist Critique of the Newest Liberal Institutionalism," *International Organization,* Summer 1988, vol. 42, no. 3; and Peter Cowhey, "The International Telecommunications Regime, Political Roots," *International Organization*, Spring 1990, vol. 44, no. 1; Eckart Kehr, from "Englandhass und Weltpolitik: Eine Studie über die innenpolitischen und sozialen Grundlagen der deutschen Außenpolitik um die Jahr hundertwende," from *Der Primat der Innenpolitik*, vol. 19, 1965.
4. See Robert Axelrod, *The Evolution of Cooperation*, 1984; See also Glenn H. Snyder and Paul Diesing, *Conflict Among Nations: Bargaining, Decision Making, and System Structure in International Crises*, 1977.
5. Axelrod, 1984, p. 8.
6. Putnam, Summer 1988, p. 449.
7. Putnam, Summer 1988, p. 431.
8. Putnam's "negotiated win-sets" are a conceptual vehicle derived from basic arguments in the game theory literature; See especially Snyder and Diesing, 1977, p. 522.
9. Putnam, Summer 1988, p. 433.
10. See Peter B. Evans, Harold K. Jacobson, and Robert D. Putnam, eds., *Double-Edged Diplomacy: International Bargaining and Domestic Politics*, 1993.
11. See Andrew Moravcsik, "Introduction: Integrating International and Domestic Theories of International Bargaining," in Evans, et al., 1993, pp. 3–42.
12. Moravcsik, 1993, p. 15.
13. Putnam, Summer 1988, p. 436.
14. Richard C. Eichenberg, "Dual Track and Double Trouble: The Two-Level Politics of INF," in Evans, et al., 1993, p. 69.
15. Peter B. Evans, "Building An Integrative Approach to International and Domestic Politics: Reflections and Projections," in Evans, et al., 1993, p. 400.
16. Putnam, Summer 1988, p. 437.
17. Evans, in Evans, et al., 1993, p. 399.
18. Evans, in Evans, et al., 1993, p. 411.
19. Janice Gross Stein, "The Political Economy of Security Agreements: The Linked Costs of Failure at Camp David," in Evans, et al., 1993, p. 83.; Eichenberg, in Evans, et al., 1993, p. 51; Helen Milner, "The Interaction of Domestic and International Politics: The Anglo-American Oil Negotiations and the International Civil Aviation Negotiations, 1943–1947," in Evans, et al., 1993, p. 217.
20. Authors from Evans, et al., argued that elites operated on the basis of complex policy preferences. They defined these as a statesman's "acceptibility-set,"

reflecting: "1) the statemsman's interest in enhancing this domestic position, perhaps by pursuing the median domestic interest; 2) an effort to mobilize an optimal response to international imperatives, regardless of domestic factors; or 3) individual policy preferences about the issues in question, perhaps stemming from idiosyncratic first-image factors like past political history or personal idealism." See Moravcsik, in Evans, et al., 1993, p. 30.

21. See Theodore Lowi, "American Business, Public Policy, Case Studies, and Political Theory," *World Politics*, July 1964, vol.16; See also Margaret Karns and Karen Mingst, *The United States and Multilateral Institutions*, 1990, p. 210; and Gerhard Lembruch and Phillipe C. Schmitter, eds., *Patterns of Corporatist Policy Making*, 1979.
22. Evans, in Evans, et al., 1993, p. 405.
23. Arguments about the importance of consensus building and coalition building can be found in comparative politics and comparative foreign policy studies. For example, domestic structuralists argued in the the 1970s and 1980s that domestic coalitions drove foreign economic policy making. Katzenstein and Gourevitch suggested that "the domestic structure of the nation-state is a critical intervening variable without which the interrelation between international interdependence and political strategies cannot be understood." Recently, Snyder made a convincing case that consensus- and coalition-building are the key to international conflict and cooperation. He argued that international conflict could result from domestic coalition efforts to secure power at the cost of state overexpansion. See Peter J. Katzenstein, *Between Power and Plenty*, 1978, p. 22; Peter Gourevitch, "The Second Image Reversed: The International Sources of Domestic Politics," *International Organization*, Autumn 1978, vol. 32, no. 4; See also Jack Snyder, *Myths of Empire: Domestic Politics and International Ambition*, 1991.
24. Putnam, Summer 1988, p. 448.
25. Theoretical work that linked domestic political actors to international cooperation was first introduced by institutionalists like David Mitrany, *A Working Peace System*, 1943; Karl Deutsch, *Political Community in the North Atlantic Area*, 1957; Chadwick F. Alger, "Analytical Approaches: Functionalism and Integration," *International Social Science Journal*, vol. 29, no. 1, 1977; Ernst B. Haas, *Beyond the Nation-State: Functionalism and International Organization*, 1964; Haas, *The Uniting of Europe: Political, Social, and Economic Forces, 1950–1957*, 1958; and Karl W. Deutsch, *Political Community and the North Atlantic Area: International Organization in Light of Historical Experience*, 1957; For a recent version of this argument, see Peter Haas "Knowledge, Power, and International Policy Coordination," *International Organization*, Winter 1992, vol. 46, no. 1.
26. Relevant comparative works include: Gerhard Loewenberg and Samuel Patterson, *Comparing Legislatures*, 1988; Val Lorwin, "Segmented Pluralism: Ideological Cleavages and Political Cohesion in Smaller European Democracies," *Comparative Politics*, January 1971; G. Bingham Powell, "Political Cleavage Structure, Cross-Pressure Processes, and Partisanship," *American Journal of Political Science*, February 1976, vol. 20; Recent work rooted in comparative analysis includes Beverly Crawford, "German Foreign Policy After the Cold War: The Decision to Recognize Croatia," Center for

German and European Studies, Working Paper 2.21, August 1993. Relevant comparative foreign policy works include: Richard C. Snyder, H. W. Bruck, and Burton Sapin, "Decision-Making as an Approach to the Study of International Politics," *Foreign Policy Analysis Project Series*, 1954, no. 3; Robert Jervis, *Perception and Misperception in World Politics*, 1976; Graham T. Allison, *Essence of Decision: Explaining the Cuban Missile Crisis*, 1971.

27. Stoltenberg, quoted in the *New York Times*, October 2, 1986, p. 17F.
28. This hypothesis was derived from works on political parties and their role in policy making such as Kenneth H. F. Dyson, *Party, State, and Bureaucracy in Western Germany*, 1977.
29. See Maurice Duverger, *Political Parties*, 1954.
30. Works in this category tend to look at the role of elites in the domestic political arena, and some works have been extended to examine ties between party organizations and foreign policy; See Emil J. Kirchner, "Genscher and What Lies Behind Genscherism," *West European Politics*, April 1990, vol. 13, no. 2.
31. Ideas for this interpretation of factionalism drawn from Kenneth Janda, *Political Parties*, 1980.
32. See R. J. Hofferbert and Hans Dieter Klingemann, "The Policy Impact of Party Programmes and Government Declarations in the Federal Republic of Germany," *European Journal of Political Research*, 1984, vol. 18.
33. Toyozo Tanaka, "Breakup of the Tanaka Faction: End of an Era," *Japan Quarterly*, October/December 1987; See Paul H. Brass, *Caste, Faction, and Party in Indian Politics*, 1987; See also Efraim Inbar, *War and Peace in Israeli Politics: Labor Party Positions on National Security*, 1991.
34. See Clay Clemens, *Reluctant Realists: The Christian Democrats and West German Ostpolitik*, 1989; Mujal-Leon Eusebio, "The West German Social Democratic Party and the Politics of Internationalism in Central America," *Journal of Interamerican Studies and World Affairs*, Winter 87/88, vol. 29; Thomas Poquntke, "Unconventional Participation in Party Politics: The Experience of the German Greens," *Political Studies*, vol. 40, June 1992; Gene E. Frankland, "The Role of the Greens in West German Parliamentary Politics, 1980–1987," *The Review of Politics*, Winter 1988, vol. 50; and Herbert P. Kitschelt, "Organization and Strategy of Belgian and West German Ecology Parties: A New Dynamic of Party Politics in Western Europe?" *Comparative Politics*, January 1988, vol. 20.
35. See R. K. Alderman and J. A. Cross, "The Timing of Cabinet Reshuffles," *Parliamentary Affairs*, 1987, vol. 40, no. 1.
36. See Arend Lijphart, ed., *Parliamentary Versus Presidential Government*, 1992; Vernon Bogdanor, ed., *Coalition Government in Western Europe*, 1983, pp. 1–15.
37. Somewhat surprisingly, there are few systematic studies of the relationship between efforts to maintain governing coalitions and foreign policy behavior. Geoffrey Pridham notes that despite the prevalence of coalitions, "they have been surprisingly neglected in both theoretical and empirical work." Pridham, "Coalition Behavior and Party Systems in Western Europe: A Comparative Approach," *Parliamentary Affairs*, July 1987, vol. 40, no. 3.
38. Lothar Wilker, "Foreign Policy in the *Bundestag*," in Uwe Thaysen, Roger Davidson, and Robert Gerald Livingston, eds., *The U.S. Congress and the German Bundestag*, 1990, p. 51.

39. Jean Blondel and Jean-Louis Thiebault, "The Study of Western European Cabinets," *European Journal of Political Research,* 1988, vol. 16, p. 117. This approach was also taken by a number of scholars of German politics and society who carefully examined the *innenpolitische* developments that affect foreign policy behavior. Studies by German scholars like Haftendorn describe some relationship between coalition politics and foreign policy "room to maneuver." Recent scholarship (for example, Boutwell's *The German Nuclear Dilemma*, 1990) has continued the examination of the interparty politics that can affect foreign policy behavior. Finally, it is worth noting that examples of this type of argument can be applied to many different parliamentary democracies, including a study by Dishkin and Galnor of coalition politics in Israel and its effect on foreign policy toward Egypt; See Herbert Döring and Gordon Smith, eds., *Party Government and Political Culture in Western Germany*, 1982.
40. Studies of interest groups in the United States tend to focus on their structure and role in the realm of domestic policy-making (i.e., Ornstein and Elder, 1978), while the few works on German interest groups and their influence on foreign policy focus on the important impact of economic cartels, or big industries, on foreign policy decisions (i.e., Müller-Rommel, 1990; Engholm, 1975; and Heinze, 1981). Also, recent categorization and analysis has been conducted on interest groups in Israel (Yishai, 1992), the United States (McFarland, 1991), and France (Wilson, 1983); See Yael Yishai, "Three Faces of Associational Politics: Interest Groups in Israel," *Political Studies*, March 1992, vol. 40; Andrew S. McFarland, "Interest Groups and Political Time: Cycles in America," *British Journal of Political Science*, July 1991, vol. 21; See also Frank Lee Wilson, "French Interest Group Politics: Pluralist or Neocorporatist?" *American Political Science Review*, December 1983, vol. 77, no. 4.
41. Katzenstein, "The Third West German Republic: Continuity in Change," *Journal of International Affairs*, Summer 1988, vol. 41, no. 2.
42. Snyder, *The Myth of Empire*, 1990, p. 32.
43. Wilson, October 1983.
44. Gerhard Lehmbruch and Phillipe C. Schmitter, eds., *Patterns of Corporatist Policy Making,* 1979, p. 6.
45. Risse-Kappen, 1994, p. 257; See also "Public Opinion, Domestic Structure, and Foreign Policy in Liberal Democracies," *World Politics*, July 1991, no. 4.
46. William Zimmerman, "Issue Area and Foreign Policy Process," *American Political Science Review,* 1978, vol. 67, p. 1208.
47. For an interesting comparison of the effects of public opinion versus domestic structure on foreign policy, see Risse-Kappen, July 1991, no. 4; See also Warren E. Miller and Donald E. Stokes, "Constituency Influence in Congress," *American Political Science Review*, 1963 vol. 57, no. 1; For an alternative perspective, see Brian Page and Robert Shapiro, "Effects of Public Opinion on Policy," *American Political Science Review*, 1983, vol. 77.
48. See John Mueller, *War, Presidents and Public Opinion*, 1973; Thomas Graham, *American Public Opinion on NATO, Extended Deterrence, and the Use of Nuclear Weapons*, 1989.
49. Other examples of comparative works that focus on the importance of national and regional elections include: Karl H. Cerny, *Germany at the Polls: The Bundestag Election of 1976*, 1978; Rainer-Olaf Schultze, "Föderalismus als

Alternative? Überlegungen zur territorialen reorganization von Herrschaft," *Zeitschrift für Parlamentsfragen*, 1990, vol. 3; See also Heino and Ursula Kaack, eds., *Parteien-Jahrbuch 1973/74*, 1974.

50. Kurt T. Gaubatz "Election Cycles and War," *Journal of Conflict Resolution*, June 1991, vol. 35, no. 2.
51. William Quandt, "The Electoral Cycle and the Conduct of Foreign Policy," *Political Science Quarterly*, 1986, vol. 101, no. 5.
52. Benjamin Page and Robert Shapiro, "Effects of Public Opinion on Policy," *American Political Science Review*, 1983, vol. 77, no. 1.
53. Risse-Kappen argues that public opinion can directly affect the choices of top decision makers "by changing policy goals or how those goals are prioritized, by narrowing the range of options and/or means to implement goals, or by winning symbolic concessions in the sense of changed rhetoric rather than policy reforms." The public may also indirectly affect policies by "influencing the coalition-building processes among the elites. . . . It can strengthen or weaken the positions of bureaucracies or single actors within the government. Public opinion and the activities of public interest groups may lead to changes and/or realignments within or between political organizations such as parties." He concludes that these indirect effects on policy are difficult to trace and are therefore easily overlooked. However, their impact may be as important as the aforementioned direct influences." Risse-Kappen, 1991, p. 482.
54. Christopher Layne, "Kant or Cant: The Myth of Democratic Peace," *International Security*, vol. 19, no. 2, Fall 1994; Bruce Russett, *Grasping the Democratic Peace: Principles for a Post–Cold War World*, 1993; and Jack S. Levy, "Domestic Politics and War," *Journal of Interdisciplinary History,* Spring 1988, vol. 18.
55. Charles F. Hermann, "Political Opposition as Potential Agents of Foreign Policy Change: Developing a Theory," paper presented at the 28th annual meeting of the International Studies Association Convention, Washington, D.C., April 14–18, 1987; this framework also has roots in earlier works on macro-micro linkages from Rosenau and "social distance" arguments presented by Patrick J. McGowan and Howard Shapiro, in *The Comparative Study of Foreign Policy*, 1973, p. 40.
56. See Joe D. Hagan, *Political Opposition and Foreign Policy in Comparative Perspective*, 1993.
57. See Robert Keohane, *After Hegemony: Cooperation and Discord in the World Political Economy*, 1984; Also see general structuralist arguments from: Kenneth Waltz, *The Theory of International Politics*, 1979; Robert Gilpin, *War and Change in World Politics*, 1979; Robert Axelrod, *The Evolution of Cooperation*; See also Stephen Krasner, *International Regimes*, 1982.
58. See Michael Brecher, Blema Steinberg, and Janice Stein, "A Framework for Research on Foreign Policy Behavior," *Journal of Conflict Resolution*, vol. 13, 1969; Brecher et al., *The Foreign Policy System of Israel: Setting, Images, Process*, 1972; See also Knorr's definition that "national security concerns arise when vital national values (i.e., core values) are perceived as being threatened by adverse foreign actions or events." Klaus Knorr, "Economic Interdependence and National Security," from *Economic Issues and National Security*, Klaus Knorr and Frank N. Trager, eds., 1977, p. 8; See also David Baldwin, *Economic Statecraft*, 1985.

59. Brecher, et al., 1969, p. 82.
60. The case study method provides the type of substantive, qualitative information that informs hypotheses about the relationship between domestic political conditions and foreign policy decisions about cooperation. This method allows one to trace the decision-making process and the causal pathway leading to cooperation or defection in the post-commitment politics phase. In comparing across cases, however, the problem of richness of many variables and a limited number of cases—a classic problem in international and comparative politics—remains.
61. This method "has become a respectable, legitimate research strategy that can contribute to theory development." Also, this method allows the construction of significant, middle-range theories about the domestic political conditions that facilitate or obstruct foreign policy cooperation in international organizations; See Alexander George, *Case Studies and Theory Developement: The Method of Structure, Focused Comparison*, in P. G. Lauren, ed., *Diplomacy: New Approaches in History, Theory and Policy*, 1979.
62. See Arend Lijphart, "Comparative Politics and the Comparative Method," *American Political Science Review*, 1971, p. 1264.
63. Lijphart, 1971, p. 1261.
64. Nevertheless, conclusions from such studies are necessarily provisional because of the constraints built into the method. The method deals selectively with only certain aspects of the historical case and it supports only the development of contingent hypotheses; See Alexander George, "Case Studies and Theory Development." Paper presented to the Second Annual Symposium on Information Processing in Organizations, Carnegie-Mellon University, October 15–16, 1982; See also Arend Lijphart, "The Comparable Cases Strategy in Comparative Research," *Comparative Political Studies*, vol. 8, no. 2, 1975, pp. 158–177.

2 GERMANY AND THE EUROPEAN COMMUNITY, 1975–1978

This chapter is divided into two sections, both of which explore different domestic political conditions in the post-commitment phase that influenced German support for international agreements in the 1970s. The first section describes Chancellor Helmut Schmidt's decision in 1975 to withdraw German support for the European Regional Development Fund in light of domestic opposition to the plan. The second section explores how conditions in the post-commitment phase enabled Schmidt to support the establishment of the European Monetary System just three years later.

DEFECTION: THE EUROPEAN REGIONAL DEVELOPMENT FUND

The European Regional Development Fund (ERDF) was one of the most important programs under consideration in the EC during the 1970s. The ERDF was designed to provide economic stimulus through Community development grants to those regions designated as "low-growth." Combined with plans to enlarge the Community and to create a European Monetary Union, the fund was part of a new wave of efforts to achieve equitable levels of development in Europe.[1]

West German government officials gave their support for the establishment of a ERDF on several occasions. The fund concept was first introduced at the 1969 Hague summit as a long-term program to raise levels of development throughout Europe. German Chancellor Willy Brandt supported the fund as a way to lend stability to the European Monetary Union plan, and EC leaders unanimously agreed that some type of fund should be established within four years. At the Paris summit three years later, Brandt's finance minister, Helmut Schmidt, voted with other members of the EC to establish the fund by December 31, 1973. When Schmidt became chancellor in May 1974, he expressed continued support for the ERDF program.[2]

German leaders who supported the development fund idea, however, did not carefully analyze its financial implications for their own government, nor did they take an accurate reading of domestic political support for the plan. As time passed, it became clear that many officials in the Finance and Economics Ministries and in the party organizations had deep reservations about the organization and purpose of the fund. After a series of debates in Brussels and Bonn, German government leaders reneged on previous commitments to support the fund in May 1975.

Elite Decision Authority

Leaders in the West German government who voted to renege on the ERDF plan in 1975 included representatives from a coalition of the Social Democratic Party (SPD) and the Free Democratic Party (FDP). Key decision makers on Europe policy included: Chancellor Helmut Schmidt (SPD), Foreign Minister Hans-Dietrich Genscher (FDP), Economics Minister Otto Graf Lambsdorff (FDP), Finance Minister Hans Apel (SPD), and Agricultural Minister Josef Ertl (SPD). Economic policy factions in the major party in government were represented by the moderates, including Chancellor Schmidt, Justice Minister Hans-Jochen Vogel, and parliamentary representative Horst Ehmke. Moderates tended to support EC programs that might have long-term benefits for Germany, and each offered their support for the ERDF early on. Finally, their views were challenged by fiscal and monetary policy conservatives in the party, including Finance Minister Apel and Parliamentary State Secretary Hans Matthöfer, who opposed the development fund on the grounds of serious cost and management concerns.[3]

Historical Development of the ERDF

The ERDF concept first began to receive the attention of Community leaders in the late 1960s. EC leaders articulated a collective goal for the fund at this time: to provide long-term, equitable economic development for Europe with relatively small grants of funds.[4] Experts suggested that the fund would facilitate other Community plans to achieve economic union or monetary union, as well as helping with larger problems by aligning policies in the new European market. By the early 1970s, many European leaders saw the ERDF as vital to foster the goals of stability and long-term economic growth in the Community.

But the fund was much more than just one piece of a larger mosaic of EC integration efforts; it was also a reaction to growing disparities in per capita income and standards of living in the Community. In 1970, the gap in the gross domestic product (GDP) per capita between the ten richest and the ten poorest regions in the EC was three to one. Workers in the industrial heart of West Germany were much more prosperous than rural farmers in the Netherlands; merchants in Paris lived far better than tradesmen in Scotland, and so on. The relative prosperity of the Community in the 1970s would also be affected by widening Community membership. When Greece became an EC member in 1972, for example, the overall ratio of GDP per capita between rich and poor regions dropped to five-to-one. Europe also faced related problems including a very high level of labor migration from the poor to rich sectors.

The countries most in need of an economic boost in the 1970s included Ireland, Italy, and Great Britain. Other countries had regions that were in need of some type of economic stimulus, including southern and western France, northern Belgium, and northern Denmark. The relative underdevelopment of these regions and countries had naturally created a number of direct problems in aligning economic and trade policy in the Community, as well as indirect problems with health care, social welfare programs, and unemployment.

The Federal Republic of Germany and the ERDF

West Germany experienced tremendous economic growth in the 1960s, establishing itself as one of the most prosperous countries in the EC and as an economic engine for many of the region's economies. Germany extended its interests to other member states of the Community through trade and direct investment. In 1970, Germany had one of the highest rates of private investment in other countries in the region, investing 3.8 billion *Deutschmarks* (DM) in Luxembourg, DM 1.56 billion in Italy, DM 0.2 billion in Greece, DM 0.3 billion in Portugal, and DM 2.7 billion in the Netherlands. German private investment facilitated long-term development in Europe that, in turn, produced profit for German industries.[5]

When Willy Brandt became the first Social Democratic chancellor of West Germany in 1969, foreign policy took on a decidedly European focus. With the support of top political leaders in the German government, Chancellor Brandt began to articulate a focus on European cooperation and more active EC integration policies. This was significant because the SPD had generally opposed European integration in the late 1950s. But once in government, party leaders including Brandt, *Bundestag Fraktion* leader Herbert Wehner, and Finance Minister Schmidt began to support European integration plans based on their belief that there was latent domestic support for European economic cooperation.

Brandt's foreign policy agenda allowed for consideration of all of these issues. At the 1969 EC summit at the Hague, the German government supported the creation of a European monetary system plan, encouraged discussions about a regional development fund, and championed the enlargement of Community membership. EC leaders voted unanimously to set up programs for a European Monetary Union that would eventually lead to the "surrender of sovereignty on currency questions" and the creation of a central banking authority that could control monetary and perhaps even fiscal policy.[6] They also agreed that the stability and effectiveness of the monetary system was contingent on equitable levels of development—calling on the European Commission to draw up plans for a fund to be established within four years.

The "First Enlargement" plan of the Community would bring in Great Britain and Ireland as new members.[7] British Prime Minister Edward Heath seized the opportunity at the conference to make a connection between the development fund and the enlargement question, arguing that it was crucial for the Community to create some sort of development program that he could then use as leverage to overcome domestic political opposition against membership back home. According to one expert, Heath made the creation of a regional fund a high priority in order "to head off the possibility of financial loss from membership and to produce tangible benefits for the British people as quickly as possible."[8]

German Domestic Constraints

Some leaders at the Hague summit supported the creation of a ERDF because their countries would receive needed support. Others, including Chancellor Brandt and French President Pompidou, supported the fund because of its long-term benefits for European economic integration. But when these leaders returned home from the Hague summit, press reports began to surface in Germany and France that were quite critical of the fund because of its "dangerous financial implications." In response to critics, Brandt did express some concerns about the open-ended commitment of the ERDF, and Pompidou said that continuing economic problems at home might limit France's ability to support a regional development fund. Both leaders were cognizant of a rising tide of opposition among nationalist and conservative supporters who were concerned that programs like the ERDF would erode their sovereignty. At subsequent EC meetings, representatives of Germany, France, Belgium, and Holland pulled back and articulated their support only for a "sharply bounded and carefully monitored" fund.[9]

EC member governments continued to debate the prospects for establishment of a regional development fund for several years.[10] Throughout this period, Germany's Europe policy was managed by the Foreign Ministry, and Walter Scheel met on a regular basis with his counterparts from other EC governments. Inside the Foreign Ministry, Europe policy was overseen by a Parliamentary State Secretary. It is worth noting that during the early discussions of the ERDF proposal, two SPD leaders served as State Secretaries—Hans Apel (1972–1974) and Hans-Jürgen Wischnewski (1974–1976)—and both were more conservative on questions of future integration than were their respective foreign ministers. The conservative Parliamentary State Secretary Hans Apel was also a political ally of Finance Minister Schmidt and would later become Schmidt's finance minister. These Parliamentary State Secretaries were able to participate in cabinet sessions in the Brandt government and were able to have a direct impact on Europe policy. Thus, while it appeared to outside observers that the German government supported the ERDF between 1969 and 1972, conservative voices were gaining strength in Bonn.

Bureaucratic struggles over ERDF further complicated the government's stand on the fund. Officials from the Economics Ministry sought to influence Foreign Ministry policy on this question based on the justification that its own *Referat* division was responsible for domestic development policy. Officials argued that the plan was more in line with the interests, knowledge, and experience of Economics Ministry administrators. At the same time, Finance Ministry officials expressed concerns about the proposed size of the ERDF and were reluctant to sanction any major spending initiative that would represent only a net payout by the German government. Both Finance and Economics Ministry officials were much less pro-ERDF than their counterparts in the Foreign Ministry, and a shift of program oversight to these offices ultimately had a serious impact on Germany's Europe policy.

Differences over Europe policy also arose between the parties in government in the early 1970s. Junior party leaders (FDP) controlled the Foreign Ministry, the Economics Ministry, and the Agricultural Ministry at this time, but Social Democrats knew that the FDP had been divided over the question of European integration for years. Foreign Minister Scheel expressed some concern that a European development fund was just another program that went against the grain of the liberal party ideology. Scheel also saw the plan as a diversion from *Ostpolitik* and challenged Brandt that he was choosing "European integration over German unity."[11] Overall, the government was unable to focus its attention or position on the establishment of a regional fund in the period from the Hague conference to the Paris summit (1969–1972). The default position for the German government on ERDF thus became continued, but purposefully vague, support for the ERDF plan.

German Elections and the Paris Summit, 1972

In late 1972, national elections were held in West Germany that marked a turning point in the way that the Brandt government approached Europe policy. Brandt gave a speech in the *Bundestag* after the Social-Liberal coalition victory in mid-January 1973 that defined the new government's policy priorities and central interests. The chancellor stated that "European integration would be the government's primary goal" in the second term. Finance Minister Schmidt echoed his chancellor's speech in subsequent statements to the press, but he added the word *pragmatic* to describe plans to align

EC monetary policy and levels of development. The finance minister stated that the Germans would support further integration so long as the EC would impose some standards of financial relations on other member states in the organization.

The Paris summit of October 1972 offered these leaders an opportunity to act on their new platform, but once again, discussions about the fund were intertwined with concerns about the enlargement plans of the Community and monetary policy coordination. Countries that sought entry into the Community at that time were states with a large number of problem regions; each had large regions with very little industrial development, infrastructure, and employment possibilities. Italian and British officials again warned that they did not have the "political support to move forward" on the proposal for a European Monetary Union without such a fund.[12] In response, Chancellor Brandt and Finance Minister Schmidt put forward a nine-point social program that would support the creation of a development fund, address enlargement concerns, and move forward on an EC monetary union. Brandt stressed that a regional structural policy should be implemented hand-in-hand with the development of a European Monetary Union.[13] After some debate, a summit communiqúe was issued that stated that "a high priority should be given to the aim of correcting in the Community, the structural and regional imbalances which might affect the realization of economic and monetary union." Perhaps most importantly, leaders agreed unanimously that an ERDF would be established by December 31, 1973.[14]

Once again, leaders had to return home to gain confirmation and support for the development fund. Once again, the progress on ERDF made at the Paris meeting was soon derailed by domestic political opposition in the more prosperous states. Chancellor Brandt had made a commitment at Paris to move forward on this plan, but he returned home to face serious debates about the size and control of the development fund. German government officials were very concerned about the size of the fund and preferred to dictate EC policy by simply making a set, limited offer of German support for the fund. Officials in the Economics Ministry favored a small fund that would offer a few, very concentrated economic stimulus packages. Foreign Ministry officials believed that the ERDF should be larger and designed to offer many grants to promote development (dubbed the "watering-can" approach to regional development).[15]

This debate came to a head at a cabinet meeting on February 11, 1973. Economics and Finance Ministry officials argued that the German contribution to the fund should be quite small and that the fund should operate on the principle of concentrated, package grants. Foreign Minister Scheel argued that the fund would be of greater benefit if it followed the watering-can approach. Chancellor Brandt was persuaded by Schmidt's arguments in his formulation of a compromise. German leaders agreed that a fund should be created with a base value of 50 million European Units of Account (EUA) for the first three years of its existence. Furthermore, they decided to support the concentrated package approach for the fund in subsequent EC ministerial discussions.[16]

Meanwhile, discussions about the size and shape of the fund had finally reached the ministerial level in Brussels in the spring of 1973. The European Commission produced a report that proposed a development fund totaling at least 2,250 million EUA—*more than 40 times as large as the German government supported in the February cabinet meeting.* The Commission also presented a formula for calculating member state contributions that showed that Germany should donate 630 million EUA to the fund. And this proposal called for the implementation of a watering-can approach for the fund, so that almost 50 percent of the total area of the Community could eventually be considered eligible for aid.[17]

The Thomson Report

In spite of lukewarm reviews for the Commission proposal across Europe—and muted anger inside the German government at its size and scope—Community officials forged ahead in developing plans for the fund. One important step was the 1973 release of the Thomson Report, a European Commission study of the disparities in the Community, which addressed a number of issues. It began by legitimizing the ERDF as grounded in the Treaty of Rome objective to achieve a "continuous and balance expansion in economic activity." So long as regional imbalances in the community existed, certain elements of market and growth potential "went untapped." Therefore it was argued, the whole EC economy, was held back by economic problems in the weak regions. The report argued that regional disparities, if left unresolved, would pose a threat to the common market and so to the basis of the Community itself. Putting the point rather bluntly, it stated that "no community could maintain itself, nor have meaning for the peoples which belong to it, so long as some have very different standards of living than others."[18]

Most importantly, the report defined those regions in the Community that were in need of help, so-called "problem regions." It developed a list of criteria that would technically define what countries would be eligible for a percentage of the proposed ERDF. The criteria included that areas must already be benefiting from the regional polities of the member states of the EC, and the areas must have a "GDP per head less than the Community average."[19] But according to addenda to the report, the problem regions also had to demonstrate at least one of the following characteristics: 1) heavy dependence upon agriculture and possessing few manufacturing activities; 2) heavy dependence upon declining industries such as coal mining or textiles; or 3) suffering persistent underemployment due to fundamental structural problems. Recognizing the complexity of the formula the Thomson Report had created, the Commission released a map that identified the problem regions and their particular circumstances. The map was subsequently used to facilitate debate in the Commission and Council settings.[20]

The report also made a connection between the existence of regional disparities and the potential to create a European Monetary Union in the future. This was a direct appeal to governments of relatively prosperous states like Germany and France to consider the implications of development problems for monetary union. Because a monetary union meant that states would surrender their sovereign control of certain instruments including exchange rates and money flow, the report emphasized that poor states needed some incentive like the development fund to support monetary union.[21]

Resistance to the ERDF Plan

The size of the European Commission proposal and the scope of the Thomson Report both had a profound impact on Germany's Europe policy. First, the size and shape of the spring Commission proposal came as a great surprise to German leaders. Second, Germans saw the Thomson Report as a heavy-handed proposal that demanded too much of the prosperous states. But instead of staging dramatic protests, Chancellor Brandt and key leaders made a conscious policy decision in the fall of 1973 not to support the creation of the ERDF for the near term. During a September 1973 interview,

Parliamentary State Secretary Hans Apel referred to problems with getting "any realistic proposals" out of the European Community.[22]

In Brussels in November 1973, the German government announced that it would no longer engage in negotiations over the establishment of the development fund.[23] One expert suggested that Brandt and other German leaders believed that they had very little to lose by taking this step at this time. Subsequently, the German cabinet supported the postponement of a final decision on ERDF in a December meeting.[24] Accounts of Economics Ministry meetings over the future of ERDF also showed deep reservations about the policy program.[25]

That same month, EC leaders met for a summit in Copenhagen.[26] German and French representatives at the summit refused to consider a development fund along the lines of the Thomson Report plan, and they made comments that the EC proposals were way out of line with expectations.[27] Parliamentary State Secretary Apel ultimately did offer a concession that Germany would support the ERDF at a base level of 750 million EUA. But this German offer was quickly ruled unacceptable by other European leaders, and Apel said that member states "expected too much of the German government." He later argued that "We [Germans] are not the paymasters of the Community," and that German friendship could not be bought.[28] As a result of these stormy debates, there was very little movement in the Community on ERDF in the winter months of 1973–1974.

Leadership Changes

As the European Commission continued to finalize plans for the development fund, important leadership changes were under way in the three most powerful states in the Community. In the British national elections, the Labor party put together enough votes to defeat the Conservatives and establish a minority government. French President Pompidou died in early 1974, and Giscard D'Estaing took over. And in May 1974, Chancellor Willy Brandt resigned as chancellor (due to a political scandal) and was replaced by SPD party leader Helmut Schmidt.

Germany's position toward questions of European integration and policy coordination changed after Schmidt took over. Schmidt appeared less likely to compromise on German national interests than was Brandt, and Schmidt was very aware of the drag that EC contributions put on the German federal budget. Up until he became chancellor, Schmidt had been working on a Finance Ministry report for the SPD *Präsidium,* in which he warned against any major West German financial sacrifice to the EC. He had concluded that Germany should not contribute any more to the EC budget until other governments reformed their Europe policies providing more financial support for the organization.[29] Also, Schmidt named Hans Apel, a known critic of the ERDF, to be the new finance minister.

Chancellor Schmidt was committed to some elements of the EC, however, and he emphasized that stable and efficient Community programs were very important. In an address to the *Bundestag* shortly after taking office, Schmidt stated that he would support "fiscally responsible" European policy so long as other member states carried their own load. He explicitly stated that Germany should continue to support social policies like the ERDF program that would benefit many members of the Community. Development programs instituted through the EC, he argued, would provide a way to coordinate market policy, improve working conditions, and provide wage agreements.[30] But fund effectiveness would be determined by the amount of financial resources involved—not the potential gains from Community aid.

Proponents and opponents of the ERDF lined up to compete for the new chancellor's attention. By this time, those ministries controlled by the Free Democratic Party (the Foreign and Economics ministries) had developed constituencies that supported the concept of a carefully monitored ERDF for the Community. On the other side of the issue stood Finance Minister Apel and his supporters, who had developed a serious distaste for the budget burdens the ERDF would represent for West Germany.

In spite of cross-pressures inside the German government, Schmidt and other new European leaders did forge ahead in support of ERDF for at least five important reasons:

1. They believed that there was latent domestic support for the program as an extension of social policy.
2. They saw a development fund as a necessary step toward monetary policy coordination.
3. They knew that this was not a highly salient issue for their respective publics and therefore was unlikely to become too politicized.[31]

4. Schmidt fostered a personal relationship with French President Giscard d'Estaing, and they strongly agreed about Franco-German responsibility for the management of regional problems—including renegotiation of the British contract with the Community and the formalization of ERDF proposals. To that end, they sponsored a series of bilateral talks to discuss the growing divisions between net-contributors and net-beneficiaries in the Community.
5. Plans for the upcoming EC summit in Paris in December 1974 added a sense of urgency to German-French collaboration on Europe policy, and leaders sought to cement some sort of unified position on many issues ahead of time. Some leaders even suggested that a settlement on the ERDF proposal was likely. Foreign Minister Genscher went on the record suggesting that the German government was in agreement that a "slimmed-down ERDF" could be finalized at the summit.

Schmidt continued to court French support for the plan and to work with the British to pave the way for future cooperation on such issues as the establishment of the ERDF.

President d'Estaing, Chancellor Schmidt, and other European leaders finally gathered for a summit on the matter in Paris in December 1974. In fact, the Irish and Italian governments had threatened to boycott the summit unless other leaders promised that progress would be made on the ERDF. French and German leaders, interested in recapturing the lead on development policy and other matters, agreed to debate the fund with the idea that the slimmed-down ERDF proposal would dominate discussions.[32]

After two days of serious deliberation at the Paris summit, European leaders unanimously resolved that a slimmed-down ERDF with a financial foundation of EUA 1,300 million should be established by early 1975. The compromise plan also included a dilution of the watering-can principle, a reduced commitment of funds expected from the EC's largest economies, and even a promise to grant 6.4 percent of the fund to German regions in need of development assistance.[33]

This compromise agreement was significant for several reasons. First, many states in need of aid were given less of an allotment than they had requested. Second, the proposed size of the fund was reduced dramatically through debate at the summit—far below the size anticipated by the Thomson Report and earlier Commission proposals. The size of the fund was to be only half of what was already considered by less-developed member states to be "inadequate."[34] And at the same time, some German government officials including Finance Minister Apel were disgruntled at the compromise because the fund was many times larger than what they had originally proposed.

Post-Commitment Political Conditions

German leaders returned from Paris with different attitudes about the development fund compromise.[35] Subsequent bureaucratic struggles over ERDF details actually became real public struggles for control over European policy in early 1975. Key officials in the Finance Ministry, including Minister Hans Apel, argued loudly that the proposed ERDF was too costly and unwieldy. These officials were joined in their concern by local and *Länder* officials who feared that they would have to pay for the ERDF program.[36] Generally, *Länder* leaders and officials in the Finance Ministry believed that if any type of fund were to be created, West Germany should receive some money from it.

However, many officials in the Economics Ministry, Foreign Ministry, and the *Kanzleramt* supported the Paris compromise on ERDF and believed that Germany should not expect to draw funds from the program. Economics Minister Lambsdorff and Foreign Minister Genscher both articulated their support in early 1975 for the ERDF. They saw the plan as an important step toward other goals in the Community, including monetary union.[37] Economics Ministry leaders subsequently turned their attention to promoting efficiency in the fund operation.[38]

Chancellor Schmidt faced dissension in the elite decision authority relative to the ERDF compromise plan. Differences emerged inside the SPD over technical issues associated with the ERDF. While the chancellor was on the record supporting the program, leaders like Finance Minister Apel and regional leaders opposed the program. In December 1973, Parliamentary State Secretary Apel had rejected British demands to create a very large ERDF at the Council of Ministers session in December 1973, and he continued to oppose any large-scale ERDF in 1974 and 1975. Later, several Social Democrats in the *Bundestag* went on record with their concerns that the proposed ERDF would really be too much of a burden on the German government.[39]

These challenges to Schmidt's support for the development fund served as catalysts for other problems inside the SPD in 1975. There were serious rifts in the leadership between *Fraktion* leader Herbert Wehner, party leader Brandt, and the chancellor. Throughout the winter months of 1974–1975, Schmidt responded to a series of direct challenges to the stability of his own party and the government. Issues of concern in that period included the upcoming 1976 national election campaign, differences in his party about goals and concerns, and regional election losses.[40] The Social Democrats lost 2 percent of their popular support in the *Landtag* elections in Rheinland-Pfalz on March 9, 1975. And SPD leaders had not forgotten regional losses in the fall 1974 in Niedersachsen, Hessen, and Bayern.[41] Schmidt and others referred to these losses as symptomatic of a rough period for the Social Democrats.[42]

There were also signs of problems between the Social Democrats and the Free Democrats related to the ERDF issue. While Foreign Minister Genscher was on the record supporting the plan, he did not appear to take the lead in promoting the plan inside the government. This loss of leadership actually slowed the progress of the fund idea through the German government and the EC. To some extent, this was a function of division and uncertainty within the Free Democratic Party itself relative to questions of European policy. By early 1975, there were reports of differences between FDP party leader Martin Bangemann and Genscher about how much to support the Social Democratic programs. Differences with the SPD were expressed at an important FDP party conference in Stuttgart in January 1975, where leaders basically argued that the FDP's liberal policy preferences were being overridden by the Social Democrats.[43]

These developments led to numerous press reports in mid-May that there was a cabinet crisis underway. Basically, it was argued, the leadership clout that Schmidt had enjoyed faded away with differences over coalition policy. Quarrels became public in May 1975, when Genscher said in an interview that he was concerned that the FDP "was not the first consideration" of the leadership. The Foreign Minister was concerned by what he interpreted as a loss of credibility in German foreign policy on the ERDF and other questions.[44] Also, many references were made to the consideration that the 1976 election was rapidly approaching. One FDP leader, Werfred Maihofer, went on the record saying that Schmidt's mannerisms in cabinet meetings in the spring of 1975 had spoiled interparty relations.

However, rumors of a cabinet crisis did not correspond to changes in public attitudes. Even though the government faced internal political problems and economic stagnation, public support for the Social Democrats increased strongly in the period leading up to the March 1975 decision on the ERDF. According to *Institut für Demoskopie* surveys, the SPD gained about 7 percent in the polls between March 1974 and March 1975.[45] Records suggest that Schmidt ultimately interpreted popular support as policy-making latitude on the ERDF question.[46] An FDP leader summed up the situation well in May 1975 when he said that "everyone feels a new [political] wind . . . but no one can tell what direction it is coming from. . . . Perhaps there is just no definitive direction for the wind." Political cross-pressures existed at all levels of the government, which ultimately affected the government decision on the ERDF.[47] Figure 2.1 summarizes political conditions in Germany relative to the ERDF.

Germany Moves Away from the ERDF

Chancellor Schmidt held several conferences with key government leaders in the early months of 1975 to encourage better foreign and domestic policy coordination. Schmidt was aware of problems with

Conditions	Case Study Analysis Questions	Coding
Major Party Unity	A. Few Different Statements B. Few Different Positions C. Serious Disputes	Dissensus
Coalition Consensus	A. Few Different Statements B. Few Different Positions C. Very Serious Disputes	Dissensus
Symmetry of Effects	A. Symmetrical B. Some Public Impact C. Some Sectors	Symmetrical
Election Results	A. Highly Influenced by Elections B. Results Have Negative Impact C. Elections Offer No Support	Highly Influential
Popular Support	A. Yes, Upcoming Elections B. Very Positive Polls C. Polls Offer Intense Support	Strong Support

Figure 2.1 Summary of domestic political conditions in the ERDF case.

the coordination of European policy, and he sought to streamline the policy-making process to prepare for the fall opening of a new government session. These meetings also led to discussions of the ERDF, and leaders raised concerns about waning support in the polity.

A special cabinet meeting was held on March 24, 1975, in which members of the elite decision authority worked to formalize a German position on the ERDF program.[48] During the meeting, FDP leaders reportedly made open challenges to the SPD on differences of opinion with regard to government social, agricultural, and spending policies. One report of the meeting indicated that Economics Minister Lambsdorff, Agricultural Minister Ertls, Finance Minister Apel, and Foreign Minister Genscher debated the German stance on a number of key economic issues.[49]

Cabinet leaders decided at this meeting not to support any EC efforts to establish the ERDF in the short term. The primary consideration behind this decision was leaders' concerns about the long-running debate with the EC about the proposed size of the fund.[50] Any government support for the ERDF would be only for a loose, unstructured program with an indefinite commitment of resources. Schmidt, Genscher, and Economics Minister Lambsdorff appeared to hold out the hope that other European leaders would publicly fight the creation of the fund as well. Schmidt subsequently described the ERDF as "merely a mechanism for redistributing finance clothed in a pair of bathing trunks with regional policy painted on them."[51]

Aftermath of the Decision

German leaders' hopes that friends would join in their crusade against ERDF in the spring 1975 were quickly dashed. The cabinet decision was subsequently challenged by many European leaders, including French President d'Estaing. He called on Community members to hold a special meeting in Paris in June 1975 to discuss progress on economic union, to resolve ongoing problems in the Community, and to attempt to rebuild support for an ERDF program. At the Paris meeting, German leaders declared their opposition to the ERDF in its present form, forcing British and French leaders to lobby hard for the Germans to reconsider. Primarily, the British and French leaders argued that the program was essential for any consideration of monetary union and that it would benefit less-developed German regions.[52]

Away from their constituencies, Chancellor Schmidt and other German leaders were convinced that they could turn the positive elements of the ERDF into political capital to gain support for a European Monetary System. In turn, Schmidt got French and British support for future plans for monetary coordination. German leaders finally agreed on a compromise plan whereby they would not disagree with the formalization of plans for the ERDF in the future and they would have a veto right over any ERDF expenditures through the annual EC budget.[53] Ironically, by 1988 the same development fund that had barely gotten off the ground in the 1970s was viewed as so successful that European leaders voted unanimously to double its size over a five-year period.

COOPERATION: THE EUROPEAN MONETARY SYSTEM

European leaders began to consider plans for a common monetary system in the 1960s. After years of debate over a blueprint for the system, German Chancellor Helmut Schmidt actively promoted the creation of a European Monetary Union (EMU) in 1978, with the goal of coordinating community-wide currency exchange, fiscal policies, and monetary policies to pave the way for full economic integration.[54] Specifically, the plan would modify the existing "snake in the tunnel" arrangement for setting the value of European currencies in order to encourage a free flow of capital, goods, services, and labor across borders. By the end of 1978, EC leaders had agreed to a compromise European Monetary System (EMS), which consisted of four main elements: 1) a "basket" of currency that would determine the value of the new European Currency Unit (ECU); 2) an exchange-rate mechanism; 3) credit provisions among the participating central banks; and 4) a pooling of reserve assets among the members.[55]

The EMS agreement has been heralded by some scholars as the "first major act of German leadership in the history of the European Community." In fact, Chancellor Schmidt's vocal support for a monetary union plan at a series of summit meetings in 1978—in Copenhagen in April, the Group of Seven (G-7) summit in July, and the Luxembourg European Council summit in December 1978—created real momentum for the establishment of the program in the EC. He touted the EMS repeatedly as a system of "fixed but adjustable exchange rates" and as a way "to promote exchange rate stability, trade, economic coordination, and Community growth."[56]

At the same time, Schmidt's leadership efforts on EMS were bolstered by a climate of domestic political support for government policies in Germany. The chancellor was described in this period as an "astute tactician, a self-confident technician, and an electorally secure politician" who seized an important opportunity at the right time. In the following sections, the history of efforts to create a monetary union and the domestic political wrangling behind German foreign policy in 1978 and 1979 are examined.[57]

Elite Decision Authority

The elite decision authority responsible for the decision to support the EMS included many of the same leaders who were involved in the ERDF decision: Chancellor Schmidt (SPD), Foreign Minister Hans-Dietrich Genscher (FDP), Economics Minister Otto Graf Lambsdorff (FDP), Finance Minister Hans Apel (SPD), and his successor Hans Matthöfer, who took over the post in February 1978. Once again, economic policy factions in the major party in government were represented by the moderates who favored some cooperation with EC programs, including Chancellor Schmidt, Justice Minister Hans-Jochen Vogel, and parliamentary representative Horst Ehmke; and conservatives including Finance Ministers Apel and Matthöfer, who resisted most major contributions to the EC on the grounds that they were too costly.

Historical Background of the European Monetary System

When the EC was formally established, leaders were interested in promoting long-term cooperation and regional stability. The founders began their work by addressing problems with the free movement of capital, goods, services, and the labor force. By the late 1960s, many trade and tariff barriers in Europe had been removed and experts began to focus more attention on the connection between monetary cooperation and trade. Some argued that in order for the Community to substantially improve its economic conditions, a free flow of goods must be accompanied by a standardized monetary and currency coordination program. They drew legitimacy for this effort directly from the Treaty of Rome, which prescribed the establishment of a stable exchange rate and called for the coordination of monetary policy.[58]

European leaders took the first important step toward the development of a common monetary system at the Hague summit in 1969, where they formally recognized that economic growth in Europe had been slowed by problems with the mix of currencies and exchange rate instability.[59] They issued a communiqûe in support of the creation of a European monetary system and assigned Luxembourg's Prime Minister Werner to chair a new, high-level group on monetary union.

Debates in the Werner Group (as it became known) in 1970 were dominated by two different groups with distinct views on monetary union. On one side, the "economists" like German Economics Minister Schiller argued that policy coordination was necessary and that a "convergence of the inflation rates of other countries to their own" was likely.[60] On the other side, "monetarists" included representatives of Luxembourg and France, who argued that exchange rates should be stabilized and there should be an effort to strengthen the monetary personality of the EC in international negotiations. Specifically, these groups were divided over what the transition from the existing system to a future one would look like, and they debated "whether the Community would move towards the irrevocable fixity of parities and the elimination of margins of fluctuation before the system of economic policy coordination had proved its effectiveness."[61]

Economists and monetarists were eventually able to reach a compromise in the Werner Group.[62] It submitted a final report in October 1970, which called for a complete coordination of monetary policy in three stages over the next ten years. The plan called for the Community to create a central monetary policy control organization that would also align exchange rates. Subsequent efforts to institutionalize the programs advocated by the Werner Group included the Smithsonian agreement of December 1971. Economics ministers announced a community-wide attempt to stabilize economic and fiscal conditions by creating a "snake in the tunnel" system to provide narrow margins of fluctuation from a standard currency (the U.S. dollar), to be implemented in March 1972.

Unfortunately, the Smithsonian snake system failed to control wide fluctuations in currency exchange rates.[63] Government leaders in Britain, Luxembourg, and Denmark announced in July 1972 that they would take control of their currency exchange rates out of the tunnel program.[64] Even after promising to remain in the snake system at the October 1972 Paris summit, the Italian and

French governments left the snake program, and the remaining members agreed to float against the *Deutschmark* as in the past. From 1972 to 1978, critics characterized the snake as "little more than a *Deutschmark* zone"—a small consortium of the Benelux countries, Denmark, and Germany.[65] The small countries participated because of the importance of stable exchange rates for their open economies and the relative weight of their trade relations with Germany, but the system as a whole took on a very asymmetric quality. This actually benefited German economic interests, and most banking, business, and agricultural leaders in Germany were quietly satisfied with the system. The snake contributed toward a relative undervaluation of the *Mark*, while at the same time it did not impose any additional constraints in the conduct of the German monetary policy.[66]

By the mid-1970s, it became clear to many Community leaders that the first real attempt to develop a European monetary policy coordination system had failed. Fewer leaders of EC member states spoke publicly in support of the snake, and the larger goal of developing an EMU seemed to fade away. According to one critic, the EMU concept thereby "became the biggest non-event of the 1970s."[67]

Changing the Status Quo

Despite earlier efforts, real momentum for a change in this arrangement only began to build in late 1977 as the result of several well-timed developments. First, the new European Commission President, Roy Jenkins, became so frustrated by economic stagnation in his first six months in office that he began to pressure governments to consider a "relaunching of monetary integration." Jenkins believed that monetary policy coordination represented the most viable possibility for enhanced European cooperation in the short term, and he was willing to fight for progress in the Community. Second, European leaders also began to consider a "second enlargement" of the Community at this time, with the governments of Spain and Portugal seeking membership. Enlargement would entail institutional change and general reorientation for the EC, and this was seen as a prime opportunity for those who favored an EMS package to push it through. Expected disparities in currency value and general economic performance compelled many leaders in the Community to reconsider the EMS.[68]

Perhaps the most important factor on the road to the establishment of the EMS was leadership. In early 1978, the concept drew the attention and support of two key leaders in the Community, Chancellor Schmidt and French President d'Estaing. In Schmidt's memoirs, he provided some insight about his motivation for supporting the EMS at the time. On a personal level, Schmidt was influenced by Roy Jenkins' leadership, and he was inspired by reading the memoirs of Jean Monnet in late 1977. At a government level, Hans Matthöfer became the new finance minister in February 1978 and openly supported EC monetary policy reform. At the regional level, Schmidt saw that the snake system benefited his own economy and wanted more for the Community. Schmidt said later that the EMS system was all about "overcoming a preoccupation with national authority."[69] Finally, the chancellor turned his attention to the EC "because of the disorders that had emerged in the Atlantic Community [relative to intermediate-range nuclear weapons and European security] and the threat that these disorders represented to Germany."[70]

D'Estaing proved to be the best kind of French leader, according to Schmidt, because the pursuit of the EMS was not directed at undermining the U.S. role in Europe so much as bolstering the European situation. The two leaders often conferred in preparation for major international summits, and they exchanged views on ideas about leadership and policy innovation. Schmidt and d'Estaing agreed on strategies for the promotion of the EMS plan by coordinating their efforts in light of the difficult domestic political obstacles that they would have to overcome if the system was to work efficiently. Ultimately, their discussions of strategies would prove to be pivotal in overcoming the very sectorized decision-making process on Europe policy in Germany.[71]

However, Chancellor Schmidt kept his decision to support EMS secret from all but his closest advisers for a few months because of concerns that the *Bundesbank* and other actors might try to derail the plan before it really gained momentum. Schmidt was very aware of opposition to monetary policy coordination from the *Bundesbank* and many German financial experts, who had already suggested that it would mean a "loss of sovereignty" through a transfer of control to supranational authority.[72] He believed, however, that he could eventually gain confirmation for the plan from these and other domestic political actors based on concerns about unemployment, slow economic growth, and the high currency exchange rate for the *Deutschmark*. He also knew that small- and medium-sized businesses in Germany would support a fixed exchange rate system that would promote European business collaboration.

Finally, Schmidt perceived external pressure from American officials to exert some economic power to promote the EC economic recovery from the years of recession in the mid-1970s. Schmidt and his finance minister Matthöfer were concerned that the United States might reinflate its currency on the world market and wreak havoc on EC currencies if they did not do something. A common monetary system seemed in order because they were concerned that it appeared that the *mark* might be considered an international reserve currency, which would have an effect on the latitude of the German polity and economy.[73]

Formulation of a European Monetary System, 1978

In January 1978, Chancellor Schmidt announced that the next summit of the G-7 leaders would meet in Bonn. But preparations for the conference illuminated a growing tension between the German and American vision of the proper response to the global economic downturn. In February, U.S. Treasury Secretary Blumenthal came to Bonn to appeal to the German government to work to stimulate Western economies and threatened that President Carter might skip the Bonn summit unless the Germans would provide an economic stimulus to pull the West out of an economic recession. Schmidt and other German leaders rebutted that the Germans should not be seen as the economic locomotive for Europe. German-American relations thus worsened during the first few months of 1978.[74]

Political and economic conditions did seem ripe in early 1978 for Schmidt and the German government to consider changes in economic and monetary policy that might stimulate European economic growth. Disagreements with the United States seemed to convince Chancellor Schmidt to go public with his support for the EMS, and he recognized that it would be important for him to take on a leadership role in the EC in order to get the program established. According to some analysts, Schmidt became convinced of "the merits of the EMS only when the U.S. seemed incapable of action."[75]

Schmidt informed Commission President Jenkins of his interest in leading the charge on EMS at a meeting in Bonn on February 28, 1978, and he told French President d'Estaing soon thereafter. Schmidt and d'Estaing had developed a very close personal relationship, and they soon began plotting a strategy for the implementation of the EMS in the spring months. The strategy was subsequently endorsed and developed in discussions with the French president at Rambouillet on April 2, 1978, and created an entirely new political situation. One scholar notes that "from then on, the question was not whether there would be a new European monetary system but what form it would take and when it could come into existence."[76]

At the level of Community relations, Schmidt's most serious challenge was how to convince other large economies especially Britain, to join a new monetary policy system. The British Labor Government wanted to avoid any deflationary pressures in this period, and any new exchange rate mechanism would produce such pressures. Further, Britain had had a traumatic experience with earlier attempts under the Bretton Woods system to keep fixed the exchange rate of the pound sterling.

Presentation of the EMS Plan

Helmut Schmidt and Giscard d'Estaing formally introduced the EMS plan at a European Council meeting in Copenhagen on April 7–8, 1978. Their proposal was that the EMS be founded on many of the same principles of the existing snake, but structured so as to encourage a freer flow of capital, goods, services, and labor across boundaries. The system would consist of four main elements: 1) the creation of a European Currency Unit (the ECU); 2) an exchange-rate mechanism; 3) credit provisions among the participating central banks; and 4) a pooling of reserve assets among the members.[77]

One important new creation of the system was the ECU, consisting of fixed amounts of each EC currency, including those not participating in the exchange rate mechanism. ECUs were to be the official reserve asset and the official common means of currency and exchange. Schmidt argued that the Community should create a "zone of monetary stability in Europe" that would allow for a "convergence of economic development." The EMS would also involve regulation and careful control of monetary policy with the *Deutschmark* as a standard for establishing future exchange rates.[78]

The substance of the EMS proposal was important, but so was the style of its presentation in this case. Schmidt first presented the proposal in a very informal setting during an after-dinner Council discussion. This forum was chosen by Schmidt for two reasons. First, representatives of the German Finance Ministry, the *Bundesbank*, and the Economics Ministry (routine participants in formal Council sessions) would *not* be present at the dinner. In other words, Schmidt consciously chose to bypass these leaders in his bid to get Community support for the EMS plan. Second, Schmidt had a deep-seated commitment to high-level resolution of problems and saw the EC policy development bureaucracy as much too slow and cumbersome.

Schmidt and d'Estaing proposed the establishment of a panel of three economic experts to deal with this important issue—giving careful consideration to the EMS initiative and reporting directly back to the leaders of the European Council. Schmidt's nominee for the panel was the chief economic adviser in the chancellor's office who operated independently from the executive agencies that formally held the responsibility for economic and monetary policy. The *Bundesbank*, Finance, and Economics Ministries could only then react to EMS proposals and their impact on the German polity.[79]

Coming Home from Copenhagen

Germany took over the rotational presidency of the European Political Cooperation council in July, and Schmidt and Finance Minister Matthöfer announced that they were ready to adjust the German growth rate in return for progress on trade and monetary policy issues.[80] In addition, Economics Minister Lambsdorff (FDP) appeared to have concluded that as U.S. pressure mounted and the domestic political climate shifted in 1978, he could not "fight the tide [and] should turn it to his advantage."[81] Thus, Lambsdorff, Matthöfer, Schmidt, and other leaders agreed to forge ahead on EMS.

Chancellor Schmidt also sought to nip domestic political opposition to EMS in the bud by holding a series of special meetings with those groups in Germany who might oppose the plan. On July 5, 1978, the chancellor held a four-hour meeting with a group of about 20 industry, finance, and trade union leaders and was able to convince them to support the plan.[82] Schmidt called a special cabinet meeting in Bonn a week later to air differences on the EMS proposal and invited *Bundesbank* President Emminger to voice concerns. Emminger argued that the EMS would mean a return to a Bretton Woods–type fixed exchange rate system and that Germany might lose control over monetary and economic policy. In turn, Chancellor Schmidt assured Emminger that Schmidt would not support any EMS program that would lead to a loss of sovereignty.[83]

The only opponents to the plan that Schmidt was not able to quiet were opposition Union party leaders, including Franz Joseph Strauss, who called on the *Bundesbank* and the economics minister to block the EMS plan and warned of dire consequences if it was not stopped.

Having overcome serious domestic political opposition, the German government encouraged the Community to move ahead on monetary policy alignment.[84] A European Council meeting was held in Bremen in early July to discuss EMS proposals. There, Commission President Jenkins joined forces with Schmidt and d'Estaing to win a new endorsement of the EMS by EC leaders. British leaders, however, remained concerned that the EMS might reduce prospects for Community growth in exchange for German economic dominance. In the end, minor concessions garnered British support for EMS in the unanimous vote taken at that meeting.

Schmidt and d'Estaing continued their fight for EMS at the Bonn G-7 summit in mid-July. They argued that the system would make Europe a strong "zone of stability in the world." But President Carter and Japanese officials expressed some concern about the European monetary system idea and its implications for wider G-7 relations. One analyst who witnessed summit proceedings said that Japanese and American representatives ("with quiet encouragement from British Prime Minister Callaghan") closely questioned proponents about the details of the EMS.[85] Monetary policy issues ultimately took a backseat to other concerns at the summit, and the final communiqúe simply stated that "We are united for the implementation of a strategy for growth, industry and inflation."[86]

The Commission Finalizes the EMS

Support for a monetary system increased throughout Europe as 1978 wore on, and President Jenkins tasked the European Commission to draw up a detailed monetary system in consort with government officials from member states. These officials developed an EMS structure that would provide for day-to-day and long-term monetary stability. They agreed to create a common reserve fund to provide for market intervention, and each member state would be required to allocate 20 percent of its reserves to a central reserve pool. The ECU would act as a reserve asset and a means of settlement; and in the Exchange Rate Mechanism of the EMS, it would offer fixed, though adjustable, bands of exchange for participating currencies."[87] Thus, the system was designed to be more flexible than the old snake plan, and was oriented around the creation of the ECU, which would be established based on a standardized basket of national currencies from member states in the system. The new program also recognized that some countries would be relatively less able to support shortfalls in currency levels, and therefore a system for providing short-term loans within the context of the EMS would be established.

Many intergovernmental consultations were held on the proposed system as it was being finalized. By late 1978, the leaders of Germany, France, Luxembourg, the Netherlands, Belgium, and Denmark had all indicated their support for the proposed EMS to commission President Jenkins. The leaders of Italy and Ireland indicated that although they had "some reservations," they would support the program. British leaders argued that they could not support the EMS and would not participate in the program. Nevertheless, the *Pound* was included in the basket of currencies from which the value of the ECU would be established.[88]

Post-Commitment Political Conditions

Chancellor Schmidt clearly gambled in early 1978 when he took the lead on EMS. This began to pay off, however, as the EMS gained support in the German domestic political arena. Schmidt successfully convinced many German leaders, the *Bundesbank*, and the public that the new system was the key to long-term economic stability.

At the cabinet level, Schmidt did not hold consultations with officials, nor did he order a special study of EMS proposals by ministry officials until the summer of 1978. This meant that at the level of intraparty politics, Schmidt did not promote open debate about the initiative. Finance Minister Matthöfer provided needed support for the plan, but other Finance Ministry officials held onto reservations about the arrangement. These reservations were primarily focused on concerns about the budget, structure, and control to be vested in the new EMS.

Chancellor Schmidt experienced some resistance on EMS from leaders in the junior party in the months leading up to a final government decision. Foreign Minister Genscher tacitly supported the monetary system, but Schmidt had more trouble garnering support from Economics Minister Lambsdorff in this period. Press reports support the argument that Lambsdorff and Genscher differed on this plan. Lambsdorff and other Economics Ministry (predominately

FDP) officials opposed any radical restructuring of the existing European monetary system.[89] When the chancellor tried to garner FDP support for all aspects of the EMS plan in the summer 1978, the leadership stalled to see how much popular support there was for the plan before committing to it.[90] In dealing with the ministry, Schmidt worked carefully to avoid the scrutiny of those agencies and officials tasked to focus on Germany's Europe policy. Thus, Schmidt dedicated himself to pushing the EMS through the German government without the benefit of established support in the *Referat* or other agencies of the Economics Ministry.

The *Bundesbank* was also an important actor in the process, and bank president Emminger expressed concerns about the system in early 1978.[91] Even though Schmidt garnered the support of Emminger through a series of contacts in the summer, some bank officials continued to fight against the plan. They focused on reviewing and critiquing the technical aspects of the arrangement and released reports in 1978 indicating their concern that the EMS was "structurally flawed" and that the German government would likely end up bearing the burden of the new arrangement. *Bundesbank* leaders were particularly concerned about the creation of the European Monetary Fund as the central European institution to provide short-term loans to countries experiencing capital shortfalls in the currency arrangement. The Fund threatened the legal autonomy of the *Bundesbank,* and it was, therefore, one of the main subjects of criticism.[92] Bank officials were concerned that without British participation in the EMS arrangement the program would ultimately revert back to the existing minisnake.

Chancellor Schmidt did allow small changes to the proposed EMS program as a response to criticisms from the *Bundesbank*. The bank proposed a technical change in the program that would allow all participants in the arrangement to withdraw their currencies in case of severe crisis, and Schmidt reluctantly agreed to such a provision in October. The bank also elicited guarantees from Schmidt and other European leaders that Great Britain would commit itself to future involvement in the EMS. In turn, German banking officials gave their support to the plan. For example, Wilfried Guth, president of the *Deutsche Bank*, spoke out in favor of the EMS as a way to "stand against the loss of a strong dollar base and to provide direction for the international monetary system."[93]

Schmidt was able to garner some support for the EMS from German trade unions like the *Deutsche Gewerkschaftsbund* (DGB).

In 1978 DGB leaders expressed their interest to the press and directly to Schmidt in favor of the creation of an EMS. These interest group leaders gave their support for the system based on several factors: 1) The proposed EMS would allow for smoother flows of goods, capital, and labor across borders; 2) The EMS meant a further cooperative venture between Germany and the European Community, thus enhancing the prospects for coordination and collaboration; and 3) European monetary cooperation meant that there was an increased potential for German exports and strength in the German economy.

Schmidt also enjoyed strong public support for his government policies in this period. Schmidt's image as defender of German national interests and stability received a great boost when he successfully managed a hostage crisis involving a German passenger jet in Mogadishu, Somalia in October 1977.[94] He became even more popular in Germany by manipulating U.S. and European governments on the stimulus initiative question in 1978. By the late summer 1978, the editors of *Der Spiegel* printed a retrospective of Schmidt's career in which they described Schmidt's public image as "dynamic as Napoleon" and being at the "zenith of his political career."[95]

This was reflected in public opinion polls and the SPD's performance in regional elections. The Social Democratic party experienced a steady increase of 5 percent in public support in the period leading up to the October 1978 decision on EMS, according to Allensbach Institute surveys. The SPD also made important gains in regional elections in Hamburg (a 6.5 percent increase in support) and in Bayern (1.2 percent gain).[96] Social Democratic leaders linked these gains to perceptions of policy-making latitude and government stability, leading to an environment conducive to cooperation. Finally, the Hessen *Landtag* elections scheduled for October 1978 became an important testing ground for Schmidt's popularity. The chancellor participated in the campaign and played up the party's responsibility for developing and promoting the EMS arrangement. The election was seen by many analysts as a judgment of the progress of SPD policies, because a Conservative win would have granted a two-thirds majority in the *Bundesrat.* thus limiting the government's room to maneuver. Even though public opinion polls taken shortly before the election suggested that the Conservatives and the Social Democrats were in a dead heat, Hessen's SPD Ministerpresident, Holger Börner, won the election by 0.9 percent.[97] Figure 2.2 summarizes the domestic political conditions in the EMS case.

Conditions	Case Study Analysis Questions	Coding
Major Party Unity	A. No Different Statements B. No Different Positions C. No Disputes	Consensus
Coalition Consensus	A. Few Different Statements B. Few Different Positions C. Serious Disputes	Dissensus
Symmetry of Effects	A. Symmetrical B. Some Impact C. Some Sectors	Symmetrical
Election Results	A. Highly Influenced by Elections B. Results Have Positive Impact C. Elections Offer Support	Influential
Popular Support	A. Yes, Upcoming Elections B. Polls Are Very Positive C. Polls Offer Intense Support	Strong Support

Figure 2.2 Summary of domestic political conditions in the EMS case.

Germany Supports the EMS

Consensus emerged in Europe that the EMS was a European way to soften the blow of regional economic problems, and it would help to ameliorate inflation problems and related currency crises. Most leaders joined the growing wave of support for the EMS program, and they justified their support for the EMS to the opposition based on the necessity to bandwagon or be left behind. French President d'Estaing described the EMS in November as a "useful external constraint on domestic economic policy," which meant that participation was essential. British officials suggested that they would continue to negotiate on participation in the EMS. And in November 1978 President Carter even spoke publicly about the rapid devaluation of the dollar on world markets, implying that the EMS program and related economic stimuli were needed for the sake of U.S. and world economic health.[98]

Buoyed by the Hessen election victory and regional support for the plan, Schmidt met with the French president in Aachen, Germany, to align a final Franco-German position on the EMS. The chancellor returned from Aachen and scheduled a *Fraktion* meeting and a cabinet session to finalize the EMS. This cabinet session was to include representatives from the Economics and Finance Ministries, as well as the *Bundesbank*. In fact, Schmidt made his position on the EMS very clear before the cabinet meeting. In a press statement after his return from Aachen, he said that "we are now ready to bring something into being that will have a great political significance for the whole rest of the century."[99]

The final cabinet debate over the EMS was reportedly not very contentious. Even the *Bundesbank* officials in attendance were comfortable with the plan and the compromises reached to that point. The cabinet decided to support an EMS initiative inside the German government and to pursue the plan in the EC. Schmidt was able to gain the support of all members of the elite decision authority for the plan. In turn, Schmidt prepared to finalize the EMS at the upcoming December European Council meeting.[100]

From Formal Decision to Implementation

Unfortunately, developments at the European Council meeting did not go as most European leaders had planned. Several contentious issues emerged that stymied progress on the EMS, including balance of trade disparities in the Community and a flap between France and Germany over an exchange rate system for agricultural prices. The German government was unwilling to completely give up the Monetary Compensatory Amounts (MCA) system, and other leaders wanted to tie MCA reform to any type of larger monetary policy reforms. Subsequently, several state representatives actually vetoed the possibility that there could be an inauguration of the EMS at the December meeting, arguing that without a solution to the MCA dispute, the EMS could not be established by January 1, 1979.[101]

After a series of back-channel negotiations, a "gentlemen's agreement" was reached at a Council of Agricultural Ministers meeting on March 6, 1979 that paved the way for a final vote on the EMS. EC leaders voted to establish the EMS in May 1979, and the first phase of the plan was set to go into effect on January 1, 1980. The achievement of the EMS can, at least partly, be attributed to the leadership ability of Chancellor Schmidt in overcoming the skepticism and opposition of German financial establishment in West Germany. Schmidt was in an unusually strong situation because he was knowledgeable about the facts and figures of the EMS, he had support for the plan from key

European leaders, and he was an electorally secure politician in late 1978. Clearly, the EMS represented an important achievement on the road to European economic integration.

NOTES

1. See David Keeble, P. Owens, and C. Thomson, *Centrality, Peripherality and EEC Regional Development: The Influence of Peripheral and Cental Locations on the Relative Development of Regions,* 1982.
2. Jacques Van Ypersele and Jean-Claude Koeune, *The European Monetary System*. Brussels: Commission of the EC, European Perspectives Series, 1984, p. 31; See also Simon Bulmer and William Paterson, *The Federal Republic of Germany and the European Community,* 1987, p. 130.
3. See Simon Bulmer, *The Domestic Structure of European Policy-Making in West Germany,* 1987; Also see Bulmer and Paterson, "The Federal Republic of Germany," in J. Lodge, ed., *Direct Elections to the European Parliament* 1984, 1986.
4. H. W. Armstrong and J. Taylor, *Regional Economic Policy and Its Analysis,* 1978, p. 221.
5. Geoffrey Denton, "Regional Divergence and Policy in the Community, with Special Reference to Enlargement," chapter 7 in Mark Hodges and W. Wallace, eds., *Economic Divergence in the European Community,* 1981, p. 14; See also *Der Spiegel,* no. 46, 1975.
6. Armstrong and Taylor, 1978, p. 193.
7. D. W. Parsons, "Notes on the Regional Development Fund," *The Political Quarterly,* vol. 48, no. 2, April–June 1977, p. 178.
8. Introductory Notes to Hague Summit Proceedings, *Europa Archiv: Zeitschrift für Internationale Politik: Beitrage und Berichte,* 1972, Deutsche Gesellschaft für Auswärtige Politik.
9. Parsons, April–June 1977, p. 181.
10. Commission of the European Communities, 1973, OJ C86 and OJ C106.
11. See Stephen George, "Regional Policy," in J. Lodge, ed., *Institutions and Policies of the European Community,* 1983, p. 203; See also Commission of the European Communities, 1973, Reports, OJ C86 and OJ C106.
12. Wayne Sandholtz and John Zysman, "1992: Recasting the European Bargain," *World Politics,* vol. 42, October 1989.
13. See *Jahrbuch der Europäischen Integration 1972,* Brussels, 1973.
14. "Deutsche Initiative für Massnahmen zur Verwirklichung einer Europäischen Sozial- und Gesellschaftspolitik," from *Bulletin,* October 20, 1972, p. 16.
15. Bulmer and Paterson, 1987, p. 216.
16. *Der Spiegel,* no.7, 1973, pp. 41–44.
17. Commission of the European Communities, 1973, OJ C86 and OJ C106.
18. Commision Report of the European Communities, *Report on the Regional Problems of the Enlarge Community,* COM (73) 550 (The Thomson Report), Brussels: European Communities, 1973.
19. Paul Lützeler, *Western Europe in Transition: West Germany's Role in the European Community,* 1986, p. 158; See also *Journal of Common Market Studies,* 1975.

20. See The Thomson Report, 1973.
21. Lützeler, 1982, p. 191.
22. *Bundespresse-Agentur,* Press Release, Bonn, September 27, 1973.
23. *Bundespresse-Agentur,* Press Release, Bonn, November 15, 1973.
24. *Bundespresse-Agentur,* Press Release, December 19, 1973.
25. See *First Annual Report on the Regional Development Fund,* 1975, Com (76) 307, June 1976, p. 10
26. D. W. Parsons, April–June 1977, p. 179.
27. *Bundespresse-Agentur,* Bulletin, November 15, 1973.
28. Apel also said about the plan, "Nor do I offer my wife money to be faithful"—a reference to the link between ERDF and continued EC membership; See Transcript from *Taggeschau,* BPA Press Release, December 18, 1973; BPA Press Release, December 19, 1973.
29. *Die Zeit,* May 17, 1974, p. 4.
30. See government policy declarations, May–June 1974, from *Europa Archiv: Zeitschrift für Internationale Politik: Beitrage und Berichte,* 1974, Deutsche Gesellschaft für Auswärtige Politik.
31. Other changes represented in the British government's call for a renegotiation of the Treaty of Rome relative to the U.K.'s legal obligations within the community. Thinly veiled threats on the part of the British government in this period to consider withdrawing its membership from an organization created a groundswell of support for an EC summit to address these issues. However, states like Italy and Ireland argued that they would be involved in the 1974 Paris summit, but only if there was prior commitment by member states to the establishment of a European Development Fund; See Commission of the European Communities (1975), "European Regional Development Fund," First Annual Report, Bulletin of the European Economic Communities, supplement 7/76, Brussels.
32. Lützeler, 1982, p. 195.
33. The European Community released a European Regional Development Fund Inaugural Report in 1975 that stated: "the underlying gap between the richer and the poorer regions remains as intractable as ever." Commission of the European Communities, Brussels, 1975, p. 5.
34. *Bundespresse-Agentur,* Press Release, Bonn, November 15, 1973.
35. See Armstrong and Taylor, *Regional Economic Policy and Its Analysis,* 1978.
36. Bulmer and Paterson, 1987, p. 208.
37. Lützeler, 1982, p.209.
38. Ibid, 1982, p. 208; See also D. Keeble, P. Owens, and C. Thomson, 1982, p. 62.
39. Commission of the European Communities, Brussels, 1975.
40. *Der Spiegel,* "Ich haben mein Leben lang ungern gepfuscht," 1975, no. 44, p. 61.
41. Data drawn from Suzanne S. Schüttmeyer, "Die Ergebnisse der Landtagswahlen 1946–1990," *Zeitschrift für Parlamentsfragen,* vol. 21, no. 3, October 1990, pp. 464–472.
42. Schüttmeyer, October 1990, p. 470.
43. *Der Spiegel,* "Freidemokraten: Zeichen von Resignation," 1975, no. 3, p. 19.
44. *Der Spiegel,* "Koalition: Spass vorbei," 1975, no. 22, p. 24.
45. Elisabeth Noelle-Neumann, *The Germans: Public Opinion Polls, 1967–1980,* 1981, pp. 214–215.

46. Schüttmeyer, October 1990, p. 470.
47. *Der Spiegel,* "Tendenzwende: Jeder fühlt den neuen Wind," 1975, no. 2, p. 31.
48. Author's Interview, Hans-Dietrich Genscher, April 29, 1993.
49. *Der Spiegel,* "Hosen Runter, Steuern Rauf," 1975, no. 32, pp. 28–34.
50. Author's Interview, Hans-Dietrich Genscher, April 29, 1993.
51. See Commission of the European Communities, "European Regional Development Fund," *First Annual Report, Bulletin of the European Economic Communities,* supplement 7/76, Brussels, 1975.
52. *Der Spiegel,* "Konjunktur: Hoch kommt vor der Wahl," December 12, 1975, no. 49, p. 31.
53. Commission of the European Communities, The Regions of Europe, COM (80) 816, Brussels, 1980; See also Neill Nugent, *The Government and Politics of the European Community,* 1991, p. 36.
54. Werner Weidenfeld, "Basic Questions of European Integration Seen from a German Point of View," chapter from Paul Michael Lützeler, *Western Europe in Transition: West Germany's Role in the European Community,* 1986.
55. *Jahrbuch der Europäischen Integration 1979,* Bonn 1980, chapter 2.
56. See "Resolution of the European Council of 5 December 1978 on the Establishment of the European Monetary System and Related Matters," Brussels: European Commission, 1978, pp. 303–308.
57. Van Ypersele and Koeune, 1984, pp. 40–71.
58. Loukas Tsoukalis, *The Politics and Economics of European Monetary Integration,* 1977, p. 92 and 264; See also Michele Fratianni and Jürgen von Hagen, *The European Monetary System and European Monetary Union,* 1992, p. 8.
59. Stephen George, *Politics and Policy in the European Community,* 1991, pp. 20–116; See also Andrew Shonfield, *International Economic Relations of the Western World,* 1959–1971, 1976.
60. The Hague communiqúe also addressed a fledgling program idea in the community—the creation of a regional development fund to help improve potential future markets and to create a level playing field; See also Michele Fratianni and Theo Peeters, eds., *One Money for Europe,* 1978.
61. Shonfield, 1976, p. 154.
62. Unfortunately, other factors had evolved in this period that confounded some of the efforts of the Werner Group. In particular, a devaluation of the French *Franc* coupled with a revaluation of the *Deutschmark* caused some concerns among German leaders about the real implications of the EMS. Other ideas were floated by the Werner Group that would have had an impact on the German government, including an idea to provide subsidies for countries that might be hurt by monetary policy coordination efforts; Werner Weidenfeld, in Lützeler, *Western Europe in Transition: West Germany's Role in the European Community,* 1986; See also Nugent, 1991, p. 70.
63. D. C. Kruse, *Monetary Integration in Western Europe: EMU, EMS and Beyond,* 1980, pp. 59–64.
64. Kruse, 1980, pp. 79–84; See also Francesco Giavazzi, Stefano Micossi, and Marcus Miller, eds., *The European Monetary System,* Cambridge, 1988.
65. Ludlow, 1982, p. 81.
66. Tsoukalis, 1977, p. 50.

67. Peter Ludlow, *The Making of the European Monetary System,* 1982, pp. 136–148.
68. Tsoukalis, 1991, p. 74; Arguments based on a review of OECD, *Main Economic Indicators,* Paris; *OECD Economics Surveys: Germany, 1977.*
69. Schmidt, *Menschen und Mächte,* 1987, p. 168.
70. Heinz Stadlmann, *Frankfurter Allgemeine Zeitung,* October 14, 1978, p. 1.
71. "Wehner: Das Ende ist nähe," *Der Spiegel,* March 7, 1978, no. 10, p. 21.
72. Schmidt, *Menschen und Mächte,* 1987, p. 168.
73. Peter Katzenstein, "The Third West German Republic: Continuity in Change," *Journal of International Affairs,* vol. 41, no. 2.
74. Robert D. Putnam and Nicholas Bayne, *Hanging Together: The Seven-Power Summits,* 1987, p. 73.
75. Ibid., 1987, p. 82.
76. *Der Spiegel,* "Vielleicht eine Chance," November 6, 1978, no. 45, p. 24; See also A. M. El-Agraa, *The Economics of the European Community,* 1990, chapter 3.
77. *Jahrbuch der Europäischen Integration 1979,* Bonn 1980, chapter 2.
78. Giavazzi and Pagano, *European Economic Review,* no. 32, 1988.
79. *Der Spiegel,* May 4, 1978, no. 16, p. 27.
80. Jocelyn Statler, "The European Monetary System: From Conception to Birth," *International Affairs,* vol. 55, no. 2, April 1979, p. 206.
81. Economics Minister Lambsdorff publicly signaled his conversion supporting tax cuts, in a June statement made during a visit to Washington. Hearing reports of this, Schmidt smiled triumphantly at one senior aide—apparently indicating a position favored by Schmidt for some time; Derived from "Konjunktur: Ein bißchen mehr Inflation?" *Der Spiegel,* September 14, 1978, no. 30, pp. 26–32 [author's translation].
82. *Frankfurter Allgemeine Zeitung,* June 26, 1978, p. 3.
83. *Frankfurter Allgemeine Zeitung,* July 13, 1978, p. 2.
84. *Bulletin der Europäische Gemeinschaften,* Supplement 3/79, Brussels: EC Information Office, p. 153.
85. Putnam and Bayne, 1987, p. 94.
86. *Der Spiegel,* "Konjunktur: Ein bißchen mehr Inflation?" September 14, 1978, no. 30, p. 29.
87. Nugent, 1991, p. 255.
88. George, 1991, p. 168.
89. Bulmer and Paterson, 1987, p. 34.
90. *Der Spiegel,* "Vielleicht eine Chance," November 4, 1978, no. 45, p. 27.
91. The federal bank retained authority in matters related to control of the money supply and general currency exchange. Constitutionally, the bank stood as an autonomous structure because of problems with control of monetary policy from the Weimar years; See Kirchner and Schwaiger, *The Role of Interest Groups in the European Community,* 1981.
92. George, 1991, p. 87.
93. *Der Spiegel,* "Vielleicht eine Chance," November 11, 1978, no. 45, p. 26; See also Werner Weidenfeld, "Basic Questions of European Integration Seen from a German Point of View," from Paul Michael Lützeler, *Western Europe in Transition: West Germany's Role in the European Community,* 1986.
94. Fratianni and von Hagen, 1992, p. 28.

95. "Kanzler Schmidt: Dynamisch wie Napoleon," *Der Spiegel,* August 28, 1978, no. 32, p. 19.
96. Elisabeth Noelle-Neumann, *The Germans: Public Opinion Polls, 1967–1980,* 1981, pp. 214–215; See also Infratest, Marplan, Wildenmann, Allensbach, and INFAS poll results—which all found that the CDU or the SPD had about 45 percent of the support; Reported in *Der Spiegel,* September 26, 1978, no. 40, p. 63; INFAS asks a feeling thermometer, and Schmidt had grown from June 1976 to August 1978 from 45 percent to 58 percent popularity approval rating.
97. "Hessen-Wahl: Es ist unser Kopf, der wackelt," *Der Spiegel,* September 11, 1978, no. 40, p. 71.
98. "Dollarsturz: Züge einer griechischen Tragödie," *Der Spiegel,* October, 24, 1978, no. 44, p. 140; See also Wayne Sandholtz and John Zysman, "1992: Recasting the European Bargain," *World Politics,* 42, October 1989.
99. *Der Spiegel,* "Helmut Schmidt: Zurück zu Europa," September 7, 1978, no. 39, p. 21.
100. Ludlow, 1982, p. 194.
101. Monetary policy aspects of revision in MCAs can be seen in Deutsche Bundesbank, *Kosten und Nutzen der deutschen EG-Mitgliedshaft,* Bonn, 1982.

3 GERMANY AND NATO, 1979–1982

COOPERATION: THE NATO DUAL TRACK PLAN

NATO leaders formulated plans to modernize intermediate-range nuclear forces (INF) in Western Europe in the late 1970s in response to the changing international security environment. Alliance members voted unanimously on the "Dual Track" plan in December 1979, which called for the following: 1) negotiations between U.S. and Soviet representatives to reduce the numbers of INF in Europe; and 2) the deployment of modernized INF in Europe if the negotiations produced no agreement by 1983.[1]

Chancellor Helmut Schmidt, Foreign Minister Genscher, and other German leaders strongly supported the NATO Dual Track plan. Schmidt actually brought the issue of INF modernization to the formal NATO agenda through an important speech in October 1977. Later, German representatives supported a communiqúe at an April 1978 NATO High Level Group (HLG) meeting recognizing the need for an "evolutionary adjustment in NATO's intermediate-range nuclear forces."[2] And in January 1979, Schmidt, President Carter, British Prime Minister Callaghan, and French President d'Estaing finalized the Dual Track plan at a Nuclear Planning Group (NPG) meeting in Guadeloupe.[3]

The evolution of the Dual Track plan was not, however, without controversy. Chancellor Schmidt had to overcome serious rifts inside his own political party and in the domestic political arena to uphold this German commitment to the alliance. The story of the NATO plan provides some interesting lessons about the post-commitment politics of security issues in the late 1970s.

Elite Decision Authority

The elite decision authority for the November 1979 cabinet decision to support the Dual Track plan included some of the same leaders who had been involved in the establishment of the EMS. The cabinet was comprised of a coalition of Social Democratic Party (SPD) and the Free Democratic Party (FDP) leaders, and included Chancellor Helmut Schmidt (SPD), Foreign Minister Hans-Dietrich Genscher (FDP), and Defense Minister Hans Apel (SPD). Further, the SPD had factions of leaders with different perspectives on security policy. Moderates, including Chancellor Schmidt and Defense Minister Apel, supported cooperation with NATO and a strong conventional and nuclear deterrent in Western Europe. Liberals, including party leader Willy Brandt, *Fraktion* leader Herbert Wehner, Saarland President Oskar Lafontaine, and party leader Egon Bahr, emphasized detente and were concerned that NATO cooperation could damage Germany's relations with the Soviet bloc.

German Security Policy and the NATO Plan

Helmut Schmidt came into the *Kanzleramt* in 1974 concerned about how the U.S. government was handling European policy in general, and security concerns in specific. He was the author of two important works on national security policy and deterrence, and as Defense Minister under Willy Brandt, had been responsible for initiating the defense ministry's publication of the annual *White Paper* on German defense policy and strategy.[4] While Brandt's *Ostpolitik* efforts had improved inter-German relations, Schmidt believed that superpower arms control efforts had actually undermined European security.[5] In his first year in office, he even suggested that the United States and the Soviet Union had entered into "condominium through arms control negotiations" and had "systematically ignored concerns about European security" in the 1970s.[6]

Schmidt was determined to change the way that European security issues were handled by the superpowers, and with support from Defense Minister Apel and Foreign Minister Genscher, he stepped up his campaign to alert NATO allies to new security threats.[7] Most German leaders shared Schmidt's perception of the strategic imperative of addressing force imbalances in Europe at the time.[8] This could be achieved, they believed, either through arms negotiations or the enhancement of NATO strength to meet the Soviet threat.[9] This threat was discussed quite openly in the German Defense Ministry's 1976 *White Book,* which recognized several new medium-range Soviet nuclear systems including the new three-warhead, highly accurate SS-20 nuclear missiles, *Backfire* bombers, *Delta*-class submarines, and the Warsaw Pact's 600 older, medium-range ballistic missiles.[10] The *White Book* also called attention to the Soviet's overwhelming superiority in fighter aircraft in theater, and numerical advantage in the numbers of tanks, armored troop carriers, and other forces.

By 1977, Schmidt had become the most outspoken European proponent of some sort of balance in alliance conventional troops and theater nuclear systems.[11] German leaders were convinced by this time that back-channel appeals to the U.S. government about defense concerns were being systematically ignored.[12] Accordingly, the chancellor used NATO forums to try to push the United States to respond to European security concerns. NATO government leaders met to debate a Long-Term Defense Program (LTDP) in May 1977, and Schmidt pushed allies to consider emerging intermediate-range nuclear threats. He stated that "Soviet strategic and theater force increases had initiated a third phase for the alliance," in which new defense options must be considered.[13] The final, ten-point LTDP for improving NATO forces remained focused on conventional forces, but it did call for the eventual modernization of some intermediate-range nuclear systems in Europe. Later, at an October 1977 meeting of the Nuclear Planning Group, NATO defense ministers bowed to German pressure to attend to European security concerns and created the HLG. The group was tasked to address high-urgency programs on European defense strategy. Nevertheless, in the fall 1977, German government leaders were not satisfied that all efforts had been explored to promote European security.[14]

INF on the Public Agenda

Chancellor Schmidt brought European security concerns to the public agenda through his famous October 1977 speech at the International Institute for Strategic Studies in London. Schmidt emphasized that superpower negotiations had created a situation where the balance of strategic nuclear weaponry was no longer as significant as conventional and theater force imbalances. He criticized the U.S. government for its neglect of European security concerns in arms control negotiations to date. Schmidt was particularly concerned that the United States was willing to negotiate away cruise missiles and omit references to the *Backfire* bombers and SS-20s in the Vladivostock formula. And he focused a great deal of his discussion on the potential enhancement of NATO deterrent strategy and other measures to restore the cohesion of the alliance. This could be carried out, Schmidt argued, through the modernization of its theater nuclear forces. But he emphasized the modernization of intermediate-range nuclear forces was an alternative to a lack of progress in the Mutual Balanced Force Reduction MBFR and Strategic Arms Limitation Talks (SALT).[15]

This speech was significant for several reasons. First, the substance of what the chancellor was saying was truly novel relative to past strategy debates in the alliance. Schmidt called into question the entire notion of extended deterrence in the alliance, and he pushed for a European nuclear deterrent. These statements went against long-standing NATO strategy concepts, and he emphasized existing regional imbalances without assuming that the overall balance could be compensated through strategic forces or other U.S. commitments. His call for the NATO alliance to maintain "the balance of full deterrence strategy," or a "Euro-strategic parity" in forces, was unique. In addition, Schmidt went public with his concerns by criticizing the U.S. negotiation strategy and the general objectives of the Carter administration's security policy.[16] This move came in the face of efforts by the Carter administration to keep the concerns in private, and within official NATO channels.[17] In an interview, Schmidt later admitted that

> The London speech was a reaction against being rebuffed twice by the White House in the course of 1977, telling them publicly in front of an audience that I understood what I was talking about, that it was not a good approach to let these missiles and weapons that were targeted against Europe, and not against America, be left out of negotiations as being of negligible quantity or quality.[18]

In many ways this speech was the genesis of NATO efforts to redress European security imbalances and to modernize INF systems.

NATO and European Defense Strategy, 1978–1979

The events of 1977, highlighted by Schmidt's October speech, helped to force the hand of the NATO allies to consider nuclear force modernization. Alliance relations in 1978 and 1979 were dominated by debates about the future of European security concerns in both the United States and Europe. The special HLG meetings produced real progress on intermediate-range nuclear weapons modernization plans. The HLG was made up of government representatives from the United States, Britain, France, and Germany, with the mandate to discuss security issues and with the authority to report back to the NPG in order to establish legitimate policy recommendations. The HLG met numerous times to design a report recognizing the "need for an evolutionary adjustment in NATO's TNF (Theater Nuclear Forces) that would provide more in-theater long-range capability than at present."[19]

In all of these meetings, German diplomats supported theater nuclear force modernization, and NATO leaders worked on a credible strategy of selective nuclear options. NPG members called for new land-based systems to prevent decoupling and enhance political relationships, and discussions began to center on the development of a highly accurate, mobile, long-range follow-on to the Pershing IA. Finally, NATO defense ministers met in Brussels in May 1979 to discuss issues raised by the HLG, and they issued a communiqúe stating that the allies were prepared to modernize their own intermediate-range systems if the Soviets remained unwilling to discuss their SS-20 and *Backfire* deployments.[20]

Support for INF Modernization in Germany

Meanwhile, Chancellor Schmidt and officials in the Defense and Foreign ministries continued to encourage support for INF modernization at home. The Defense Ministry's 1978 *White Book* highlighted the risk associated with the growing preponderance of Soviet medium-range missile systems. And subsequent statements to the press by Chancellor Schmidt and Foreign Minister Genscher repeated concerns that European security was being ignored by the United States, and that "gray zone" weapons, like the SS-20, presented serious disequilibria of forces in the region. As time wore on, leaders began to talk publicly about modernizing the land-based Pershing IA deployed in Germany and bringing cruise missiles into Europe to enhance nuclear deterrence.

Efforts to develop a unified stand on INF modernization in the German government during this period were influenced by the actions of the Soviet and American governments. Soviet intransigence on this issue helped to foster elite consensus in Germany in favor of INF modernization. In May 1978, Soviet General Secretary Brezhnev visited Bonn and claimed that military equilibrium existed in Europe, further underscoring the different perceptions of the European security environment held by leaders of the two alliances. Schmidt tried to counter the Soviet leader's assertion in several meetings, expressing the German and Western concern about the accumulation of conventional and nuclear potentials. At the end of the summit, Schmidt attempted to get Brezhnev to admit that Soviet efforts were challenging the foundation of detente. Brezhnev agreed on a hollow declaration that committed both sides to "pursue the principles of parity and detente."[21]

Ironically, attempts by the Carter administration to respond to European security concerns in the late 1970s actually undermined elite and public support in Germany for INF modernization plans. One example of this was the U.S. plan to develop and deploy enhanced radiation weapons (ERW, or the "neutron bomb") in Europe as an immediate and tangible sign of the U.S. commitment to defend its allies.[22] In spite of opposition to the plan from German religious organizations, liberal politicians, and intellectuals, Schmidt announced to the *Bundestag* on March 13, 1978, that his coalition government was willing to deploy these systems when they were ready. But before a NATO compromise on ERW could be finalized on March 20, Carter decided unilaterally to cancel production of the systems on "moral grounds." Schmidt and other European leaders subsequently protested that they had risked great political capital to gain support for the program and claimed that the United States was once again "selling out" European security.[23]

Instead of promoting alliance unity, the neutron bomb affair actually damaged European support for subsequent NATO nuclear modernization plans and strengthened a popular movement opposed to nuclear weapons on European soil. In Germany, the ERW debacle helped to polarize the Social Democratic party into security policy factions. Schmidt, Defense Minister Apel, and their supporters stood firmly on the more moderate side of the issue—supporting moves to enhance the long-term security of Western Europe including the deployment of modernized nuclear weapons. But a strong left wing of the party, led by *Fraktion* member Egon Bahr, party leader Herbert Wehner, and party leader Willy Brandt, saw ERW as a dangerous precedent—preferring arms reduction or disarmament as the best routes to peace.[24] This left wing of the SPD eventually gained a strong public following during the INF modernization debates from 1979 to 1983.[25] It soon became apparent that the debate over INF modernization would be a test of Helmut Schmidt's leadership ability and of alliance cohesion.[26]

Buildup to the Brussels Summit

Carter administration officials recognized the problems they had created in the alliance with the ERW decision, and they decided to move quickly to regain momentum on the issue of INF systems. Carter ordered his representatives at the HLG meetings to garner support for a plan for eventual nuclear force modernization if arms control initiatives failed. In June 1978, the president also created an interagency study group known as PRM-38, Long-Range Theater Nuclear Capabilities and Arms Control, charged with developing concrete recommendations that the United States could take to NATO HLG meetings.[27]

With the support of the U.S. government, the HLG was able to reach consensus in favor of theater nuclear force modernization by February 1979. NATO leaders agreed that the NATO alliance should develop a two-tiered policy of "deployment with an arms control option." Formal proposals included: modernizing through basing ground-launched cruise missiles; a modified version of the Pershing IA called the Pershing IIXR; committing a new contingent of sea-launched cruise missiles; or the deployment of an improved version of the FB111A.[28] Early on, U.S. and German government representatives expressed support for a combination of the Pershing II and cruise missiles, which could provide mobility, accuracy, and utility against troop and supply contingents.

Progress toward the completion of a plan to modernize NATO intermediate-range nuclear systems continued in 1979. At a special summit for the leaders of key NPG member states in Guadeloupe on January 5–6, British Prime Minister Callaghan, French President Giscard d'Estaing, Chancellor Schmidt, and President

Carter discussed a number of European security concerns. Leaders agreed on an outline of the Dual Track plan, including a goal for deployment of new nuclear systems in Europe no later than 1983. President Carter agreed that the United States would develop and deploy modern, intermediate-range nuclear weapons in Western Europe in conjunction with a second track for arms negotiations. Schmidt received a verbal guarantee that new systems would be deployed in several member states and not just in Germany.[29]

A few months later, another meeting of the NPG was held at the Homestead Air Force Base in Florida, where Defense Minister Apel argued strongly that a number of NATO allies should agree to the deployment of the ground-launched cruise missiles (GLCMs) on their soil to avoid the "singularization" of Germany. Alfons Pawelczyk, the SPD spokesman on arms and security issues, also supported the stationing of sea-launched cruise missiles in theater as part of the package. Ultimately, the NATO group agreed at the Homestead meeting to deploy between 200 and 600 theater nuclear weapons and to form a "special group on arms limitation" to work on negotiation strategies for dealing with the Soviets on INF. Finally, the NPG formally tasked the HLG to develop specific recommendations for theater force modernization and to present these at the fall 1979 meeting of the NPG to be held in the Netherlands.[30]

Changes in the International Security Environment

On June 18, 1979, Soviet General Secretary Brezhnev and U.S. President Carter signed the SALT II agreement, which put a cap on the number of nuclear warheads each superpower could possess. Before the signing, President Carter reassured NATO allies that Euromissiles would be addressed in planned negotiations of the SALT III treaty.[31] With the symbolic solidification of the strategic balance in the signing of the SALT II Treaty, it appeared that the German government was resolved to work to enact the Dual Track decision. During the September 1979 HLG meeting, Defense Minister Apel pressured other European leaders to accept a modernization formula that would include deployment of 464 cruise missiles in five NATO countries and 108 Pershing IIs on German soil.[32]

Finally, the Soviet leadership began to recognize that modernization was a real possibility and that the new systems would be a serious threat to Warsaw Pact and Soviet security. Foreign Minister Gromyko and Secretary General Brezhnev began to make diplomatic appeals to the German government and other Europeans to postpone the Dual Track decision. On October 6, 1979, Brezhnev gave a speech in East Berlin in which he announced a Soviet unilateral reduction of forces in East Germany, a freeze on the deployment of new Soviet INF systems, and a call for negotiations over other regional concerns.[33] Ultimately, this eleventh-hour attempt to convince the Germans and NATO that the Soviets were willing to negotiate on INF systems had little effect on perceptions in the West, or on the final outcome.[34]

Post-Commitment Political Conditions

As the INF modernization plan took shape, German government leaders turned more attention to the development of public support for such a plan. In 1978 and early 1979, German government representatives including Chancellor Schmidt, Foreign Minister Genscher, SPD arms control expert Alfons Pawelczyk, Union party *Fraktion* leader Kohl, and Christian Socialist Union (CSU) party leader Strauss all pledged formal support for the NATO Dual Track plan. This was not, however, a guarantee of widespread support for the plan throughout the German polity.[35]

Factionalism inside the SPD became even more of a concern for Chancellor Schmidt as his government approached a final decision on support for the Dual Track plan. Throughout 1979, the chancellor and defense minister faced increasingly vocal criticism of their support for INF modernization. Chancellor Schmidt was particularly concerned by the loss of support for INF modernization from his party's left wing, including Willy Brandt, Oskar Lafontaine, Erhard Eppler, *Fraktion* leader Herbert Wehner, Egon Bahr, and others. These leaders wanted to develop a new, more political concept of arms control, favoring negotiations over INF modernization at all costs. Schmidt and his supporters faced severe criticism in *Bundestag* debates throughout 1979.[36]

Dissensus in the major party was at a high point during the SPD Special Party Congress held in Berlin from December 3–7, 1979. This congress was jointly called by Schmidt and Brandt to address the central question of the course of German security policy. But before the congress even started, there were disagreements between the security policy factions over the wording of an SPD political platform to be voted on in Berlin. A working group to discuss security policy comprised of Alfons Pawelczyk, SPD defense expert Karsten Voigt, and Karl Kaiser (a Schmidt adviser) produced a draft of the section on security policy in October. The give-and-take between the chancellor's supporters and his opponents in the party eventually produced a document that called for a German Dual Track solution combining both arms control and serious defense efforts.[37]

At the Berlin conference, deep divisions in the SPD over security policy came to the surface. Schmidt worked hard to garner the support of a majority of the party for the government's stance on INF modernization. But he faced a direct offensive from the leaders of the left, Brandt, Bahr and other younger SPD leaders who pushed for further arms control efforts. Voigt argued that the Dual Track proposal would only lead to an ever-increasing spiral of an arms race.[38] Brandt went on record at the conference in support of a deferment of the actual deployment decision "until 1983 or 1984, when arms control efforts with the Soviets had been seriously pursued" and when NATO systems themselves would actually be deployed.

Factionalism was so severe that at one point during the Berlin congress, Schmidt actually threatened to resign as the party's candidate for chancellor in the 1980 election unless leaders agreed to support INF modernization. Schmidt reportedly told a session of the party executive, behind closed doors, that he was "no longer prepared to shoulder the burden of government without a clear mandate from the conference."[39] The chancellor apparently calculated that he had a great deal of personal political influence and that he could withstand the scope of opposition given that elections were ten months away. Ultimately this ploy was successful, and he was able to get endorsement of his preferred policies, especially on the contentious issues of INF modernization. The struggle between Schmidt and left-wing members of the SPD was evident even in the title of the final party congress resolution on the subject: "Peace and Security Policy: Security Policy in the Context of Peace Policy."[40]

Relations between parties in the coalition were characterized by a somewhat different dynamic. Basically, the key player in the FDP on security policy issues was Foreign Minister Genscher. Beginning in 1977, Genscher had made public statements that supported Chancellor Schmidt's position on arms modernization and negotiations. The foreign minister subsequently demonstrated his support for modernization of INF systems in articles and *Bundestag* debates.[41] In a report for *NATO Brief*, he argued that the Soviet arms buildup was a challenge to western security. He made the case that Soviet deeds did not match their words in the theater nuclear force buildup. On several other occasions in 1978 and 1979, Genscher termed the SS-20 "a weapon of political intimidation directed against the nonnuclear Federal Republic of Germany."[42]

In fact, Genscher appears to have been the closest politician (in terms of policy preferences) to the chancellor on the Dual Track plan. This actually led to rifts between the left wing of the SPD and the Liberal party leadership. There were reportedly direct confrontations between FDP leader Möllemann and SPD leader Wehner, and there were indirect attacks on the foreign minister from Wehner and others in 1979. Mutual enmity arose between some leaders of the two parties because of these conflicts.[43]

Differences of opinion inside the government were also reflected in the German polity. Regional elections in 1979 produced mixed results for the Social Democrats. The most immediate election, in Bremen in October, brought about a 4.2 percent increase in public support for the SPD relative to the most recent election.[44] However, less-proximate regional elections in Rheinland-Pfalz produced a 2.7 percent loss of support for the SPD in March 1979.[45] In Schleswig-Holstein in April 1979 the SPD lost support, but had gained some support in Berlin in March elections.[46] Because the operationalization schema developed for case analysis does not incorporate a category for mixed results, averaging the results of the elections suggests a slightly negative impact on the decision context.

According to Eurobarometer polling data, the majority of West Germans in the late 1970s exhibited general support for the NATO alliance and concern about the imbalances created by Soviet armament.[47] In April 1979, polls showed that a majority of Germans felt that, at a general level, it was very important to "work closely with the U.S." The Social Democrats experienced a small gain of 1 percent in popular support in the period leading up to the final decision on the Dual Track plan, according to *Institut für Demoskopie* surveys. However, they experienced a slow, steady decline in support between June and December 1979, and the proportion of German citizens who supported specific NATO programs began to shrink. By November 1979, *Allensbach* surveys showed that many Germans had reservations about nuclear force modernization in Europe. Thus, the veneer of general support in Germany for NATO tended to obscure the growing opposition to specific programs, such as nuclear modernization in Europe.[48] Figure 3.1 summarizes Germany's domestic political conditions in the Dual Track case.

Conditions	Case Study Analysis Questions	Coding
Major Party Unity	A. Repeated Different Statements B. Many Different Positions C. Very Serious Disputes	Intense Dissensus
Coalition Consensus	A. Repeated Similar Statements B. No Different Positions C. No Disputes	Consensus
Symmetry of Effects	A. Intensely Symmetrical B. Direct Public Impact C. Many Sectors	Symmetrical
Election Results	A. Highly Influenced by Elections B. Results have Negative Impact C. Elections Offer Little Support	No Support
Popular Support	A. Yes, Upcoming Elections B. Polls have Positive Impact C. Polls Offer Support	Support

Figure 3.1 Summary of domestic political conditions in the Dual Track case.

German Support for the Dual Track Plan

In spite of the uncertain political climate, Schmidt had received a vote of support from his own party organization at the Berlin congress, and he turned his attention to achieving a final government decision on INF modernization. On December 9, 1979, Chancellor Schmidt called a cabinet meeting in which the members of the German security policy-making team were assembled.[49] At this meeting in the *Kanzleramt*, members of the elite decision authority participated in serious discussions about the Dual Track, which centered on two aspects of the issue. First, Schmidt reiterated that the Soviet Union had continued to deploy new SS-20s at a rapid pace, further undermining the strategic situation in which the West Europeans found themselves. The chancellor clearly saw a strategic imperative for INF modernization. Second, Foreign Minister Genscher and Schmidt evaluated the willingness of the Soviets to negotiate on these systems versus the importance of close cooperation with the alliance. Genscher stressed that German support of the Dual Track plan was essential if they were to stay involved in the alliance at such a crucial phase of its development. The upcoming Brussels summit was designed, in part, to celebrate 30 successful years of alliance cooperation and stability.[50]

Members of the elite decision authority decided to forge ahead with plans to support the NATO Dual Track decision that would be addressed the next week in Brussels. The leaders explicitly approved of the proposed wording for the agreement and of the structure of the Dual Track plan finalized at a meeting of NATO defense ministers in the Hague in mid-November.[51] Accordingly, German leaders all agreed to offer a strong show of support for the Dual Track plan at the Brussels summit.

The Dual Track Decision and Its Aftermath

The NATO 30th anniversary summit was held in Brussels on December 10–12, 1979. The most important development of the summit meeting was a special session of the defense ministers and foreign ministers during which the Dual Track decision was reached. On December 12, the allies agreed that NATO would deploy 572 intermediate-range nuclear weapons, which could strike targets in western parts of Soviet Union, if no agreement was reached in negotiations over these systems.[52] Of these weapons, 108 would be Pershing IIs, deployed only in Germany, and 464 would be ground-launched cruise missiles, deployed in Germany, Great Britain, Italy, Belgium, and the Netherlands.[53] Domestic political uncertainty in Belgium and Holland kept leaders from making commitments on deployment, but leaders agreed on the Dual Track plan pending authorization from their governments. The modernized systems would be deployed if superpower negotiations did not achieve a settlement by the summer of 1983.[54]

The Dual Track commitment was somewhat of a cathartic experience for the NATO alliance. In Germany, the first debate over INF was held on December 14, 1979, when the government leaders formally presented the Dual Track decision to the *Bundestag*. Foreign Minister Genscher presented the government's position in favor of the Dual Track plan, and most Union party, SPD, and FDP leaders spoke in favor of some aspect of the decision.[55]

As time passed, however, the Dual Track plan led to heightened East-West tensions and domestic political problems in Germany. Ultimately, between 1979 and 1983, the *Bundestag* held more than 35 debates over the decision, which increased in intensity as time for deployment drew near. Chancellor Schmidt continued to struggle to maintain a policy consensus, in the face of growing opposition from left-wing leaders like Bahr, Brandt, and Wehner. Eventually, intraparty factionalism, very large public demonstrations against INF modernization, economic problems, and a loss of respect from the FDP party all contributed to Chancellor Schmidt's downfall in late 1982.

On October 1, 1982, Schmidt was voted out of office through a constructive vote of no-confidence in the *Bundestag*, and Helmut Kohl became chancellor of a Conservative-Liberal coalition. The new chancellor pledged to uphold the Dual Track policy in NATO, and modernized INF systems were deployed in West Germany one year later.

DEFECTION: NATO SANCTIONS AGAINST THE SOVIET UNION AND POLAND

The imposition of martial law in Poland in December 1981 represented a very dangerous turn of events in Eastern Europe. NATO allies responded to this challenge by threatening to impose heavy economic sanctions on the Polish and Soviet governments if they did not lift martial law immediately.

At first, West German government leaders went along with NATO sanctions plans. In early January 1982, Chancellor Schmidt and Foreign Minister Genscher recognized the Soviet role in the crackdown and called for allied cooperation in response to the challenge in Poland. Later, German officials also supported the North Atlantic Council decision to establish economic sanctions on Poland and the Soviet Union, and they pledged not to undermine allied responses to the crackdown during a meeting of the Coordinating Committee for Export Controls (COCOM). However, strong domestic opposition eventually forced government leaders to renege on these commitments and support the construction of a high-volume natural gas pipeline from Siberia to Western Europe.

Elite Decision Authority

The elite decision authority for the case study of the February 1982 decision not to cooperate with NATO sanctions and to complete the Siberian natural gas pipeline deal included many of the same leaders who had supported the NATO Dual Track decision in 1979. Chancellor Helmut Schmidt (SPD), Foreign Minister Genscher (FDP), and Defense Minister Hans Apel (SPD) were all key players. In addition, security policy factions in the major party in government were represented by several leaders, including Helmut

Schmidt and Defense Minister Apel in the moderate wing of the party. This group was challenged on the left by party leader and former chancellor Willy Brandt, *Fraktion* leader Herbert Wehner, Saarland President Oskar Lafontaine, and party leader Egon Bahr.

Energy and Security Policy in the 1970s

Detente and *Ostpolitik* initiatives in the 1970s led to the enhancement of East-West trade in many product categories. This was especially the case for the energy sector. Many Western firms, such as Caterpillar Tractor, Dresser Industries, and International Harvester, began exporting energy equipment to the Soviet Union, providing compressors, pipe layers, and other key materials for the development of the Soviet infrastructure and the exploration of energy reserves.[56] German firms were particularly well-suited to provide industrial machinery and know-how for the energy sector. According to one estimate, the West Germans were tripling U.S. interests in the Soviet bloc market for all goods by 1980, doubling the French interests, and quadrupling the Italian and British interests in the region.[57]

While oil remained the primary source of energy for industrialized countries, the Europeans had begun to seriously explore the utility of natural gas as an alternative energy source in the 1960s. Europeans looked first to local sources of natural gas, and the German government signed its first deal to purchase gas from the Netherlands in 1969. But the Soviets also possessed vast, untapped natural gas fields in Siberia and regions near the Ural Mountains. By 1979, the German government was importing 18.2 percent of its natural gas from the Soviet Union, Italy was importing 24.8 percent, and France was importing 13.9 percent from the same source.[58]

The relatively rapid increase in imports of natural gas from the Soviet Union demonstrated the mutual benefits of trade for the East and West. European leaders saw the economic ties as integral to fostering better political relationships in the region. Helmut Schmidt believed that strong economic relations and trade ties were the best way to manage conflict and help isolate any political debates that might emerge between the blocs.

The Soviet invasion of Afghanistan in late December 1979, however, changed the way that some Western countries viewed relations with the East—and served as a foreshadowing of events in Poland two years later. The Carter administration responded to the Soviet invasion by calling for NATO military maneuvers in the North Atlantic and Indian Oceans, a trade embargo against the Soviet Union, and a boycott of the 1980 Moscow Olympics. Chancellor Schmidt ignored critics inside Germany and authorized German participation in the NATO naval maneuvers and the Olympic boycott.[59] But the German government did not support the institution of a trade embargo against the Soviet Union in 1980, and Schmidt and Genscher worked to minimize the effects of this rift on the stability of the European security environment. In the end, U.S. exports fell by more than 50 percent in 1980 as a product of the embargo, but Germany, France, and Britain filled this vacuum by increasing their exports to the East bloc by more than 30 percent.[60]

The Pipeline Deal

In 1980, German leaders met with Soviet General Secretary Brezhnev and signed several new trade agreements. One was an outline plan to construct a natural gas pipeline between Siberia and Western Europe. Plans were hatched by European government leaders, major corporations, and Soviet government representatives to construct a natural gas pipeline from the Yamburg gasfield north of the Arctic Circle in the Soviet Union through Poland and East Germany to the West. Chancellor Schmidt had supported the use of alternative energy supplies in Western Europe, and in 1980 he argued that "economic prosperity should not be sacrificed for environmental purity."[61]

In essence, the pipeline plan had all the elements of the "deal of the century" for Western Europe and the Soviet Union.[62] West European firms would contract to supply 56-inch diameter steel pipe, turbines, compressors, and related technology to the Soviets for the construction of the 3,000-mile pipeline.[63] The pipeline grid was to be constructed so that gas would eventually go to Germany, France, Italy, Belgium, and Ireland. The plan was designed so that equipment contracts arranged with Western European firms would be distributed roughly proportional to planned natural gas purchase/consumption rates. Western credits would be paid off by the Soviets in the form of gas deliveries, to be made after completion of the pipeline in 1984, and the gas deal was to be valid for 20 years.

Many European firms became involved in this deal. Representatives of the West German firm AEG-Kanis began to negotiate a contract for a number of turbines that would support gas extraction and energy production. The German corporation Mannesmann was in line to become the main supplier of wide-diameter pipe for the project and signed a preliminary contract with the Soviets worth over $2 billion.[64] A French firm, Creusot-Loir, began to negotiate a contract to produce and install a number of compressor stations; a British firm, the John Brown Corporation, completed a deal to produce turbines for the project; and an Italian firm also secured a large contract for compressor stations and turbines.[65]

Chancellor Schmidt and other European leaders came out in support of the pipeline arrangements. But U.S. government leaders reacted negatively to the pipeline plan and commercial deals from the outset. Reagan administration officials made it clear that they did not approve of the pipeline plan without serious restrictions. U.S. officials expressed concern that the pipeline would make Western allies, and especially West Germany, "dangerously dependent on Soviet natural gas supplies."[66] There were predictions that the Soviet share of the Western gas imports would rise so dramatically in the following ten years that Western European countries would become highly dependent on Soviet gas and therefore subject to significant Soviet political leverage. U.S. Assistant Secretary of Defense Richard Perle charted the dangerous relationship between Soviet natural gas and the vital sectors of West European economies—steel, chemicals, and automobiles. Perle said he feared that Soviet pressure on the Europeans would ultimately lead to a "Finlandization of Europe."[67]

The Group of Seven (G-7) summit in Ottawa, Ontario, Canada, in July 1981 represented the first official forum in which President Reagan could directly address this issue. In spite of their differences, G-7 leaders found some common ground in the final summit communiqúe, where they pledged to ensure that "our economic policies continue to be compatible with our political and security objectives." Reagan also convinced allies to participate in a high-level COCOM meeting to "undertake a systematic review of the Western export control system."[68] Analysts saw the agreement for a consultative group meeting of the COCOM leadership as a serious step toward a change in the way that the Western industrialized leaders approached trade ties with the Soviet Union. However, scholars have since argued that by agreeing to meet in such a session, European leaders were signaling their willingness to negotiate on the pipeline deal.[69]

Nevertheless, Schmidt and Foreign Minister Genscher clearly did not come away from Ottawa with the feeling that they had obligated themselves to change course on the pipeline project. They continued to support the completion of formal contracts in the pipeline deal in the summer and fall months of 1981. Contracts were formalized by a consortium headed by the German corporation, Mannesmann, and with Creusot-Loire on September 29, 1981, to produce and deliver turbines and compressor stations. These two corporations also were named the general contractors for the entire pipeline project. Soon afterward, British, Italian, and Belgian companies signed contracts for turbines, compressors, heavy equipment, refrigerator stations, and other materials. Finally, the contracts for wide-diameter pipe for the project worth more than $1 billion were signed with German and Italian firms.[70]

In response, the Reagan administration tried a new carrot-and-stick approach to convince the Europeans to cancel the pipeline project. The carrot came from a U.S. delegation sent to Western Europe in November 1981 that offered to sell large amounts of American coal to Europe at reduced prices. The delegation also encouraged the Germans and others to accept increased shipments of natural gas from Scandinavia—even though agreements had not yet been secured with third country suppliers.[71] The diplomatic stick was the government's increasingly vocal opposition to the European natural gas pipeline deal, including efforts to cast this issue as a national security threat. For example, Reagan administration officials cited a CIA study released in October 1981 that argued that natural gas exports from the pipeline would earn the Soviets a badly needed $8 billion in hard currency annually.[72]

U.S. efforts to broadside the pipeline deal were rebuffed by Europeans, and the German government in particular, for several reasons. Chancellor Schmidt and other leaders came out strongly against the U.S. offer as invalid and flawed. German leaders believed very strongly that the pipeline deal was an avenue for Western Europe to work its way out of some serious economic problems at the time. Europe faced high unemployment rates and an economic recession. German exports were on the decline, and Social Democrats were concerned about declining public support for their programs measured in *Institut für Demoskopie* surveys.[73] Therefore, European leaders responded by noting that any new energy deal with the United States would provide only a fraction of the total energy resources needed in Western Europe. They criticized the

United States for allowing farmers to continue to make grain sales to the Soviet Union even after the invasion of Afghanistan. At least one U.S. firm, Caterpillar Tractor, was directly involved in the pipeline operation, and Schmidt argued that the Reagan administration had done little to crack down on that aspect of the deal.[74]

The Declaration of Martial Law in Poland

The declaration of martial law in Poland in December 1981 had a significant impact on East-West economic and political arrangements. The crackdown actually resulted from a series of developments in Poland in the 1970s and early 1980s, including the emergence of civil unrest, increased activism by the Solidarity labor movement, and even Soviet threats to invade Poland to restore order. After a series of failed edicts to quiet the protest movement and eliminate challenges to Communist rule in Poland, General Jaruzelski declared martial law on December 12, 1981. This included outlawing the Solidarity movement, banning public protests and other forms of dissent, and deploying of 56,000 Polish and Soviet troops to enforce the new state of law.[75]

The crackdown caught many Western leaders by surprise, and it came at a particularly bad time for the NATO alliance, which was caught up in debates over the Siberian natural gas pipeline, INF modernization, and other strategic issues. Nevertheless, President Reagan and the U.S. government took the lead in challenging developments in Poland. Reagan interpreted martial law as "serious repression, conducted with the full knowledge and support of Moscow."[76] After a series of high-level administration meetings, the president stated on December 17, 1991, that the West would not "stand idly by while martial law was imposed in Poland with clear signs of Soviet involvement." Reagan later outlined the plan for the imposition of strong economic sanctions on Poland and the Soviet Union, and he requested that U.S. allies join in the plan. The president called for cutting the planned $740 million in foreign aid pledged to the Polish government, the cancellation of plans to reschedule Warsaw's debt to the West, suspension of $100 million in agricultural assistance, and the withdrawal of Poland's right to fish in U.S. waters.[77] He also called for an embargo of the sale of any material, equipment, or technology on the U.S. Commodity Control List to the Soviet bloc, and he pledged to use "whatever diplomatic and economic influence necessary"—with support of

U.S. allies—to prevent the military crackdown in Poland from becoming permanent.[78]

The American government articulated a broad plan to counter Soviet and Polish repression. U.S. officials failed to coordinate this plan for an economic sanctions package with allies, however, and European governments responded more cautiously to the imposition of martial law. For one, Chancellor Schmidt initially declined to implicate the Soviet Union in the crackdown. Schmidt and other German leaders were concerned because they had sunk significant costs in economic and political relationships with the Eastern bloc.[79] On top of that, Schmidt was operating in an uncertain domestic political environment, and he was concerned about relations with the Free Democrats and continuing economic problems. European leaders reminded members of the media that the U.S. government had carefully avoided the imposition of a grain embargo on the Soviets in the wake of the invasion of Afghanistan.[80]

On December 18, 1981, the chancellor finally did speak out on the events in Poland. He gave a televised speech before the *Bundestag* in which he decried the imposition of martial law and introduced a resolution calling for the "liberation of all prisoners" in Poland as well as the "restoration of the freedoms arrived at through a course of reform and renewal . . . and resumption of the dialogue with the patriotic forces of the Polish people willing to engage in reforms."[81] Officially, the *Bundestag* resolution called for the suspension of German economic aid to Poland for "as long as the measures of suppression of the current regime against the Polish people remain in force."[82]

Allied Response to the Crackdown

Western leaders continued to speak out against Soviet and Polish actions. NATO leaders held an emergency meeting on December 14, 1981, where they ruled out the use of force to respond to the crackdown and agreed to employ diplomatic and economic tools to push a negotiated settlement of the crisis with Polish and Soviet governments. This consensus in the alliance prompted Reagan administration officials to announce a wide-ranging sanctions program on December 29, 1981. Sanctions were oriented around two objectives: 1) compelling the Soviet and Polish governments to end repression; and 2) convincing allies to consider a complete reorientation of Western export policies. In essence, administration officials saw energy trade as something of a linchpin in the entire Soviet economic relationship with the West.[83] The sanctions package included cutting off the export of computers, electronic equipment, and other high-technology items, and increasing the regulation on port arrangements. Perhaps the most important element of the sanctions package was the increased restrictions on the transfer of materials needed for the construction of the Siberian natural gas pipeline. The United States called for a broadening of licensing requirements for equipment that could be used in refining and transmission of oil and gas. The extension of controls for the sanctions list covered a planned Caterpillar pipe layer that the Soviets valued at over $80 million and contracts signed by General Electric in connection with the Siberian pipeline, worth $175 million. In sum, sanctions reflected both a short-term response to the crackdown and an effort by the Reagan administration to pursue long-term policy goals related to the energy trade.[84]

On January 3, 1982, Chancellor Schmidt and Foreign Minister Genscher held a special meeting with U.S. leaders in Washington to discuss the crisis and larger questions of East–West trade. Schmidt expressed concern that the involvement of Western Europe in sanctions against Poland and the Soviet Union would have a number of detrimental effects on the political and economic environment, including getting "hopes up in Poland . . . making them risk their lives for nothing."[85] Genscher reiterated the vested German interest in maintaining good relations with the Polish government, part of a long-developing foreign relations program couched in *Ostpolitik*. Nevertheless, Schmidt and Genscher agreed to the wording of a joint communiqúe issued at the meeting, which explicitly recognized that the Soviet Union was involved in the crackdown and called for Western economic sanctions.[86]

NATO leaders also came together in early January 1982 for another emergency meeting to discuss their responses to the crackdown in Poland, and they established an official alliance response to the crisis. Leaders agreed to a communiqúe condemning the Soviets for their "active support for the systematic suppression in Poland."[87] They also agreed to the imposition of some selected economic sanctions against both Poland and the Soviet Union, but not explicitly against the Siberian gas pipeline."[88] And in return for a reduction of U.S. diplomatic pressure for endorsement of the sanctions package, European leaders pledged not to undermine U.S. policy and to devise and implement their own sanctions at some point in the future. The final summit communiqúe stated: "Soviet actions towards Poland make it necessary to examine the course of future economic and commercial relations. . . . The Allies will also reflect on longer-term East-West economic relations, particularly energy."[89] Thus, Secretary of State Haig and other Reagan administration officials interpreted this meeting as a success, and it paved the way for a very important January COCOM meeting.

The special COCOM review session was held a few weeks later; it represented the first high-level review of the COCOM embargo lists in 24 years. Discussions at the meeting centered on the rules for collective multilateral Western trade controls. European leaders approached this COCOM session with mixed feelings about how rigid export controls should be in the wake of the crackdown in Poland. But the Reagan administration came to the COCOM table with strong predispositions to establish rigid controls on exports, especially in the energy sector.[90] As a result, COCOM representatives, including German officials, accepted that the consortium structure should be reconceptualized, and that a new protection list should be adopted. Members agreed to "harmonize" their licensing procedures in order to avoid disputes over interpretations of key lists and to improve general trade monitoring and enforcement. But while Reagan administration representatives wanted to establish even tighter control criteria that would include the denial of exports of turnkey plants and technology to defense priority sectors, the Europeans thought this was asking for too much of a shift in alliance export control strategy.[91] Many European economic and foreign ministry officials argued that COCOM already did well to balance economic and security interests and thus it was unnecessary to complicate the process by adding a military subcommittee in COCOM that would facilitate stronger defense department participation.[92] During the session, one German Economics Ministry official characterized as "unthinkable" that other states would change their organizational procedures to satisfy U.S. interests.[93]

European leaders pledged their support to uphold the sanctions package and to restructure COCOM export controls in January 1982, but several developments challenged allied consensus soon thereafter. First, corporations that would be affected by the sanctions packages and export controls launched a new campaign to complete the pipeline deals. Several French firms worked to sign contracts with the Soviets, taking the lead in bucking NATO and COCOM sanctions. In late January, the French government announced that it had ordered 280 billion cubic feet a year of Soviet natural gas to be delivered through the proposed pipeline.[94] Several German firms, including Mannesmann, also began to appeal to their government for support in challenging the U.S. sanctions package. Meanwhile, U.S. leaders responded quickly and harshly to such moves. Pentagon officials publicly brought pressure on the Europeans to impose sanctions against the pipeline, stating that they would be reneging on commitments if they failed to do so. Some Pentagon officials warned that the United States could delay the project "indefinitely by preventing American companies and their Western European affiliates from supplying equipment for the pipeline."[95]

Post-Commitment Political Conditions

While Schmidt and other government leaders promised to cooperate with NATO sanctions, there were serious domestic political pressures to continue the construction of the pipeline in 1982. In Bonn, Schmidt faced increased opposition from across the political spectrum to his handling of the Polish crisis. Early in the crisis period, Schmidt had estimated that he had relatively strong support inside his own party for these policies, but this changed when Schmidt took a tougher stance on the sanctions question after a meeting with President Reagan in early January 1982. In fact, this issue became linked with other economic and foreign policy problems faced by the government. A cartoon appearing in the *Frankfurter Allgemeine Zeitung* in September 1981 summed up Schmidt's perceived relationship with his own government during this period. It showed Schmidt as Gulliver, tied down by many different concerns including the left-wing opposition from inside his own party to his security policy stance. An accompanying article suggested that the SPD faced a serious party crisis and said that "open conflict has broken out among the leaders of the SPD in the last six months."[96] Key party opponents at this time included *Fraktion* leader Herbert Wehner, party leader Brandt, and Saarland President Oskar Lafontaine who were openly opposed to any move that would exacerbate tensions between Germany and the Soviet Union. In late 1981, one close adviser to Brandt warned that "chancellors come and go, but the leader of the party stays in place."[97]

Schmidt also faced challenges from the regional branches of the SPD, which demanded changes in German security and foreign policy. On February 7, 1982, party leaders at three regional SPD conventions voted to disavow and challenge existing national SPD party programs.[98] Leaders of regional party organizations were very concerned that the Schmidt government had drifted too far to the political right and that relations with the Soviet Union and East bloc would be jeopardized by that drift. The idea that Germany would support harsh NATO economic sanctions against the Soviets came to symbolize the ideological distance between the party offices in Bonn and members in the region.

Within a month of his meeting with President Reagan, it appeared that Schmidt had begun to lose confidence in his own ability to reign in party support for the sanctions plan and at the same time tackle serious economic problems at home. In an unusual move, Schmidt asked for, and won, a vote of confidence in his coalition government from the *Bundestag* on February 6, 1982. Nevertheless, this and other developments undermined any image of stability in the Schmidt government. The situation soon became so bad that the chancellor announced a cabinet reshuffle in early March 1982. As part of this restructuring, Finance Minister Hans Matthöffer, Labor Minister Herbert Ehrenberg, and others were replaced. Schmidt announced that his long-time political ally, Manfred Lahnstein, would become the new Finance Minister.[99] Officially, Schmidt sought to reestablish some legitimacy for his party's economic policies, but the chancellor also saw the need for a fresh image of his government to deal with continuing problems and crises, such as Poland.

Problems for Schmidt inside his own party were coupled with the general erosion of FDP support for the government. According to some reports, interparty relations had deteriorated to a point where the junior party leadership considered withdrawing from the coalition government as early as September 1981.[100] Reports surfaced that the inner consensus of the coalition had fallen apart in this period due to differences over the proper responses to economic problems and concerns about the ability of the SPD leadership to manage crises. Schmidt and SPD leaders worked very hard to secure the support of the FDP for a package of initiatives to improve the economy, but consensus was hard to achieve. The package that received FDP support included plans for a tax increase, and it was reported that Foreign Minister Genscher and FDP party leader Lambsdorff "got what they wanted" in the deal.[101]

Thus, the proper response to the Polish crisis was clearly viewed through the perceptual lens of economic recovery by some German leaders. Foreign Minister Genscher and Economics Minister Lambsdorff were very concerned that long-term German economic and military security was challenged by forces outside and inside the government. The Siberian pipeline deal was obviously seen by Lambsdorff and others as beneficial for the German economy. And by February 1982, rifts between the FDP and SPD had become so serious that Genscher publicly warned that "in two or three months, we will have a different constellation of leadership." FDP leaders were particularly concerned about their performance in upcoming regional elections in Hessen, Niedersachsen, Hamburg, and Bayern.[102]

With respect to interest groups, Schmidt faced direct appeals from key sectors of the German economy on the sanctions issue. For example, *Bundesbank* officials lobbied the German leadership in late December and January not to become involved in large-scale sanctions against Poland or the Soviet Union. The banking sector was very concerned about the implications of such a move for German economic health.[103] Pressure also came from several large firms directly involved in the construction of the Siberian natural gas pipeline. Officials from several corporations, including AEG-Kanis and Mannesmann, lobbied coalition leaders very hard to appeal for a continuation of the pipeline program. This lobbying effort did not fundamentally challenge the ruling coalition, but it represented significant, outside pressure on the government.[104]

Finally, Schmidt had to deal with mixed signals on the question of NATO sanctions and the proper German response to the crisis among the citizenry.[105] The results of the March 1982 *Landtag* elections in Niedersachsen and public opinion polls reflected the loss of public confidence in government policies. The SPD lost 6 percent of the popular vote from prior elections, leading to a collapse of the regional coalition government. Also, the SPD lost 4 percent of its popular support in the period leading up to the final decision on NATO sanctions and the pipeline, according to *Institut für Demoskopie* surveys.[106] Coupled with election losses came a series of public protests of German government security policy. Most of these protests tended to be oriented against the close ties with the United States and budding protest against INF modernization. On October 10, 1981, some 150,000 Germans rallied in Bonn. While Genscher publicly discounted the protest, some SPD leaders embraced the movement and challenged government security policy. These protests, declining support for the SPD in the opinion polls, and the serious election loss in Niedersachsen were interpreted as signs of continued losses of support for the Schmidt government.[107] Figure 3.2 summarizes Germany's domestic political conditions in the NATO sanctions case.

Germany Defects from Sanctions

Several factors actually led to a final German decision on the pipeline and sanctions questions. First, American officials warned the Germans that the alliance was "on a collision course" and "bound for disintegration" if there was no clarification of the allied response to the crackdown.[108] Second, public warnings were coupled with intensified allied pressure on the German government to cooperate with the sanctions and cancel the pipeline plans. A U.S. mission headed by Under Secretary of State James Buckley was dispatched to Bonn and other European capitals in early March to push for a final agreement. Third, a German Foreign Ministry review of government foreign policy was released in the spring. It formally faulted

Conditions	Case Study Analysis Questions	Coding
Major Party Unity	A. Few Different Statements B. Few Different Positions C. Serious Disputes	Dissensus
Coalition Consensus	A. Few Different Statements B. Few Different Positions C. Very Serious Disputes	Dissensus
Symmetry of Effects	A. Asymmetrical B. Indirect Public Impact C. Few Sectors	Asymmetrical
Election Results	A. Highly Influenced by Elections B. Very Negative Impact C. Elections Offer No Support	Highly Influential
Popular Support	A. Yes, Upcoming Elections B. Negative Polls C. Polls Offer No Support	No Support

Figure 3.2 Summary of domestic political conditions in the NATO sanctions case.

the SPD leadership for providing a "lack of coherence" in German foreign policy across the board.[109] Finally, members of the elite decision authority also sought closure on this issue in light of the need to deal definitively with other crises including unemployment and investment problems. Closure was particularly important given upcoming regional elections and concerns about the erosion of popular support for the federal coalition.

Several meetings were held in the chancellor's office in late March in which members of the elite decision authority debated key issues. The primary debate revolved around whether Germany should strive to uphold the NATO decision to support a unified sanctions programs.[110] Finally, on March 31, 1982, members of the elite decision authority held a cabinet meeting in which they decided to reject participation in the sanctions authorized by NATO. Instead, cabinet leaders agreed to uphold German commercial commitments to the construction of the Siberian natural gas pipeline.[111] Decision makers subsequently made it clear to the press that they believed economic sanctions "hurt the little man in Poland," by creating an acute scarcity of consumer goods.[112] Based on a summary of the meeting provided to the German press, coalition leaders were very concerned that they maintain strong ties with the NATO alliance and provide strong guarantees of support for the West.[113]

Aftermath of the German Decision

The decision by the German government not to support allied economic sanctions on Poland or the Soviet Union—and to continue construction of the Siberian natural gas pipeline—represented a defection from international commitments that had great symbolic importance. U.S. officials reacted very negatively to the German decision. During the G-7 summit at Versailles in June 1982, Reagan administration officials insisted that more commercial measures should be incorporated into a Western foreign policy strategy toward the Soviet Union, and this led to public confrontations between French, German, and U.S. representatives. The final summit communiqúe only called for the leaders to "pursue a prudent and diversified economic approach to the Soviet Union and Eastern Europe, consistent with our political and security interests."[114] Reagan administration officials again attempted to influence German foreign policy at a NATO summit in June, where they promised that they would not make claims of extraterritoriality that would limit the use of U.S.

technology in any production process associated with the pipeline project.[115] Nevertheless, only a few days after the summit, President Reagan announced that the U.S. government *would* claim extraterritorial application of its export controls on a retroactive basis, establishing serious violations with stiff penalties.[116]

The announcement about extraterritoriality angered Soviet and Polish officials, and it solidified the European position that the U.S. government had gone too far. After months of indirect challenges from the United States, this move was considered a serious challenge to European autonomy and prompted a relatively unified response to the move. Leaders of most European countries, except West Germany, publicly ordered their companies to ignore the U.S. government declaration and honor pipeline contracts. French Foreign Minister Cheysson said there would be a "progressive divorce [from U.S. foreign economic and security policy] because we no longer speak the same language."[117] Chancellor Schmidt was slightly more cautious, although he pledged in an interview in late June that the "pipeline will be built," regardless of U.S. decisions. Finally, in a joint session of the EC Council of Ministers, European leaders formally protested this "unacceptable interference" in its sovereign affairs. They charged that "the effect on European Community interests of the United States' measures, applied retroactively and without sufficient consultation, are unquestionable and seriously damaging."[118] Relations between the United States and Germany did not improve significantly during the summer 1982, and SPD leader Egon Bahr said that alliance relations were "at their lowest point in years."[119]

As relations continued to deteriorate, Senator Ted Stevens, the second-ranking Republican in the U.S. Senate, even introduced legislation to cut back American troops stationed in Western Europe as retaliation for noncooperation on the pipeline issue.[120] Nevertheless, European firms continued to challenge the U.S. declaration of extraterritorial authority by shipping parts for the Siberian natural gas pipeline. The cycle of response and retaliation continued with the Reagan administration laying countersanctions on Dresser-France and Creusot-Loire, one of the general contractors for the project. Subsequently, the German firm AEG-Kanis also began shipment of certain parts for the project and was subjected to countersanctions from the United States.[121]

Ultimately, the Reagan administration only relented in its efforts to block the pipeline project when a new Conservative-Liberal coalition, headed by Helmut Kohl and Genscher, took over the German government. As part of a final compromise with the Kohl government, European leaders agreed, in November 1982, to participate in three studies under the auspices of the Organization for Economic Cooperation and Development, COCOM, and NATO to review ways to strengthen controls on dual-use, high-technology goods.[122] In the end, German leaders had successfully fought the political tide in the West and held the line on *Ostpolitik* in the face of great international pressure and threats. This case study holds valuable lessons about the power of domestic political conditions in the post-commitment phase.

NOTES

1. For more information about the INF Treaty, see *Dokumente: Vertrag Zwischen den Vereinigten Staaten von Amerika und der Union der Sozialistischen Sowjetrepubliken über die Beseitigung ihrer Flugkörper mittlerer und kürzerer Reichweite*, from *Der Abbau der Mittelstreckenflugkörper*, published by the Bundesminister der Verteidigung, Informations- und Pressestab, June 1988.
2. Helga Haftendorn, *Sicherheit und Entspannung: Zur Aussenpolitik der Bundesrepublik Deutschland 1955–1982*, 1983, pp. 70–83.
3. See Wolfram Hanrieder, *Germany, America and Europe: Forty Years of German Foreign Policy*, 1989.
4. See Helmut Schmidt, *Strategie des Gleichgewichts: Deutsche Friedenspolitik und die Weltmächte*, 1969; See also the *Weissbuch 1972–73,* Der Bundesminister der Verteidigung Informations- und Presseamt, 1985, p. 34.
5. For an overview of European security environment in this period, see Gebhard Schweigler, *West German Foreign Policy: The Domestic Setting*, Washington Papers, no. 106, 1984.
6. In 1975, Schmidt's fears were confirmed when he learned that most European security issues had been glossed over during the Vladivostock negotiations between Soviet leader Brezhnev and President Ford; Schwartz, 1983, pp. 391–392; See also *Weissbuch 1984–1985,* Der Bundesminister der Verteidigung Informations- und Presseamt, 1985, p. 34.
7. *SALT and the NATO Allies*, U.S. Senate Committee on Foreign Relations, Subcommittee on European Affairs Report, Washington, D.C., U.S. Government Printing Office, 1979, pp. 1–72; See also Kelleher, 1975; See also *Handbuch*, from Der Bundesminister der Verteidigung Informations- und Presseamt, Bonn, June 1987; For background information, see Josef Joffe, *The Limited Partnership: Europe, the United States, and the Burdens of Alliance*, 1987.
8. Based on author's interview with W. R. Smyser, former official in the U.S. Embassy, Bonn, 1976–1982, September 4, 1991, Washington, D.C.
9. Brauch, 1982, p. 31.
10. *Weissbuch 1975/76*, 1976, p. 18; Other differences of opinion between the German and U.S. leaderships also contributed to a seemingly widening gulf between European and U.S. security concerns. These included the debate over

West German support costs for the U.S. airborne command aircraft, American reluctance to adopt the German 120 mm cannon for its new Abrams tank, and Bonn's insistence that Washington offset West German purchases of American weapons system by purchasing more German military goods (such as trucks and communications equipment); Jeffrey Herf, *War By Other Means: Soviet Power, West German Resistance, and the Battle of the Euromissiles*, 1991, pp. 132–165.

11. Schmidt, *Men and Powers: A Political Retrospective*, 1989, p. 139.
12. One example was the concern shared by many German government leaders (including the leaders of all parties in government) that the U.S. government would bargain away cruise missiles at the SALT II talks without receiving comparable restrictions on Soviet theater systems, especially the new and feared *Backfire* bomber and the SS-20. These concerns were borne out in a round of negotiations in mid-1977, where there was little substantive U.S.–Soviet discussion of these systems; See *NATO Final Communiqúes*, 1949–1974, Brussels, NATO Information Service, 1975; See also Helga Haftendorn, "Der Abrüstungsbeauftragte: Zur Organisation der Abrüstungspolitik in der Bundesrepublik," *Politische Vierteljahresschrift*, vol.1/1972, p. 6.
13. Schmidt, "The North Atlantic Summit Meeting," Remarks from speech, May 10, 1977, *Survival* July/August 1977, pp. 177–178.
14. Herf, 1991, p. 67.
15. Schmidt, "The 1977 Alastair Buchan Memorial Lecture," Reprinted in *Survival*, vol. 20, January/February 1978, p. 4.
16. Jeffrey Boutwell, 1990. *The German Nuclear Dilemma,* p. 73.
17. *Der Spiegel*, November 21, 1983, no. 46, pp. 29–33.
18. Quoted in Stephen Szabo, *The Changing Politics of German Security*, 1990, p. 62.
19. See Stephen Hanmer, "NATO's Long-Range Theater Nuclear Forces: Modernization in Parallel with Arms Control," *NATO Review*, February 1980, no. 28.
20. Later, Schmidt would remind the Soviets that the issue of proceeding with INF modernization and arms control could have been headed off if it had not been for the Soviet disregard of the May 1978 communiqúe as one justification for alliance deployment of INF; Herf, 1991, p. 184.
21. *Der Spiegel*, "Breschnew-Besuch: Eine dominierende Rolle," May 10, 1978, no. 18, pp. 23–27.
22. A story in the *Washington Post* said that the Carter administration had given the go-ahead to Department of Energy to begin producing enhanced radition warheads for short-range tactical nuclear delivery systems that began the ERW debate; *Washington Post*, June 5, 1977, p. 1.
23. *New York Times*, April 5–8, 1978, pp. A1; Alfred Mechtersheimer, ed., *Nachrüsten? Dokumente und Positionen zum Nato-Doppelbeschluss*, 1981, pp. 267–272; See also Dieter S. Lutz, *Weltkrieg wider Willen?* 1981.
24. These leaders publicly entertained notions of a declaration of German neutrality in exchange for German reunification and peace in the region. The left wing of the party did not support such strong ties to the United States through the alliance, and certainly would not support the development of a weapon with the destructive capabilities of the neutron bomb; See *Der Spiegel*, "NATO: Schmidt stellt sich quer," June 3, 1978, no. 22, p. 23.

25. *New York Times*, August 16, 1978, p. A7; *Der Spiegel*, "Wir Können auf Kernenergie nicht Verzichten," September 3, 1979, no. 33, p. 23; See also *Der Spiegel*, "Front Gegen den Religiösen Schwärmer," April 6, 1978, no. 13, p. 23.
26. See Hanmer, February 1980, p. 36.
27. See *The Modernization of NATO's Long-Range Theater Nuclear Forces*, Report, 1980, p. 27.
28. James A. Thomson, "The LRTNF Decision: Evolution of US Theater Nuclear Policy, 1975–1979," *International Affairs*, vol. 60, no. 4, 1984, pp. 603–612.
29. Schmidt and Callaghan favored SALT II ratification, from *Christian Science Monitor*, January 6, 1979, p. 3.
30. See Schwartz, *NATO's Nuclear Dilemmas*, 1983.
31. See *The Modernization of NATO's Long-Range Theater Nuclear Forces*, 1980, p. 27.
32. J. J. Martin, "Nuclear Weapons in NATO's Deterrent Strategy," *Orbis*, Winter 1979, vol. 22 p. 876.
33. See *NATO Review*, vol. 28, February 1980.
34. The German government reaction to this unilateral concession was initally optimistic, but guarded. While Schmidt publicly welcomed the offers and willingness to negotiate, he argued that the announcement would not fundamentally alter the strategic situation in theater. Schmidt's initial reaction was one of cautious optimism, noting that the initatives were "generally . . . very substantial." But Foreign Minister Genscher was much more cautious about the implications for this program, stating that "the decision will be taken in December and implemented." Later, Schmidt argued that without NATO action the Soviets would still be left with a very large numerical superiority in intermediate-range systems, coupled with modern and highly accurate systems; *Der Spiegel*, "Abrüstung: Aus der Ecke Raus," November 10, 1979, no. 42, p. 26; See also John Vinocur, *New York Times*, "Germans Uncertain on Brezhnev Offer," October 13, 1979, p. A1.
35. Opponents included a group of elites within the chancellor's own party, editors from German periodicals like *Der Spiegel*, *Die Stern*, and the daily *Frankfurter Rundschau*, authors and intellectuals, leaders of major peace research institutes, and many others; Brauch, 1983, p. 111.
36. See Schmidt, 1987; See also Stephen F. Szabo, *The Changing Politics of German Security*, 1990, p. 88.
37. "Materialen: Sicherhetispolitik im Rahmen der Friedenspolitik," *Leitantrag des Parteivorstands für den Parteitag in Berlin*, Bonn, Vorstand der SPD, Abteilung Presse und Information, October 9, 1979.
38. Karsten Voigt, "Schrittweiser Aussteig aus dem Rüstungswettlaug: Nach dem Berliner Parteitag der SPD," in *Neue Gesellschaft*, January 1980.
39. *New York Times*, December 5, 1979, p. 5A; The author states that Schmidt "hinted that he would resign if the delegates did not back him on the issue in a vote scheduled for December 5th, because he wants strong party support behind him when he participates in a meeting in Brussels next week." See also Schmidt, 1987, p. 114; The erosion of the SPD consensus on security issues ultimately contributed to the loss of control of the government in October 1982; See Lutz, *Weltkrieg wider Willen?* 1981.

40. *New York Times*, "Party Gives Schmidt a Strong Lift," December 7, 1979, p. A6; This article says that Schmidt won "a significant personal and political success, emerging with a clear mandate for his policy."
41. *Freie Demokratische Korrespondenz*, "Genscher: Moskau Soll Verhandlungswillen Des Westerns Ernst Nehmen," a press release from the FDP party offices, released November 4, 1979 [author's translation].
42. Hans-Dietrich Genscher, "Mittelstreckenraketen: Der Schlüssel zur Abrüstung in Moskau—Kontinuität und Berechenbarket; Der Deutschen Haltung Dürfen Nicht Gefährdet Werden," *NATO Brief*, German Version, Number 3/4, 1983, pp. 3–10.
43. *Der Spiegel*, February 22, 1979, no. 7, p. 21.
44. Data drawn from Suzanne S. Schüttmeyer, "Die Ergebnisse der Lantagswahlen 1946–1990," *Zeitschrift für Parlamentsfragen*, vol. 21, no. 3, October 1990.
45. For an analysis of this, see Barry M. Blechman and Cathleen S. Fischer: *The Silent Partner: West Germany and Arms Control*, 1988.
46. Federal Office of Statistics, Federal Office Publications, Wiesbaden, 1990, p. 278.
47. "Eurobarometer: Public Opinion in the European Community," Commission of the European Communities, December 1984, no. 22.
48. See Elisabeth Noelle-Neumann, ed., *The Germans: Public Opinion Polls, 1967–1980*, 1981, p.103; See also the Office of Research USIA, West European Opinion on Key Security Issues, 1981–1982; Tables 42 and 43 show a dramatic increase in the percentage of Germans who opposed INF modernization no matter what. For an interesting analysis of German public opinion on security issues of the time, see Richard Eichenberg, *Drifting Together or Apart?* 1986, p. 16.
49. Hanmer, February 1980, pp. 14–17.
50. Mechtersheimer, 1981, p. 276.
51. See also "Kommunique der Nuklearen Planungsgruppe der NATO," 26. Ministertagung in den Haag, *Bulletin*, no. 1412, p. 1299.
52. Drew Middleton, "When Deployed in 1980s, the New Missiles in West Europe Could Strike Soviet Union," *New York Times*, December 13, 1979.
53. Barely a week before the Dual Track decision, Holland's parliament postponed any kind of final decision, defering the decision until later; See *Der Spiegel*, "NATO: Zweifel an America," December 26, 1979, no. 51, p. 19.
54. *Bulletin*, "Kommunique der Ministertagung des Verteidigungs-Planungsausschusses," December 11–12, 1979 in Brüssel, no. 154, p. 1415.
55. "Erklärung der Bundesregierung zur NATO-Ratstagung in Brüssel," *Bulletin*, no. 154, p. 1405, Bonn, December 1979, 194. Sitzung des Deutschen Bundestages on December 14, 1979, p. 1406.
56. Marshall Goldman, *Detente and Dollars*, 1975, p. 296; See also Michael Mastanduno, "CoCom and American Export Control Policy: The Experience of the Reagan Administration," in David A. Baldwin and Helen V. Milner, eds., *East–West Trade Policy and the Atlantic Alliance*, 1990.
57. Angela Stent, *From Embargo to Ostpolitik: The Political Economy of West German–Soviet Relations, 1955–1980*, 1981, p. 169; See also Homer E. Moyer, Jr. and Linda A. Mabry, "Export Controls as Instruments of Foreign Policy: The History, Legal Issues and Policy Lessons of Three Recent Cases," *Law and Policy in International Business*, vol. 15, no. 1, 1983.
58. Jonathan Stern, *Soviet Natural Gas Development to 1990*, 1990, p. 192.

59. Michael Mastanduno, "Between Economics and National Security: The Western Politics of East-West Trade." Ph.D. Dissertation. Princeton University, 1985, p. 269.
60. According to Stent, even the pledge not to directly undermine the sanctions did not hold up. The West German firm Klockner-Werke snapped up the contract for a $311 million contract for construction of a steel mill that Armco had been forced to give up by the Carter sanctions; Stent, 1991, p. 141.
61. Schmidt, *Menschen und Mächte*, 1987, p. 83.
62. See Gary K. Bertsch, *East–West Strategic Trade, CoCom and the Atlantic Alliance*, April 1983, p. 44.
63. While the original plan was to develop natural gas production in the Yamburg oilfields, government leaders began to change the deal—suggesting that they could divert gas from the already-producing Urengoi oilfield that was 150 miles south of Yamburg. By 1978, the Urengoi field had become the world's largest gasfield, and it was seen as ready for expansion; From Stern, 1990, p. 64.
64. Mastanduno, 1985, p. 241.
65. For German firms, the deal was a welcomed opportunity. Mannesmann had been losing money during the past several years, and, therefore, at least one of its plants was entirely dependent on Soviet orders.
66. See Richard Perle's testimony before Congress, November 12, 1981, reprinted in *Defense '82*, February 1982, pp. 15–19.
67. Subsequently, the Reagan administration exploited every avenue it could to influence the Europeans against the construction of the natural gas pipeline. Administration officials brought up the issue in regular meetings of the COCOM, during NATO summits in late 1980 and early 1981, and in other fora. Soon after his election, President Reagan began dispatching high-level delegations to Europe to lobby governments to forgo the construction of the pipeline; See Mastanduno, 1985, p. 401; See also *New York Times*, August 16, 1981.
68. *New York Times*, July 19, 1981, p. A4.
69. In fact, key U.S. officals were engaged in heated debates about how best to approach the allies on the pipeline deal in the days and weeks leading up to the summit. According to subsequent reports, Secretary of Defense Weinberger stated that the United States should bring strong pressure on the Western Europeans to abandon the pipeline deal, including limiting export credits to the Europeans. Secretary of State Haig favored a more cautious route, recognizing the difficult situation the United States was in; See Mastanduno, 1985, p. 402; See also *New York Times*, July 19, 1981, p. A4.
70. Bruce W. Jentleson, *Pipeline Politics: The Complex Political Economy of East–West Energy Trade*, 1986, p. 182.
71. Caspar Weinberger, "Technology Transfers to the Soviet Union," *The Wall Street Journal*, January 12, 1982; See also the *New York Times*, January 14, 1982, p. 1.
72. See Hardt and Tomlinson, "Soviet Gas Pipeline: U.S. Options," 1982, p. 7; One extreme example of the U.S. opposition to the deal was expressed by Assistant Secretary of Defense Richard Perle in November 1981 at a Congressional hearing on the pipeline. He stated, "We believe that the increasing dependence of our European allies on Soviet energy and especially natural gas, will weaken the alliance politically and militarily." Perle went on to say that the estimates

were that $10 billion would be spent in Western Europe to import Soviet natural gas that would "finance . . . the modernization of the Soviet military and industrial establishment." Moreover, he believed the Soviets would gain a strong leverage over Western Europe because they would be dependent on the Soviets who could "cut the flow off." Perle said that the "day-to-day influence of the Soviets [over Western Europe] could flow like the gas itself;" Testimony before U.S. Congress, Senate, Committee on Banking, Housing and Urban Affairs, *Proposed Trans-Siberian Natural Gas Pipeline: Hearings*, 97th Congress, 1st session, 1981, pp. 113–117; See also Jentleson, 1986, p. 176.

73. Institut für Demoskopie, *Jahrbuch der öffentlichen Meinung*, vol. 7, 1977, p. 98.
74. Also, on November 25 Schmidt and Reagan had a long telephone conversation dealing with foreign policy in which Schmidt told Reagan about Brezhnev's visit to Bonn; and he sent Reagan further details by diplomatic route.
75. Jaruzelski explained the decision to impose martial law in a speech on Warsaw radio. He said, "We have to protect law and order, that is the only way to get out of the crisis. . . . Our country is on the verge of an abyss. . . . Our economy is a tragedy. The state structures no longer function. Everyone is on strike. . . . The government has been patient and had offered to bring the unionists into a front of national agreement." Blaming the democracy movement on the serious crisis, Jaruzelski rationalized that "We could not allow democracy to cause tragedy. . . . We had to do something before they dragged our country into civil war." Finally, Jarzelski assured the public that army rule would only be a "temporary measure." From "Poland Puts Military in Charge After Union Calls for Referendum," *New York Times*, December 13, 1981, p. A1.
76. Gwertzman, *New York Times*, December 14, 1981, p. 6A.
77. *New York Times*, January 14, 1982, p. A7.
78. A list of Soviet sanctions can be found in *East–West Commerical Policy: A Congressional Dialogue with the Reagan Administration*, Study by Joint Economic Committee of Congress, Feb. 16, 1982, pp. 66–68; See also Gwertzman, "U.S. Hopes to Prevent Military Rule in Poland from Becoming Permanent," *New York Times*, December 15, 1981, p. 6A.
79. Editorial, "Questions for Mr. Schmidt," *The Wall Street Journal*, January 4, 1982; See also *The Washington Post*, January 17, 1982, p. G1.
80. Helmut Schmidt Biography, *Men and Powers: A Political Retrospective*, 1989, p. 58; See also *Der Spiegel*, "DDR-Reise: Es is schon etwas besonderes," December 17, 1981, no. 52, p. 19.
81. *Der Spiegel*, December 17, 1981, no. 52, p. 19.
82. Vinocur, January 8, 1982, p. A8; But, according to later admissions, Schmidt said that German government officials appealed to the German citizenry to give "individual moral and materiel aid to our neighboring people, which they did very generously." Schmidt said, "I . . . knew that the Polish people were suffering from want; an increase in this misery might lead to an aggravation of the domestic crisis but would not result in freeing the Polish people. . . . More probably the opposite would ensue." Food baskets and other donations were shipped at Christmas time 1981, totaling several hundred million *Deutschmarks* in private aid; From Schmidt, *Men and Powers: A Political Retrospective*, 1989, p. 58; See also Editorial, "Questions for Mr. Schmidt," *The Wall Street Journal*, January 4, 1982; See also *The Washington Post*, January 17, 182, p. G1.

83. Mastanduno says that events in Poland were, therefore, more precipitaing than causal.... In fact, the objectives to be served by blocking the pipeline were not only more complex than a mere response to the Polish situation, but really the stimulus for dealing with and purging all remnants of detente economc cooperation; See Mastanduno, 1985, p. 175; Meanwhile, U.S. pressure on allies to cooperate was serious. In a meeting with the German ambassador, Peter Hermes, soon after the announcement of the sanctions, Reagan said that the entire Western alliance "must give Moscow a distinct answer" and it was expected that the German ambassador would set an example for the other allies. Also, an Office of Technology Assessment report of 1979 concluded that the Soviets were very reliant on Western equipment and technology for the functioning of every stage of the energy production process: computers, deep-well drill bits, refineries, pumps, compressor stations, and wide-diameter pipe.
84. Michael Mastanduno, "Strategies of Economic Containment: U.S. Trade Relations with the Soviet Union," *World Politics*, vol. 37, no. 4, July 1985.
85. Meanwhile, public pressure on Schmidt continued. The January 4, 1982, *Wall Street Journal* announced that the time had come for Schmidt to take a stand, "Mr. Schmidt's stance toward Moscow speaks of a demoralized leadership whose best vision of West Germany's future is as a Finlandized industrial vassal of a totalitarian empire" . . . another commentator said "No more Munichs!" See *The Wall Street Journal*, January 4, 1982; See also *The Washington Post*, January 17, 182, p. G1.
86. *New York Times*, February 4, 1982, p. A1.
87. In fact, three days before the NATO meeting, in accord with the declaration of sanctions, the Reagan administration had denied an export license to General Electric for $175 million worth of rotors and other parts for the compressor stations for which it was subcontractor to *AEG-Kanis* and others; See Mastanduno, 1985, p. 192.
88. *Bulletin*, "Erklärung zu den Ereignissen in Polen," January 13, 1982, no. 4, p. 21; See also *New York Times*, January 12, 1982, p. A8; All member countries voted in favor of the NATO final communiqúe, but there was some quiet dissent to the change in diplomatic tack. Only two days after the NATO meeting, West German Economics Minister Otto Lambsdorff excluded from the pledge not to directly undermine American sanctions those contracts for which American firms were only subcontractors. This meant that the compressor station contracts had to be reconfigured, but otherwise there was a general consensus in support of the plan; For Chancellor Schmidt's line on these developments, see *Bulletin*, "Erklärung der Bundesregierung zur Entwicklung in Polen und den Gesprächen in Washington and Paris," no. 5, p. 29, January 15, 1982; A speech by Schmidt before the *Bundestag*, 76th session, January 14, 1982, p. 29; *New York Times*, January 14, 1982, p. 1; See also *Washington Post*, January 17, 1982, p. G1; John Hardt and Kate Tomlinson, "Soviet Gas Pipeline: U.S. Options," Congressional Research Service, 1982, p. 13.
89. Accordingly, the Soviet and Polish governments responded harshly to the communiqúe, accusing NATO of interfering in their domestic politics. In a joint Soviet–Polish communiqúe issued at the conclusion of a visit by Poland's Foreign Minister to Moscow, the leaders combined a sharp criticism of Monday's statement by NATO with a strong appeal for maintenance of

detente. This was seen by Western diplomats as further evidence of disquiet in Moscow over the Europeans, increasingly critical attitude toward the military crackdown in Poland. The Soviet and Polish governments stated that they "strongly rejected" the statement issued by NATO Foreign Ministers, and they argued that sanctions against Poland and Soviet Union were particularly dangerous because they undermine the foundations of European cooperation; See Serge Schmemann, "Soviet and Poland Accuse NATO Allies of 'Interfering'," *New York Times*, January 13, 1982, p. A6.

90. Mastanduno, 1985, p. 68.
91. William A. Root, "Trade Controls That Work," *Foreign Policy*, no. 56, Fall 1984.
92. *New York Times*, February 4, 1982, p. A1.
93. Root, Fall 1984.
94. *New York Times*, February 4, 1982, p. A1.
95. Nevertheless, several nations made it clear that they would uphold the NATO sanctions agreement and offer a common front to the Soviet challenge. And this came in accord with continued U.S. government efforts to promote sanctions. For example, the Italian government put the question of pipeline and gas import contracts on hold as part of this initiative. Commerce Department officials told a House subcommittee that the United States believed it could stop a French company, Alstohm–Atlantique, from making gas compressors for the pipeline on grounds that it was using General Electric patents.
96. *Der Spiegel*, no. 18, 1982, pp. 16–30.
97. *Der Spiegel*, "Die SPD is doch nicht euer Eigentum," no. 41, 1981, p. 17.
98. "The most striking case came at the Lower Bavaria, Upper Palatinate convention, where the group, despite pleads by Peter Glotz, SPD national party manager, recommended that West Germany withdraw from the NATO plan to deploy middle-range nuclear missiles in Western Europe at the end of 1983"; See John Vinocur, "Schmidt Frustrated by Regional Party Votes," *New York Times*, February 8, 1982.
99. *Der Spiegel*, "Das ist ein dummes Gefühl," p. 17.
100. *Der Spiegel*, July 28, 1982, no. 31, p. 24.
101. *Der Spiegel*, "In einem halben Jahr sind wir dran," September 12, 1981, no. 37, p. 28.
102. *Der Spiegel*, "Genscher: Die SPD Läuft auf den Felgen," March 19, 1982, no. 11, p. 37.
103. *Der Spiegel*, May 14, 1982, no. 18, p. 20.
104. U.S. Department of State, Bureau of Public Affairs, October 1981.
105. Schmidt, *Menschen und Mächte*, 1987, p. 175.
106. Institut für Demoskopie, *Jahrbuch der öffentlichen Meinung*, vol. 7, 1977, p. 98.
107. Gerhard Ritter and Merith Niehuss, *Wahlen in Deutschland: 1946–1991*, 1991, p. 160; *Der Spiegel*, "Wird Die Landshafft Erleuchten," October 12, 1981, no. 40, p. 19.
108. Judith Miller, "Kissinger Says NATO Will Break Up If Something Is Not Done," *New York Times*, January 25, 1982, p. A6.
109. *Der Spiegel*, "Aussenpolitik: Feste Sprache," January 28, 1982, no. 4, p. 23.
110. It appears that in order to build German public consensus for a final decision on the sanctions and pipeline questions, Chancellor Schmidt had decided to be very vocal and forthright about the strong German connections with the

Polish people. On January 30, he gave a speech on the "day of solidarity with the Polish people" in the *Bundestag*. In this speech, the chancellor spoke out about German concerns for the Polish workers. He described the private German donations that had been collected as part of the "spontaneous act of giving" by citizens. Schmidt noted that over two million food baskets had been shipped eastward, worth a total of more than DM 100 million. Recognizing the crackdown, Schmidt stated that with Germany's friends in Europe and America, they hoped to encourage Poland to "throw off the yoke of oppression." See "Tag der Solidarität mit Polen," *Bulletin*, February 2, 1982, no. 10, p. 69; It is also worth noting that in this same period, members of EC agreed to reduce their imports of Soviet goods by only $140 million or approximately 1.4 percent; See the *New York Times*, March 12, 1982, p. A6; See also William Safire, "Helmut's Pipeline," *New York Times*, February 19, 1982, p. A31.

111. *Bulletin*, no. 30, p. 233, "Aktuelle Fragen der Sicherheitspolitik," April 3, 1982.
112. *The Washington Post*, June 4, 1982, p. 1.
113. See the reaction of Undersecretary of State Lawrence Eagleburger in *New York Times*, March 31, 1982, p. A8.
114. See the Versailles Summit June Communiqûe Text, *New York Times*, June 7, 1982, p. D6.
115. *Der Spiegel*, no. 24, 1982, "Lasst Uns Einen Neubeginn Machen," p. 17; See also the Versailles Summit June Communiqûe Text, *New York Times*, June 7, 1982, p. D6.
116. *Der Spiegel*, "Das Lästige Ding Versichern Lassen," no. 31, 1982, pp. 19–24; See also "Erdgas," no. 31, 1982, p. 23.
117. See *The Economist*, June 26, 1982, pp. 52–53.
118. In particular, European leaders also cited the fact that the United States wanted tough economic sanctions on key elements of the Siberian pipeline project and related industry, but there was no serious effort by the United States to embargo something important to its own economy—grain sales; *New York Times*, August 13, 1982, p. A21.
119. *Der Spiegel*, "Die Amerikaner Machen die Allianz kaputt," no. 30, 1982, p. 15–23.
120. *New York Times*, September 1, 1982, p. A4.
121. *The Washington Post*, June 4, 1982, p. 1.
122. The text of the November Resolution can be found in *New York Times* and *Washington Post*, November 14–15, 1982, pp. A1 and A3.

4 MIXED SIGNALS IN GERMAN FOREIGN POLICY, 1983–1985

COOPERATION: NATO MODERNIZATION OF INF SYSTEMS

The NATO Dual Track decision of December 1979 led to very serious public protests against nuclear weapons in West Germany.[1] Debates about the deployment of new nuclear systems came to symbolize division in Europe over defense strategy in the wake of detente and ultimately contributed to the demise of SPD-FDP governing coalition. Christian Democratic Union (CDU) leader Helmut Kohl took control of a new Conservative–Liberal coalition government in October 1982, and one of his first acts was to reaffirm German support for the Dual Track plan.[2] In spite of serious popular opposition and protests, leaders pushed an initiative through the *Bundestag* a year later that authorized the deployment of the modernized systems on German soil. The decision to support modernization in spite of tremendous popular opposition makes this case both puzzling and significant.[3]

Elite Decision Authority

The November 1983 cabinet decision to support the deployment of modernized INF systems on German soil was taken by a coalition of members from the Christian Democratic Union (CDU), its sister party in Bavaria, the Christian Socialist Union (CSU), and the Free Democratic Party (FDP). Within the context of the elite decision authority, neither the CDU–CSU nor FDP leaders could formally commit the resources of the regime without the support of the other party's leaders. Key leaders included Chancellor Helmut Kohl (CDU), Foreign Minister Hans-Dietrich Genscher (FDP), and Defense Minister Manfred Wörner (CDU). In addition, security policy factions in the major party in government were represented by conservatives Franz Josef Strauss (CSU) and Alfred Dregger (CSU); and moderates like Volker Rühe (CDU), the leader of the Union party *Bundestag Fraktion*.[4]

The NATO Dual Track Decision

As noted in chapter 3, the NATO Dual Track initiative was passed by a unanimous vote of foreign and defense ministers at the Brussels summit on December 12, 1979.[5] The first track was an alliance offer to enter into negotiations with the Soviet Union on these systems. The second track was a plan for NATO allies to deploy 572 modernized, intermediate-range nuclear systems if the negotiations did not yield significant progress. Of these systems, 108 would be land-based, new, and high-accurate Pershing IIs deployed solely in West Germany, and the remaining systems would be 464 ground-launched cruise missiles to be deployed in at least four West European member states.[6] These systems would have the range and accuracy to strike targets in the western Soviet Union.

In response to the NATO announcement, the Soviet government declared on December 14, 1979 that NATO had "ruined any chances for potential negotiation" on INF systems.[7] Nevertheless, German leaders provided political support to encourage both the U.S. and the Soviet leaderships to negotiate on INF. By July 4, 1980, Schmidt had drawn out an initial promise from Brezhnev that the Soviets would enter into negotiations on INF systems if "certain conditions were met."[8] After some prenegotiation, representatives of the superpowers met in Geneva in 1981 and began to negotiate the status of intermediate-range systems in the European theater.

Progress in INF negotiations was markedly affected by the Reagan announcement of the "Zero Option" in November 1981. He said that if the Soviets would agree to dismantle all SS-20s, SS-4s, and SS-5s, NATO would cancel deployment of the Pershing IIs and cruise missiles. While this presented a serious challenge to the legitimacy of the Soviet position, the plan achieved support immediately from Schmidt and British Prime Minister Thatcher and was to serve as a foundation for future negotiations.[9] The Zero Option also gained support at the Williamsburg conference for the G-7 leaders in May 1983, and NATO leaders reaffirmed their willingness to support the stationing of the new systems if the Geneva negotiations were not completed by the fall of 1983.[10]

Debates in Germany over INF

Initially, the Dual Track decision was warmly received by the German polity. In the first real discussion of the plan in the *Bundestag* on December 14, 1979, leaders of all major parties praised the move based on shared perceptions of the threat to Western security represented by the Soviet SS-20s. Union party spokesman Manfred Wörner defined the NATO plan as the best way to handle the difficult security policy position in which West Germany had found itself. Foreign Minister Genscher offered junior party support for the government's position in favor of the Dual Track plan. Even moderate Social Democrats offered early support of the move, recognizing the "strategic imperative" of the decision.[11]

But the NATO decision eventually led to serious debates in Germany about the extent of its commitment to the alliance. In fact, legislators in the *Bundestag* held more than 35 formal debates between 1979 and 1983 on German support for the plan, and public opposition to the plan increased in intensity as time for deployment drew nearer.[12] But perhaps the most important opposition to Schmidt's programs came from inside his own party organization in 1981. SPD leaders like Egon Bahr, Willy Brandt, Oskar Lafontaine, Karsten Voigt, Erhard Eppler, and Herbert Wehner vehemently voiced their opposition to the NATO plan.[13] At the same time, dissensus spread laterally in the major party as the Social Democratic party branch in Hamburg (Schmidt's hometown) voted against the Dual Track plan. All the while, Schmidt tried to maintain support for the Dual Track plan, and on at least one occasion in 1981, he had to make threats not to run as party leader in the next elections in order to gain tacit support from left-wing party leaders.[14]

Faced with serious political rifts in the SPD, much of the responsibility for supporting the NATO Dual Track plan fell to the Free Democratic leadership—and even to the Conservative opposition. In fact, by the summer of 1982 Genscher became the pivotal figure in the West German Euromissile dispute. Recognizing the situation was very serious, Genscher concluded that Schmidt no longer commanded a majority of support for the Dual Track decision inside the Social Democratic party. The neutralist ideas and leaning of the party organization toward the left put Genscher in an awkward political situation. Differences over support for the NATO plan were also compounded by very serious differences on economic policy inside the coalition.[15]

Die Wende

By September 1982, Genscher and the FDP leadership concluded that it was "necessary, for the sake of continuity in foreign policy," to break up the left-center coalition to form a new right-center coalition with Kohl's Christian Democrats. Without this shift to the right, Genscher believed that leaders would not be able to confirm or legitimate the foreign and defense policy he had shaped with Schmidt and the SPD.[16] Continuing economic problems, including rising unemployment and inflationary pressures, also threatened the base of support upon which Genscher depended.

Genscher resigned as foreign minister on September 17, 1982, taking his party out of the governing coalition and bringing the Social-Liberal coalition to an end.[17] On October 1, 1989, Helmut Kohl became chancellor after winning a pledge of support from the Free Democrats and a constructive vote of no-confidence in the *Bundestag*. As chairman of the Union party and leader of the party *Fraktion*, Kohl was in a particularly powerful position. He was a lifelong politico in the Conservative party with a strong commitment to cooperation in the NATO alliance and to deterrence of the Warsaw Pact. Kohl was also known as a skillful manager of political disputes, and Genscher believed he was well-suited to pragmatically respond to the divisive debate on INF modernization.

On October 13, the new chancellor delivered his first government statement to the *Bundestag* emphasizing continuity in foreign and security policy. He focused on the key to ties with the United States and working toward cooperation within the NATO alliance. Specifically, Kohl argued that the Soviets would only seriously enter into negotiations when they were sure that the NATO alliance would carry through with the Dual Track pledge, and he appealed to the Soviet government to accept the Zero Option. Kohl also made it clear that Genscher and other FDP leaders would remain in key ministerial posts, thus further guaranteeing continuity in German security policy.[18]

Federal Elections

Because of existing controversies over the NATO Dual Track plan, the national election campaign during the spring of 1983 was termed the *Raketenwahlkampf*, or "missile campaign," by some members of the press.[19] Genscher offered continuity on foreign policy to the coalition ticket, and Kohl offered Union party solutions to foreign policy and economic problems. But the *Raketenwahlkampf* was unusual in German politics for several reasons. First, a security policy issue dominated much of the debate and political stumping in the contest. Some analysts and leaders viewed the election more as a referendum on German support for INF modernization than as a vote on domestic issues like economic programs.[20] The Conservatives used the Soviet threat to European security as a tool to gain political support, and they promised long-term security and stability in relations with the United States. Second, the campaign occurred in an environment of great public protest over defense policy. Third, the campaign period was marked by an unusually large number of foreign diplomats who appeared in support of the Conservative-Liberal coalition—including a February 1983 visit by U.S. Vice President Bush, who preached a message of U.S.-German cooperation.[21]

Meanwhile, the SPD took a serious turn toward the political left on security policy issues. With Schmidt out of the way, Hans-Jochen Vogel became the chancellor candidate, and the party adopted the slogan "In the German Interest." The party took a stand against the INF modernization plans, in favor of French and British reductions of systems in conjunction with Soviet reductions, and in favor of generous negotiating stances at superpower meetings on INF. Some members of the party, including Saarland President Oskar Lafontaine, suggested that the Germans should withdraw their membership from the NATO alliance altogether. The party stand enjoined a number of direct proposals from, and interaction with, the Soviet leadership, which favored an SPD victory and a softening of the Western stance on INF.[22]

In national elections held on March 6, 1986, the Union party won a clear victory with 45.8 percent of vote. While economic issues were also important in this election, exit polls indicated that the future of

German security policy was a very salient issue for many voters. The results were interpreted by Kohl and other leaders as support for the new Conservative-Liberal coalition and a silent majority in favor of the coalition's security policy program.[23]

Post-Commitment Political Conditions

While the March elections seemed to temporarily quiet opponents of INF modernization, overall support in the German polity for the Dual Track plan continued to wane. *Europäische Meinungs—Neumann Institut für Demoskopie* (EMNID) studies showed that a growing percentage of Germans (around 50 percent in August 1983) were opposed to the Dual Track decision.[24] Other surveys reported that 75 percent of all Germans opposed the deployment of modernized systems and only 14 percent favored it.[25] Diffuse support for the Union party declined in the period leading up to the final decision on INF modernization, and according to public opinion studies from the *Forschungsgruppe Wahlen* and the *Institut für Demoskopie*, the Union party lost about 6 percent of its support over the course of 1983. This loss of support was reflected in Hessen *Landtag* elections in September 1983 when the Union party lost 6.2 percent of the popular vote from previous standings.[26]

Meanwhile, the peace protest movement (*Friedensbewegung*) in Germany gathered momentum, as more intellectuals and politicians came out against the plan. Massive public demonstrations against INF modernization were held in Bonn, Hamburg, London, Rome, and other European cities. And on August 27, 1983, there was a large protest march in Washington, D.C., which caught the attention of the European media and gave a great deal of hope to protesters in Germany. Perhaps most importantly, the peace movement gained support from (and momentum in) key sectors of the government, private industry, and trade unions.[27]

When the last INF negotiation round began in Geneva on September 6, there was an increased sense of urgency in the protest movements. Many famous and influential Germans were arrested in protests near a major NATO installation in Mutlangen in early September. On October 5, the German labor unions supported a five-minute work stoppage in support of INF opposition movements, and another large blockade of U.S. bases and NATO complexes occurred in coordinated protests on October 13. Finally, the *Friedensbewegungen* launched its "Central Action Week" on

October 15, which saw large-scale, organized protests by different groups, including laborers, students, religious groups, women, and politicians. The week culminated in the largest protests of the INF debate on October 22, with millions participating in mass rallies against deployment held in Bonn, Hamburg, Stuttgart, and other cities. Large protest rallies were also held at this time in other NATO countries, including the United Kingdom, Italy, Belgium, Austria, Denmark, and the Netherlands.[28]

Conditions Inside the Government

Even though millions of Germans were marching in the streets against INF modernization, most Union party and FDP leaders remained supportive of the NATO plan. There were no public statements of differences among party leaders in government on the Dual Track plan in 1983, and there was very little evidence of factionalism. This support seems to have been driven by a consensus about the long-term strategic needs for German and European security. Both FDP and Union party leaders shared a common perception of the Soviet threat from SS-20s and other weapons systems; they believed in upholding commitments to the NATO alliance; and they perceived that public opposition to their security policy programs would be short lived.

In fact, leaders of the governing coalition worked hard to demonstrate to the public that they were sensitive to security concerns, while at the same time maintaining firm support for the alliance and wider German security interests. The thirtieth *Bundestag* debate on INF modernization on September 16, 1983, was a good representation of intra- and interparty coalition consensus on this question. There, Conservative Defense Minister Wörner and party leader Heiner Geissler both offered strong support for possible INF modernization, suggesting real intraparty consensus. Foreign Minister Genscher and FDP leader Möllemann were careful to demonstrate their support for the plan, but they also acknowledged Soviet efforts to meet Western demands in arms talks. Finally, impassioned pleas to postpone or cancel modernization made by the Social Democrats indicated that the Schmidt faction of the party had been utterly defeated by the liberal elements. SPD opponents based their arguments, in part, on the legitimacy of public opposition to the plan.[29] Figure 4.1 summarizes Germany's domestic conditions in the INF case.

Conditions	Case Study Analysis Questions	Coding
Major Party Unity	A. Repeated Similar Statements B. No Different Positions C. No Disputes	Consensus
Coalition Consensus	A. Repeated Similar Statements B. Repeated Similar Positions C. No Disputes, Strong Consensus	Intense Consensus
Symmetry of Effects	A. Intensely Symmetrical B. Direct Public Impact C. Many Sectors	Symmetrical
Election Results	A. Highly Influenced by Elections B. Results Have Positive Impact C. Elections: Intense Support	Highly Influential
Popular Support	A. Yes, Upcoming Elections B. Very Negative Polls C. Polls Offer Little Support	No Support

Figure 4.1 Summary of domestic political conditions in the INF case.

Taking the First Track

Members of the elite decision authority met on October 10, 1983, and decided to authorize deployment of modernized INF systems on German soil if U.S.-Soviet negotiations failed. To support this decision, the cabinet agreed to advance the initiative authorizing deployment to the *Bundestag* for final debate on November 20. Leaders knew that final agreement had to be reached by midnight on November 21 in order to coordinate the political decision with NATO logistical planning for deployment.[30]

The decision to push the initiative through was the result of consensus about the strategic imperative of modernization and good relations inside the coalition. Union party leaders Kohl and Wörner were convinced of the need for modernization in the face of Soviet buildups, and for cooperation with their NATO allies at such a crucial juncture. Further, Conservatives believed that the West German public had no inherent right to block a government decision through public protests and maintained that the people had spoken through the 1983 elections.[31] The cabinet decision to forge ahead was solidified when the Free Democratic leadership committed its support to the plan without demanding concessions. Foreign Minister Genscher supported this decision because he believed that West Germany was in a precarious security situation. He called attention to the fact that the Soviets were claiming parity in Europe on nuclear systems when they had around 300 SS-20s, while the West Europeans had no weapons of comparable range or accuracy.[32]

Leaders also decided that major party congresses should be held several days before the final *Bundestag* debate on INF. While such plans had been in the works for some time, they were set into motion by the decision on the scheduling of the final debate. Evidence suggests that leaders were concerned about maintaining support in their parties and overcoming outside opposition before the final *Bundestag* debate.[33]

Outside opposition to INF modernization came from the Social Democrats and led to serious debates on the floor of the *Bundestag* several days before the special party conferences. On November 10–11, 1983, there were long discussions in the chambers about the deep differences between party stances on this issue. In these discussions, the Green Party leadership maneuvered to control the floor for as long as possible, forcing the *Fraktion* leadership from other parties to demand equal time. The Greens spoke of a German "veto right on deployment issues," and the Social Democratic opposition stressed the unique position of Germany as mediator between the superpowers. The defense minister countered that the German government had been trying to exert pressure but failed to gain anything. Wörner said "we have negotiated for two years, while they [the Soviets] have continued to arm themselves . . . and now it appears that overall there was no ground gained for which to continue to progress at the negotiation table." In the end, Green party representatives marched out of the *Bundestag* on more than one occasion in November.[34]

Party Congresses and the Final Debate

Each party organization held a special conference in the fall of 1983 to debate and discuss German security policy. Kohl, Genscher, and many others hoped that healthy intraparty debate would lead to solid interparty cooperation on the issue of support for INF modernization. The Christian Democratic leadership met on November 18. The Free Democrats came together in Karlsrühe on November 18–19 to discuss German security policy, and party leader Genscher apparently saw this meeting as very important for building consensus in his party on INF modernization. Scattered reports suggested that regional factionalism had begun to plague Genscher, and the *Schleswig-Holstein* FDP organization had announced to the press that it was against the current modernization plan as too "automatic."[35] In fact, some Free Democrats preferred to postpone deployment until the end of the year and to divulge information about basing to the public. But in the end, regional rumblings never affected the central party organizations' stand on the question. Genscher held the line at the meeting, essentially gaining a blanket authorization for deployment with no public disclosure about the basing of new missiles.[36] Finally, on November 18, 1983, the Social Democratic congress in Cologne found Helmut Schmidt virtually alone in trying to convince others of the serious strategic need for INF modernization in light of the Warsaw Pact threat. Driven by factionalism, the end product of the Cologne congress was a resolution entitled "Yes to a European Peace Order—No to More Nuclear Weapons."[37]

The final *Bundestag* debate on whether or not to authorize deployment of modernized INF systems was held on November 21–22, 1983. Cabinet leaders supported the Dual Track decision and the authorization of deployment of intermediate-range weapons on German soil throughout the debate. Chancellor Kohl opened the session with a strong speech in favor of deployment. He rejected any call for the inclusion of British and French missiles in the INF negotiations, and he supported a strong continued relationship with NATO in the formulation of European security policy. Finally, he justified German support for INF modernization on the basis of trust and cooperation with the United States in the alliance, stating, "I stand by the modernization decision on the basis of a close personal contact with the American president and knowing that every possibility was made in the Geneva talks to get progress."[38] Later, Defense Minister Wörner sharply challenged the opposition for its "irresponsible" foreign policy stances on the INF question, and Foreign Minister Genscher argued that German neutralism and concession to the Soviets would be a dangerous position on this question. Genscher said that "a drift of our country out of the Western alliance . . . would mean a dangerous destabilization of our security."[39] Finally, the SPD leadership countered that concessions to the Soviet leadership were not inherently dangerous and that Western moves might, in fact, be attributed as the cause for an opening of hostilities.

At the end of debate on November 22, 1983, a resolution was passed in the *Bundestag* that authorized deployment and urged the continuation of the arms control negotiations on the issue. The vote was taken along party lines, except for a small group of SPD supporters, led by Helmut Schmidt, who believed that INF modernization was necessary under current conditions. The final resolution stated:

> The German *Bundestag* believes that the Geneva negotiations on INF, in spite of great efforts by the Americans, are unlikely soon to come to some agreement.... Therefore, the German legislature supports the decision of the German government, fulfilling their duty as the second part of the NATO Dual Track decision lays out.... to begin the stationing process for INF.[40]

Soviet representatives at the INF negotiations in Geneva walked out in protest less than a day after the *Bundestag* declaration, and no date was set for the resumption of the talks. On the weekend of November 26, the first Pershing II missiles arrived in Germany.[41]

Overall, the German decision to uphold the commitment to the NATO Dual Track plan represents an interesting case of cooperation. There was elite consensus in support of the NATO plan based on a shared conception of the strategic imperative of INF modernization and for cooperation in NATO. But outside the halls of government, there was very little consensus on the question. Ultimately, major party and coalition consensus enabled elites to ignore public opinion polls and protests, and forge ahead with implementing the NATO plan. This decision was to have a marked impact on German security policy and German society during the 1980s and beyond.

DEFECTION: AGRICULTURAL POLICY REFORM IN THE EC

In June 1985, West German leaders decided to veto an EC initiative to reform agricultural policy and lower cereal price subsidies, defecting from earlier commitments they had made to the EC.[42] Agriculture Minister Ignaz Kiechle had voted to support agricultural policy reforms during a meeting of the EC Agricultural Council in March 1984, which included a call for a decrease in agricultural price subsidies for cereals by 3.6 percent, and Chancellor Helmut Kohl had reaffirmed this commitment at the Fontainebleau summit of Community leaders in June 1984. A year later, however, these same German leaders decided to renege on commitments to support EC agricultural policy reform—even though they were supporting many other integration efforts. This case study explores how such a seemingly small issue became a serious challenge to the Community in 1985.

Elite Decision Authority

The decision not to support EC agricultural price reduction plans was taken by many of the same leaders who had supported INF modernization in late 1983. This group included: Chancellor Helmut Kohl (CDU); Finance Minister Gerhard Stoltenberg (CDU); Foreign Minister Hans-Dietrich Genscher (FDP); Economics Minister Martin Bangemann (FDP); and Agricultural Minister Ignaz Kiechle (CSU). In addition, economic policy factions in the major party in government were represented by the moderates (including Kohl and Stoltenberg); and conservatives, including CSU leader Lothar Späth and Bayern Minister-President Franz-Josef Strauss.

One leader who played a particularly influential role in the political debate over EC agricultural policy was Agriculture Minister Kiechle, who began his tenure in office in 1983. Kiechle, a CSU leader from Bayern, was originally a farmer by trade.[43] This career experience made Kiechle well-suited to serve as minister of agriculture, but some analysts have suggested that his lack of direct political experience ultimately caused a great deal of trouble for the Kohl government. By the mid-1980s, Kiechle had developed a reputation for upholding farmers' interests above all other policy considerations in the government and in the EC.[44]

The Agricultural Sector in Germany

By the 1980s, West Germany had become a very powerful member of the EC, and German–EC ties began to take on a very positive and supportive tone under the leadership of Chancellor Kohl. Plans for enhancing economic integration and policy coordination in the EC were more openly discussed by key leaders than ever before in the history of the Federal Republic. However, cooperation in *some* issue areas in the Community did not always translate into cooperation in *all* areas, and agricultural policy had traditionally been somewhat more difficult to coordinate in the EC. Special legal protection and status for farmers in many European countries (in the immediate aftermath of World War II because of the serious need for agricultural production) made agricultural policy a complicated and serious construct.[45]

This was especially the case in Germany. The German farmers' political power was originally born out of the nineteenth century efforts of the *Junkers* to coordinate regional and national agricultural policies. Very early in the history of the unified Germany, feudal landlords had asked for, and received, special support from the government. This included the imposition of protective tariffs and the establishment of price regularity through government price supports. In exchange for political support, the German government continued to protect small- and medium-sized farms over the years, and price supports became a central element of German agricultural policy.[46]

After World War II, the German government rebuilt its special relationship with the farming sector and worked to establish a strong position for farmers in the wider European market. Leaders of the agricultural sector reinvigorated a farm lobby in the German Farmers Association (*Deutscher Bauernverband*, or DBV). The DBV began active negotiations with the new German government and developed a number of lateral contacts within the new Ministry of Agriculture. With the support of all major parties in government, the DBV pushed for and got a new agricultural law (the *Landwirtschaftgesetz*), which institutionalized the idea that the farm sector required "special support from the state to compensate for its natural and economic disadvantages."[47] By the 1970s and 1980s the DBV was described as the "voice of West German farmers" and had developed regional and branch organizations, multiple special divisions, and a permanent secretariat. The German farm lobby represented a strong, cohesive group that could employ organized, vocal support for (or opposition to) any government policy in the 1980s.[48]

Early Efforts to Coordinate EC Agricultural Policies

Efforts to coordinate EC agricultural policies began with the Common Agricultural Program (CAP), which was actually established in 1955 before the signing of the Treaty of Rome. Such programs were seen by most European leaders, including German Chancellor Adenauer and coalition leaders, as a "rising tide that would lift all boats" in the long term. Forming CAP meant that leaders had to conceptualize new ways to integrate domestic and foreign agricultural policies and to overcome nontariff barriers to trade such as a reduction of agricultural price supports.[49]

Nevertheless, the special position of farmers in the European economy and their strong lobby guaranteed that early versions of the CAP offered protection for the farming sector and allowed continued price supports. This arrangement guaranteed that the primary, short-term goal of European leaders in the 1950s—to promote production and distribution of food—would be met.[50] The CAP did encourage efforts to set standards for common price levels, develop a program for dealing with industrial processing technology, and garner commitments on tariff protection and transportation flows. And each stage of development of the CAP was subjected to periodic review by the Council of Ministers, in which a unanimous vote was necessary to uphold the program and new policies.[51]

Efforts to reform EC agricultural policies in the 1970s saw debates over the development and maintenance of Monetary Compensatory Amounts (MCAs). The MCA program was originally developed in the 1960s to establish an EC unit of account that was not based on the U.S. dollar. Basically, the MCA program was a border tax and subsidy plan combined, and it provided for some equity on the common market for exchange and trade value. In Germany, this system had produced strong gains for the farmers in the 1970s because of strong currency and high subsidization rates. MCAs represented an important level of stability for the German agricultural sector because the program insulated the domestic price level from the effects of national currency changes and kept it some 10 percent above the Community price level. Largely as a result of the MCA program and the stability it offered for farmers, Germany rose to be one of Europe's largest exporters by the end of the 1960s.[52]

But the MCA system was being destabilized in the 1970s by overproduction in Europe. French government officials recognized this and renewed efforts to bring about a reform of agricultural policy and the MCA system. In response, German Agricultural Minister Josef Ertls publicly stated that Germany would not support any type of immediate reduction in the subsidies offered to farmers by the MCA program. Ertls called for a gradual reform of the program through a transitional approach for realigning German price supports with CAP standards.[53] After many meetings between top legislators, leaders of the farm lobby, and members of the German elite decision authority, a compromise was finally reached in 1979. Germany agreed to phase out the the main MCA program only if the EC would retain a portion of it—the "green rate"—as a buffer for price reductions.[54]

Agricultural Policy Reform in the 1980s

Following this progress, some leaders in the EC began to pursue a new set of agricultural policy reforms in the early 1980s. German Chancellor Kohl and Foreign Minister Genscher considered monetary and agricultural policy reforms at this time based on an assessment of domestic political conditions inside Germany. In 1984, Union party leaders like Kohl and Agricultural Minister Kiechle were in agreement that gradual EC agricultural policy reforms would be in the long-term interest of Germany and the Community. They knew that the Free Democrats would generally support this position as a route to improve the long-term economic situation in Europe. But they were also aware that the German *Bauernverband* would oppose any agricultural policy reforms that would reduce farmers' incomes and would lobby cabinet leaders, *Bundestag* representatives, and regional party leaders against any plans.

Based on this assessment, in March 1984, German Agriculture Minister Kiechle quietly supported an Agricultural Council decision to phase out the last vestige of the MCA subsidy system, the "green rate."[55] At the same time, he ensured that the plan explicitly provided short-term economic compensation to farmers who were expected to lose income. German small farms stood to lose the most in terms of price supports, so the subsidy plan allowed for a tax relief package for the German farmers that would be as high as 3 percent of the German value added tax (VAT). In addition, the Council unanimously voted to support a reform program of the CAP across the board, which included a general cut in price supports for milk and other select products.[56]

At the European Council meeting in Fontainebleau on June 25–26, 1984, European leaders including Chancellor Kohl sponsored the introduction of the "Single European Act" (SEA) initiative, designed to restructure decision making and promote equitable development and freer trade. The initiative called for the use of qualified majority voting in the Council of Ministers and a clear delineation of members' veto rights. But in exchange for their support for the SEA, some European leaders demanded and received a tacit pledge from Kohl to support deeper agricultural policy reforms. Nevertheless, upon his return from the summit,

Kohl made clear that the German government would only support gradual reforms in exchange for concessions in other policy areas. He claimed that he had fought for the ceiling on German VAT relief to farmers to be raised from 3 percent to 5 percent and had demanded that this change go into effect on July 1, 1984 (instead of the agreed January 1, 1985).[57]

The progress on agricultural policy reform at Fontainebleau was viewed with skepticism and growing concern inside Germany. Representatives of the DVB and other farm lobby organizations issued a series of statements to the press condemning what they saw as a "radical change" in government policy.[58] They charged that the wine and cereals farmers would be hurt most if the German government supported changes in EC agricultural policies. A series of meetings of the regional farm associations were held in the fall of 1984, and farmers argued that EC plans were particularly unfair because farmers had already seen a dramatic drop in prices paid for their products over the last five years. Nevertheless, negotiations about CAP reform continued in the European Commission throughout 1984. Meanwhile, government leaders, farmers, and lobbyists in Germany all prepared for a pitched policy battle.[59]

The Commission Reform Plan

On January 25, 1985, the European Commission presented a formal plan for agricultural policy reform to the Community. The plan called for all EC member states to agree to cut agricultural price subsidies for cereals by an average of 3.6 percent. This meant that those relatively more prosperous states would have to cut even more than poorer member states, and early estimates were that German cereals farmers would suffer about a 4.2 percent cut in subsidies. The Commission also recommended that remaining positive MCA payments (the green rate program) in Germany and the Netherlands be drastically reduced in coordination with the elimination of remaining negative MCAs in Greece and France.[60]

Not surprisingly, there were mixed reactions to the reform plan inside the Community. French President Mitterand, British Prime Minister Thatcher, and the agricultural ministers from the Netherlands and Denmark all came out in support of the plan as a necessary, but painful, initiative.[61] But Chancellor Kohl was initially noncommittal and muted in his responses to questions about the plan. The record suggests that he was quietly pleased with the plan because it fit well with his preferred Europe policy in several ways. First, the call for reform of agricultural prices matched his governments' position that there should be a reduction of spending in the EC across the board. Second, Kohl repeated at all major summits leading up to the agricultural policy debate that his government was in strong support of the EC reform plans. Third, Kohl's leadership style allowed that his Agriculture Minister Kiechle have a great deal of latitude in agricultural policy, thus shifting much of the controversy associated with the plan off to Kiechle. Fourth, agricultural reform could be seen as contributing to progress in other areas of Europe policy—particularly elements of the SEA initiative.[62]

Foreign Minister Genscher and other FDP leaders were also noncommittal about the Commission reform proposal in the early months of 1985. Genscher expressed concerns about the "severity" of the Commission reform plan, but he also suggested that maintaining the high subsidies for cereals prices would damage progress in other areas of EC integration. While expressing concerns that the EC policy would hurt the family farms in Germany, he argued that a showdown with the EC could prompt a "difficult conflict in the government" where "a coalition struggle seemed likely."[63] In March, Genscher reiterated his unwillingness to support a veto on proposed EC agricultural reform while at the same time offering his general support for the plight of the farmers.

While other government officials reacted quietly to Commission efforts, Agriculture Minister Kiechle publicly declared war on the reform plan. He stated that he was strongly opposed to the plan and made several basic arguments against it. First, he defined the proposed cut as too severe (he characterized it as "completely unreasonable"), and expressed concern that it would harm the farming sector in Germany too deeply. Second, he said the proposed price reduction would not affect the more serious problem of overproduction in the Community. Third, he argued that a proposal for cuts in cereals prices unfairly targeted German farmers while other countries' farmers would not fare so badly. Ultimately, Kiechle stated that his primary goal remained working for the "highest prices attainable for German products," even in the face of proposed Commission reforms.[64]

Thus, it was Kiechle's statements of opposition to the plan in January that actually set the tone for the German debate about subsidy reforms. And Kiechle continued to dominate consideration of agricultural policy reform plans in the German government for the next few months. Other economic problems in Germany at the time facilitated his efforts to gather support for his stand from top Union party leaders. Conservative officials at a Union party leadership conference, including Lothar Späth, argued that Kiechle was fighting the good fight and that the EC was not being sensitive to important sectoral concerns in member countries.[65]

In a February 1985 agriculture ministry report on the plan, Kiechle argued that Germany had been flexible on the question of the reduction of Community milk prices, but he made it clear that German farmers rejected most other EC reform efforts. The collusion between the farm lobby and the government was so great in this period that the *Bauernverband* was actually able to have a section included in this report that called for a partial price increase of some 5 percent for some products.[66]

While Kiechle set the tone for the struggle, it also became clear that this was a battle he could not win. There was no sign of support for German stonewalling coming from top political leaders including Chancellor Kohl and Foreign Minister Genscher at this time. While the agriculture minister threatened that the German farm sector would block the streets of Brussels or Bonn if the EC forged ahead on reforms, there was little credence given to such threat by Commission leaders. Editorials published in February indicated that the emerging debate over prices would force Kiechle to play "price poker" in which he was bound to lose. Finally, critics charged that Kiechle had conveniently chosen to ignore what had already become a reality in 1985: Agricultural price reforms were supported in the EC and were already under way in some areas.[67]

The EC Agricultural Council Meeting

Another important event in the formalization of the German government's position on a plan to cut cereals price subsidies was the Agricultural Council meeting in Brussels on March 11–13, 1985. According to a formal report on the council session released by the German Agriculture Ministry, a number of European countries supported cereals price reductions and general agricultural policy reform, including France, Great Britain, the Netherlands, and Denmark, but Germany remained opposed. During the meeting, Kiechle argued that his country had "special agricultural concerns" and that it could not support a cut in cereals and rape oilseed prices. As an alternative, Kiechle suggested that other types of reforms be tried first, such as penalties for overproduction or setting standards of quality for cereals produced in the EC. Chancellor Kohl also defended the right of a member country to veto initiatives that would "sacrifice a country's sovereign rights" during a background briefing for journalists in Brussels. Further, Kohl stated that Kiechle was firmly in charge of German agricultural policy relative to the EC.[68]

Leaders at the Agricultural Council meeting in March were not able to reach consensus on the plan to cut cereals price subsidies, and a series of diplomatic exchanges ensued.[69] In March and April, Kiechle returned to a schedule of shuttling between Bonn and Brussels to try and resolve this issue. He began to more frequently articulate a threat that Germany would invoke a veto of the Commission plan if necessary. In a *Bundestag* speech in late March 1985, Kiechle pledged that he would accept no further negotiation or compromise on the cereals price issue after the end of March. He also reiterated that a 3.6 percent price cut for German farmers would be disastrous and unfair.[70] But, as before, this hard-line approach apparently had little or no direct support from other German government leaders. Instead, Kiechle primarily drew strength from the well of his CSU party support and from direct, continuous contact with the farm lobby and supporters within the ministry. Constantin Freiherr Heereman, the president of the *Bauernverband*, spoke in support of Kiechle's position in the debates on several occasions.[71]

By April 1985, debates in the Agricultural Council sessions had become quite confrontational, and leaders became more concerned about the implications of this agricultural price debate for Community relations. These debates underscored both the serious division among Community leaders and the growing isolation of the German position on agricultural policy reforms. Meanwhile, reports indicate that Kiechle began to receive messages from officials in the chancellor's office suggesting that the price reform debate be handled more cautiously. Foreign Minister Genscher even began to consciously distance himself from the German stand on agricultural policy reform because of concerns about its implications for the Single European Act.[72]

Nevertheless, Kiechle forged ahead with the fight against EC plans for reform and received occasional bursts of support from the *Kanzleramt*. When Kiechle appealed directly to Kohl for some leadership and support in May 1985, the chancellor sent a telex to European Commission President Jacques Delors asking him to do everything possible to deal with the special situation in which Germany found itself on the agricultural prices debate. In the telex, Kohl warned that "one of the most important member states of the Community should not be put under such pressure," suggesting that this issue might spill over into other areas of concern in the EC. The message also contained a veiled threat of the consequences of unfairly pushing Germany to cooperate with the EC.[73]

In mid-May the Commission made an effort to compromise on the issue by presenting member governments with its final offer reform plan. This plan called for a smaller drop of cereals prices by some 1.8 percent—about half the reduction discussed in earlier rounds of negotiation. Also, this compromise would recognize governments with special circumstances that would limit the cut in agricultural prices they would experience. Accordingly, a formal Council of Ministers vote on the plan was scheduled for June 14, 1985. Kiechle's response to the EC final offer was a brief consultation visit to Bonn (lasting only a few hours, and, in fact, involving no recorded meetings with government officials), and a strategy meeting with his advisers in which he decided not to budge on the issue of price reductions.[74]

Post-Commitment Political Conditions

In the prelude to the final Council of Ministers' vote on the agricultural price reform plan, German leaders became more divided over agricultural and economic policies. Controversies that arose in Bonn in this period were of two types. First, there were specific policy differences expressed by key leaders in the coalition government on the question of EC agricultural policy reform. Second, there were wider differences of opinion about how the coalition should be run and the future of foreign and domestic policies. These differences over agricultural policy became public knowledge through published interviews and indirect accounts of cabinet sessions. The official German policy toward EC agricultural policy reform (to support German farmers, reject cuts in prices paid for agricultural products, encourage quality standards, and discourage overproduction) had been developed and championed by Kiechle for many months.[75]

Kiechle's own position was that there should be aggressive German resistance to any EC overhaul of sectoral policy at all costs. But by May most coalition leaders had decided that they could no longer accept this stance because of its potential to harm other German foreign economic policy programs such as the SEA. Up to this point, other Union party leaders had been willing to use Kiechle's position as a smoke screen of their own and believed that they could appease the farmers without great political costs. But Kiechle's hard-line stance appears to have lost the support of Chancellor Kohl, Finance Minister Stoltenberg, and key junior party leaders over time. In fact, the main difference between Kohl and Kiechle was not on any of the substantive points but rather over the delivery of the messages on agricultural reform. Kohl favored quiet diplomacy and compromise instead of Kiechle's grandstanding and stonewalling. Kohl's tacit support for the possible use of a German veto on price reforms may have only derived from political calculations about the loss of support from German farmers. Ultimately, Kohl was unwilling to see agriculture as a major barrier to wider reforms of the EC, whereas Kiechle was ready to fight any and all supranational authority. The maneuvering room that Kohl granted Kiechle in the spring 1985 has since been interpreted as more of an effort to put distance between Kohl and the bold approach of the agricultural ministry.[76]

Finance Minister Stoltenberg, a strong political ally of the chancellor, also made public statements opposing Kiechle's maneuvers. But Stoltenberg's positions seems to have derived from ideas about Europe policy rather than a question about percentage points. His primary mission in the Finance Ministry had been the goal of reducing spending for Community programs, and he stood firm in the government for fiscal responsibility. Generally, he pushed for any and all governmental programs that would reduce the payments that the German government made to support and subsidize the functioning of the organization. This position stood in direct opposition to the preferential treatment that Kiechle sought for the German farming sector.[77]

By June, Kiechle's support base had really narrowed to two groups: ultraconservative CSU leaders and farmers. Bayern Minister-President Strauss sent a letter of support to Kiechle after the last round of agricultural price negotiations, which said that Kiechle's stand was important because "our party always has supported for the condition of the many farmers' family situation on the foundation of a wide relationship between their skills and general social stability."[78] Wheat farmers also had become a vocal and aggressive lobby fighting against possible cuts in the prices paid for their product. These farmers took their concerns directly to leaders in Bonn through public protests and private meetings during May and June 1985.

Differences of opinion about agricultural policy reform (and economic programs in general) inside the major party in government also contributed to larger concerns about Kohl's leadership ability in this same period. Inside his own party organization, Kohl had reportedly lost a great deal of authority by mid-1985, in part due to continuing economic problems and high unemployment in Germany. Morale in the Union party was described as "miserable" in the wake of poor election results and other problems. At the same time, the Union party had lost about 4 percent of its popular support measured through public opinion surveys. The steepest drop in support came in the first five months of 1985 and could be seen to have a very negative effect on German leaders' assessments of their political situation.[79]

Concerns began to grow about the viability of the chancellor to stand for another national election, scheduled for early 1987. Critics charged that Kohl was losing touch with the electorate, and references were made in *Der Spiegel* to the similarities between Kohl's battle for leadership in the party and the problems Ludwig Erhard had faced in the mid-1960s. Most leaders acknowledged that the coming fall would be a "critical time for Kohl to achieve as much as possible" in shaping foreign and domestic policy and building popular support for the party.[80]

Intraparty splits were compounded by differences between the parties in the coalition over agriculture policy and economic policy. Junior party leaders opposed Kiechle's stand and favored EC agricultural policy reforms as a route to enhanced cooperation in the Community. In May, Economics Minister Bangemann made several press statements expressing concern about the implications of a continued German hard-line stance.[81] In fact, there were reports that Bangemann ignored cabinet discipline and openly challenged the authority of the chancellor on economic policy plans on several occasions in the spring.[82] Foreign Minister Genscher seemed most disturbed about the implications of German stonewalling in one sector for cooperation in other areas. And Chairman of the FDP Lambsdorff indicated that the FDP and the Union parties were not in agreement about the future direction of European policies and blamed Kohl for Germany's flawed Europe policy.[83]

Overall, this was a reflection of the fact that the FDP leadership perceived it was losing a battle with CSU leaders to have serious influence over foreign economic policy. Reports emerged of Genscher trying to decouple foreign policy from the government because the FDP perceived that Kohl was "helpless and directionless" on foreign policy questions.[84] At one point, Genscher even suggested that it was really the Social Democrats who were most "in touch" on foreign and defense policy. And Lambsdorff stated quite explicitly that there should be some sort of breaking point with the major party in government on European policy because moves like the veto would do "irreparable damage" to the EC. All of these factors were seen as signs of the relative loss of support for Kohl inside the government.[85]

Outside the government, three important developments affected Kohl's political support base in the period before a final decision on agricultural policy reforms. First, lobbyists and farmers stepped up their pressure on the German government not to cooperate with an EC program that would do great harm to the agriculture sector. Specifically, *Bauernverband* chief Freiherr launched an advertisement campaign and organized farmer visits to Bonn to support Kiechle and challenge political supporters of the EC reform plan. Second, the Union party experienced a serious defeat in regional elections in Nordrhein-Westfal on May 12, losing 6.7 percent of the popular vote. In the press, his defeat was attributed to the sense among the public that the Union party was elitist—with its own agenda and way of conducting politics. According to exit polls, the Union party directly lost a good segment of the farm vote in the Rheinland, suggesting serious ramifications for the social and political contexts within which European agricultural policy would be viewed.[86]

Another influence on the domestic political arena was the release of a series of new public opinion surveys. Polls released in May 1985 showed that the Union party was continuing to lose vital political support. *Institüt für Demoskopie* studies showed that the Union party had lost more than 4 percent of its base of support in the first five months of 1985 alone. Finally, feeling thermometer surveys showed that support for Kohl as leader dropped, from January to May 1985, by almost 1 percent, while most other leaders (including Kiechle) actually gained support during this period. This was a product of both farmer opposition to EC reforms and public disaffection for debates with the EC over small percentage price reductions in subsidy payments.[87]

Overall, these developments did not create an environment in which perceived risky or controversial decisions were easily taken. Government leaders were reportedly very concerned about the upcoming regional election in Hessen, scheduled for March 1986.

And members of the media and political analysts began to speculate that there would be a serious cabinet reshuffle in late 1985 as a response to the loss of public support. Meanwhile, SPD opposition leaders seized on the controversy and spoke out against the direction of EC agricultural reforms. The SPD laid the blame for poor EC policy direction squarely on the shoulders of the Union party and Agricultural Minister Kiechle, and they argued that they could better represent the interests of the farm sector in negotiations over agricultural reform in Brussels.[88] Figure 4.2 summarizes Germany's domestic political conditions in this case.

The German Veto of the EC Reform Plan

By early June 1985, it became apparent that the positions of the European Commission and the German government were on a collision course. Therefore, EC Commission President Pandolfi called for a final *majority vote* on whether or not to change EC policy to be held at the next round of agricultural negotiations in mid-June. The timing of this was very important because it was scheduled just two weeks before the Community's Milan summit of government and

Conditions	Case Study Analysis Questions	Coding
Major Party Unity	A. Few Different Statements B. Many Different Positions C. Serious Disputes	Dissensus
Coalition Consensus	A. Few Different Statements B. Few Different Positions C. Serious Disputes	Dissensus
Symmetry of Effects	A. Intense Asymmetry B. Indirect Impact C. One Sector	Intense Asymmetry
Election Results	A. Highly Influenced by Elections B. Very Negative Impact C. Elections Offer No Support	Highly Influential
Popular Support	A. Yes, Upcoming Elections B. Negative Polls C. Polls Offer No Support	No Support

Figure 4.2 Summary of domestic political conditions in the cereals price cut veto case.

state leaders. For many European governments, the Milan summit represented the apex of a long and serious period of negotiation about many aspects of economic and political integration.[89]

In response to the Commission move, Agriculture Minister Kiechle again warned that the German government would not compromise on planned EC reductions in prices for cereals or rape oilseed. He issued a press release that said that the German delegation to the Brussels talks was prepared to invoke the Luxembourg Compromise in the voting on reform. This compromise was established in 1966 after the French government boycotted EC proceedings and effectively blocked members from unanimous consent in favor of a particular policy. That precedent left open the possibility for an EC member state to veto a decision that it felt seriously challenged "very important" or "vital national interests."[90]

With a showdown imminent, German leaders met to consider their options on June 7, 1985, in the chancellor's office. Cabinet members of the elite decision authority also met on several subsequent occasions to debate and formulate German governmental policy and contingency plans to deal with EC actions. By June 10, Kiechle had gained the support of Conservatives for a plan to veto any decision made in Brussels that would challenge Germany's vital national interests. Increasingly, leaders also agreed that Kiechle would go it alone, and Kohl, Stoltenberg, Genscher, and others would not take vocal public stands on the issue.[91] This was clearly based on the deep concern that the SEA and other questions not be sacrificed over agricultural policy squabbles.

On Wednesday, June 13, members of the Agriculture Commission gathered for a final vote on proposed policy reforms. At the point when the Agricultural Council leader Pandolfi called for a majority vote on the Commission plan to reduce cereals prices, Kiechle announced his intention to invoke the Luxembourg Compromise. Commission officials argued that qualified majority vote was legal and would need only 45 of the possible 63 votes to carry. Kiechle argued, however, that discussions over agricultural policy reform must continue until a unanimous decision was reached by the member states of the organization. This effectively represented a veto of the EC initiative and a serious effort to derail agricultural policy reform proposals.[92] In direct response to the German veto, agriculture ministers from five other member states—Greece, Denmark, Britain, France, and Ireland—declared that they "could not assess the vital national interests of another member" and would not vote.[93] The Commission plan to reduce subsidies for cereals and rape oilseed prices thus could not be formally adopted.[94]

The veto drew a mix of praise and criticism back in Germany. Kiechle's actions were especially lauded by the farm lobby. The president of the DBV said that the German move was "correct" and that farmers were in agreement that such a plan should be stopped.[95] Several prominent leaders of the CSU also came out in strong support for the move, and periodicals with traditional loyalties to southern Germany, including the *Süddeutsche Zeitung* and the *Bayernische Kurier,* expressed support for the action and lauded Kiechle as a hero.[96] Meanwhile, criticism of the move came from the *Gewerkschaftsbund*, the largest German labor union, and from a number of SPD officials.[97]

Aftermath of the Veto

The German government's response to the veto was damage control—seen in the scramble by top officials to explain how their use of the veto related to Europe policy in general. At a press conference the day after the veto, Kiechle said that Germany would continue to support EC integration and would support the enlargement of the Community to bring in Spain and Portugal as new members.[98] In a similar vein, Chancellor Kohl enunciated government support for European cooperation and optimism about the upcoming Milan summit in a speech to the *Bundestag* on the June 27, 1985. Kohl's speech also indicated a change in tack of Germany's Europe policy in preparation for the Milan summit. By stating that the coalition supported the development of a better EC decision-making process and a broadening of the organization's membership, Kohl recognized the limitations that the veto right placed upon the Community. Formally, Kohl stated that the German government was "ready to accept the Treaty of Rome in all formalities, with a widening of institutions and rules." Kohl even added that Germany was prepared to make "earnest efforts in the organization to shrink common agricultural prices."[99]

FDP leaders also tried to explain away the veto and politically distance themselves from the stand on agricultural policy. In mid-June Otto Lambsdorff recognized that the veto put Kohl in a "terrible negotiating position" for the Milan summit.[100] Genscher had been very optimistic about the Milan summit and argued that the veto represented a "serious contradiction" to most tenets of German foreign policy. He stated that "whatever in connection with the cereals price in the agricultural minister occurs, it remains true that German leaders will participate at the European Parliament in Milan in discussions about reform of the veto rule and support reform of the Treaty of Rome."[101]

Meanwhile, EC officials reacted strongly and decisively against the veto. Basically, they were determined to overturn any effort to veto such an important, substantive policy reform plan, and Commission President Delors stated that this type of individual resistance to group progress must not be permitted. On June 19, 1985, Chairman of the EC Agricultural Commission Frans Andriessen declared that prices would be reduced in the Community for cereals and rape oilseed products by 1.8 percent, in accord with the last compromise plan debated in the body. The Commission leadership justified its executive authority by arguing that it was responsible for making sure that the system and markets functioned smoothly. To this end, the EC would not recognize the veto right as valid for major issues of importance to the body.[102]

This unilateral move drew sharp criticism from certain German officials and the DVB. Kiechle expressed outrage at the decision, and even the chancellor spoke out in support of German farmers. But this new flare-up of controversy came just a few days before the planned Milan summit, and many German leaders sought to downplay the controversy in favor of the SEA initiative. Chancellor Kohl's declaration of German government policy toward Europe for the summit told a great deal about the shift in coalition foreign policy, and he sought to convey to the farm lobby that his government wanted to support sectoral interests and maximize gains as much as possible. But Kohl was also interested in articulating to his own party, his government, the opposition, farmers, and the public that the Conservative-Liberal coalition could not blindly support the interests of some particular sector of the economy. Therefore, he offered support for the use of majority voting and would support well-designed plans, including reductions in price supports on agricultural products. The coalition was not about to let an isolated farm lobby dictate the fate of European integration.[103]

Ultimately, this more conciliatory approach actually provided new impetus for compromise on agricultural policy. The political slate was cleared in time for the Milan summit, where substantial progress was made on the SEA. The European Commission bureaucracy subsequently conducted research on whether or not there was any way that the EC could formulate continued price guarantees and still attempt to retain a flexible and dynamic market for farmers and consumers.[104] And by July 1985 it appeared that the Commission was close to presenting a modified, more flexible plan for dealing with cereals price cuts.

Even Agricultural Minister Kiechle signed on to the shift in government policy emphasis. In a speech at a farm rally in early July 1985, he focused on problems of overproduction, the social and political ramifications of the coming change (clearly adopting a more European perspective). In mid-July, Kiechle invited Commission chief Andriessen to his farm in southern Germany, and private meetings helped bring about a new compromise on the issue for the entire Community. A few weeks later, the Commission proposed a price cut of an average 2 percent, with a kickback subsidy to be paid directly for farmers, and a plan that would include penalties for overproduction.[105] This compromise was hailed as a "partial victory" for all Community members, and it paved the way for talks to begin in September on more substantive policy reforms.[106] In sum, this case represents a significant example of foreign policy defection from earlier commitments to the EC and demonstrates the ways in which domestic political actors can affect the ability of state leaders to uphold commitments to international organizations.

NOTES

1. "Communiqúe—Declaration of the Brussels Summit," *Bulletin*, Bundesregierung Presse- und Informationsamt, December 14, 1979, p. 1352.
2. Helmut Kohl, *Stenographischer Bericht des Deutschen Bundestages*, Deutscher Bundestag, 9 Wahlperiode, 121 Sitzung, October 13, 1982, p. 7220; See also the pledge by the incumbent foreign minister, Hans-Dietrich Genscher, *Stenographischer Bericht des Deutschen Bundestages*, Deutscher Bundestag, 9 Wahlperiode, 121 Sitzung, October 13, 1982, p. 7231.
3. See Richard Eichenberg, "Dual Track and Double Trouble: The Two-Level Politics of INF," in Peter B. Evans, Harold K. Jacobson, and Robert D. Putnam, eds., *Double-Edged Diplomacy: International Bargaining and Domestic Politics*, 1993, pp. 45–76; See also Jeffrey Boutwell, *The German Nuclear Dilemma*, 1990, p. 54.
4. This is based on a survey of the German media from August 1982 through December 1983. These leaders were given priority in speaking to the INF debate in the *Bundestag*, based on a review of the *Stenographischer Bericht des Deutschen Bundestages* from key debates in this period; See especially the *Bundestag* debates on November 22–23, 1983.
5. *NATO Final Communiqúes 1975–1980*, Brussels: NATO Information Service, 1980, p. 123.

6. "Communiqúe—Declaration of the Brussels Summit," December 12, 1979, from *Bulletin*, Bundesregierung Presse- und Informationsamt, December 14, 1979, p. 1352.
7. See Schmidt, 1987, p. 114; The Soviets went on to formally reject the NATO proposal on January 3, 1980, arguing that the plan would destabilize European security; See also *Stenographischer Bericht des Deutschen Bundestages*, 8 Wahlperiode, 194 Sitzung, December 14, 1979, pp. 15465–15477—including speeches by Schmidt, Kohl, Genscher, Wörner, and others.
8. Helmut Schmidt, *Menschen und Mächte,* 1987, p. 116.
9. "Schmidt und Frau Thatcher begrüssen die Initiative Reagans," *Frankfurter Allgemeine Zeitung*, November 19, 1981, p. 1.
10. "Bekenntnis zum Doppelbeschluss in Williamsburg: Das Treffen harmonisch und zuversichtlich," *Frankfurter Allgemeine Zeitung*, May 30, 1983, pp. 1–2.
11. Karl Cerny, *Germany at the Polls*, 1990, p. 14.
12. Based on a review of *Stenographischer Bericht des Deutschen Bundestages* from December 14, 1979 to November 23, 1983; See also *Der Spiegel*, no. 46, November 16, 1983, p. 33.
13. For more on SPD internal opposition, see Karsten Voigt, *Wege zur Abrüstung*, 1981.
14. At a special party congress in Baden-Wurttemberg in May 1981, Schmidt again threatened to resign his post if the party organization tried to turn against the government on modernization; See "Der Kanzler kämpft für Nachrüstung, Warnungen an die Partei vor Selbstzerstörung," *Frankfurter Allgemeine Zeitung*, May 18, 1981, pp. 1–2.
15. Author's Interview with Hans-Dietrich Genscher, April 29, 1993.
16. "Die Bonner Koalition ist zerbrochen," *Frankfurter Allgemeine Zeitung*, September 18, 1982, pp. 1–2; See also the speeches by Schmidt, Kohl, and Genscher to the *Bundestag:* "Der Erklärung des Bundeskanzlers vor dem Parlament," *Frankfurter Allgemeine Zeitung*, September 18, 1982, p. 4; In fact, the move by Genscher was also taken to mollify a growing antimodernization faction within the Free Democratic Party. Some Liberals like Jurgen Mölleman announced in 1982 that they favored the development of Europe as a nuclear-free zone—a somewhat neutral initiative that gave Genscher cause for concern.
17. See *Frankfurter Allgemeine Zeitung*, September 18, 1982, p. 1.
18. Helmut Kohl's government declaration, from *Stenographischer Bericht des Deutschen Bundestages*, October 13, 1982, p. 7220.
19. See *Der Spiegel*, no. 3, January 20, 1983, pp. 31–42; However, the popular argument that this was really a campaign for INF modernization can be challenged. Exit polls taken on March 6 showed that voters listed unemployment, the environment, and pensions as concerns that were more serious than arms control.
20. Soviet Foreign Minister Gromyko came to Bonn in early January; See "Der sowjetische Aussenminister in Bonn, Genscher spricht von der Überlebensfrage Europas," *Frankfurter Allgemeine Zeitung*, January 17, 1983, pp. 1–2; Also, Kohl visited Paris and received a strong show of support from French President Mitterand; See "Mitterand Forder ein wehrhaftes Westeuropa, Friedenssicherung durch Gleichgewicht," *Frankfurter Allgemeine Zeitung*, January 21, 1983, p. 1.

21. "Bush spricht von einer Politik der ausgestreckten Hand," *Frankfurter Allgemeine Zeitung*, February 2, 1983, p. 2.
22. "Vogel: Das letzte Wort über Mittelstreckenraketenwaffen ist noch nicht gesprochen," *Frankfurter Allgemeine Zeitung*, January 14, 1983, pp. 1–2; "Lafontaine stellt die deutsche Nato-Mitgliedschaft in Frage," *Frankfurter Allgemeine Zeitung*, March 28, 1983; The shift in party position had gone so far that the general impression left with many people was that the SPD would accept a regional monopoly of the Soviet Union in order to attain peace—a dangerous, neutralist precedent. Among the critics was a group of intellectuals from the SPD, including Karl Kaiser, Director of the German Society for Foreign Policy; See Jeffrey Herf, *War By Other Means: Soviet Power, West German Resistance, and the Battle of the Euromissiles,* 1991, p. 242.
23. Allensbach Institute Survey #4031, released July 1983, p. 7; See also Kohl, *Stenographischer Bericht des Deutschen Bundestages*, Deutscher Bundestag, 10 Wahlperiode, 47 Sitzung, March 13, 1983, p. 12341.
24. Reprinted in Richard Eichenberg, *Drifting Together or Apart?* 1986, p. 158; See also Hans Rattinger, *Public Opinion and National Security in Western Europe: Consensus Lost?* 1989, p. 34.
25. Results of Allensbach Institute survey, from Elisabeth Nölle-Neumann, "Are Three-Quarters of the Germans Opposed to Deployment? The Situation is Actually More Complex," *Frankfurter Allgemeine Zeitung*, September 16, 1983, p. 1 [author's translation]; The results of these studies were subject to challenge. For example, in another set of survey results released in November 1983, principal investigator Karl-Heinz Reuband argued that the roughly 75 percent of respondents who opposed the Dual Track plan were really not opposed to actual deployment. Reuband supported the arguments of Nölle-Neumann in this regard; Karl-Heinz Reuband, "Demoskopische Verwirrungen in der Nachrüstungsfrage: Was halten die Bundesbürger vom Nachrüstungsbeschluß?" November 1983, pp. 64–78; See also Allensbach Institute Survey, recorded in Hans Rattinger and Gregory Flynn, eds., *The Public and Atlantic Defense*, 1985, pp. 47–54; See also SINUS survey results, from *Sowjetische und amerikanische Politik im Urteil der Deutschen in der Bundesrepublik*, reprinted in Hans Rattinger, "Change Versus Continuity in West German Public Attitudes on National Security and Nuclear Weapons in the Early 1980s," *Public Opinion Quarterly*, Winter 1987, vol. 51, no. 4, pp. 495–521.
26. Institut für Demoskopie, *Jahrbuch der öffentlichen Meinung*, vol. 7, 1977, p. 98; See also Forschungsgruppe Wahlen, *Political Barometer-Election Study 1986/87*, 1987.
27. Schmidt gives a good account of the protests and their implications for government decision making; See Schmidt, *Menschen und Mächte*, 1987, pp. 99–125; A chronology of protest demonstrations can be found in Stanley Sloan, "NATO Nuclear Forces: Modernization and Arms Control," Congressional Research Service Issue Brief Number #1B8 1128, Washington, D.C., August 2, 1983.
28. "Hunderttausende demonstrieren auf den Strassen für Frieden," *Frankfurter Allgemeine Zeitung*, October 24, 1983, pp. 1–2; See also *Der Spiegel*, October 28, 1983, no. 43, pp. 25–34.
29. See the positions of key leaders during an intense *Bundestag* debate on June 15, 1983 and later on June 23. See speeches by Hans-Dietrich Genscher, *Stenographischer Bericht des Deutschen Bundestages*, Deutscher Bundestag, 10

Wahlperiode, 13 Sitzung, June 15, 1983, pp. 700–814; and another intense series a week later; See "SPD Präsidium stellt sich hinter Brandt," *Süddeutsche Zeitung*, October 26, 1983; See also *Stenographischer Bericht des Deutschen Bundestages*, Deutscher Bundestag, 11 Wahlperiode, 4 Sitzung, September 21, 1983, pp. 1118–1162.

30. This decision was particularly significant in light of the original NATO timetable for modernization. The original plan was that states would authorize deployments of modernized INF systems by August 1983 if negotiations failed. The gradual slip from August to the end of the year was the result of production delays and necessary time for political manuvering in some NATO member states. Nevertheless, the timing issue was a bone of contention for the alliance, and the German leadership felt it important to act as definitively and quickly as possible; see *Stuttgarter Zeitung*, "Streit um Bundestagsdebatte spitzt sich zu," October 26, 1983.
31. CDU Documentation Series, "Rechtspositionen in der Diskussion um den NATO-Doppelbescluss," no. 36, November 10, 1983.
32. Hans-Dietrich Genscher, "Mittelstreckenraketen: Der Schlüssel zur Abrüstung in Moskau—Kontinuität und Berechenbarkeit; Der Deutschen Haltung Dürfen Nicht Gefährdet Werden," *NATO Brief*, German Version, Number 3/4, 1983, pp. 3–10; See also Genscher's party position as defined in *Stenographischer Bericht des Deutschen Bundestages*, 10 Wahlperiode, 23 Sitzung, September 16, 1983, p. 1578.
33. Klaus Dreher, "Termin und Dauer Der Bundestagsdebatte über die Nachrüstung heftig umstritten," *Süddeutsche Zeitung*, October 20, 1983, p. 1; See also "Genscher sucht die Rückendeckung der FDP für die Sicherheitspolitik der Bundesregierung," *Frankfurter Allgemeine Zeitung*, November 2, 1983, p. 1.
34. Rudiger Moniac, "Schroffe Gegensätze im Bundestag," *Die Welt*, November 12, 1983, p. 1.
35. "Genscher sucht die Rückendeckung der FDP für die Sicherheitspolitik der Bundesregierung," *Frankfurter Allgemeine Zeitung*, November 2, 1983, p. 2.
36. Ibid., 1983, p. 1.
37. "Das Schiff verlässt den Lotsen," *Der Spiegel*, November 14, 1983, no. 46, p. 26; "Materialen: Sicherheitspolitik im Rahmen der Friedenspolitik," *Leitantrag des Parteivorstands für den Parteitag in Berlin*, Bonn: Vorstand der SPD, Abteilung Presse- und Informations, October 6, 1979.
38. *Stenographischer Bericht des Deutschen Bundestages*, November 21–22, 1983, pp. 2321–2322.
39. Manfred Wörner, "Erklärung der Bundesregierung zum Doppelbeschluss der NATO und Stand der INF-Verhandlungen," *Bulletin*, no. 127, Bonn, November 22, 1983, pp. 1157–1171.
40. Text from Bundestagdrucksell 10/620; 10 German Bundestag, 36 Seating on November 22, 1983, s.2590; See also "Der Bundestag billigt die Stationierung "Das Bündenis bedroht niemanden," *Frankfurter Allgemeine Zeitung*, November 23, 1983.
41. "Erste Pershings in Mutlangen," *Süddeutsche Zeitung*, November 28, 1983, p. 1.
42. See *General Report on the Activities of the European Communities: 1984*, Brussels: European Community Information Service, 1985.

43. Ignaz Kiechle, *Und Grün Bleibt Unsere Zukunft*, 1985, p. 11 [author's translation].
44. At a public appearance in 1987, Kiechle displayed the intensity that sometimes affected his political interactions. In a speech, he encouraged the farm lobby to defend their interests with "uncompromising severity," regardless of "incautious external pressures." From *Bulletin*, March 25, 1987, p. 225; See also *Der Spiegel*, ed., no. 11, 1985, p. 19 [author's translation]; See also Hans-Jürgen Mahnke, *Gefragt: Ignaz Kiechle*, published by Dagmar Zirnbibl-Verlag; 1985.
45. See Michael Tracy, *Agriculture in Western Europe,* 1982.
46. See Simon Bulmer, *The Domestic Structure of European Policy-Making in West Germany*, 1987; See also Thomas Risse-Kappen, "Public Opinion, Domestic Structure, and Foreign Policy in Liberal Democracies," *World Politics*, vol. 43, July 1991; And Aurelia George, "The Politics of Interest Representation in the Japanese Diet: The Case of Agriculture," *Pacific Affairs*, vol. 64, Winter 1991/92, pp. 506–528.
47. Ignaz Kiechle, *Und Grün Bleibt Unsere Zukunft*, Stuttgart-Seewald Verlag, 1985, pp. 43–47; See also the *Landwirtschaftsgesetz*, September 1955, p. 565.
48. See H. Priebe, "German Agricultural Policy and the European Community," from K. Basevi, *West Germany: A European and Global Power*, 1980, pp. 139–150.
49. James Pearce, *The Common Agricultural Policy*, 1981, pp. 7 and 56.
50. Rosemary Fennell, "Reform of the CAP: Shadow or Substance?" *Journal of Common Market Studies*, vol. 26, no. 4, 1975.
51. See Edmund Neville-Rolfe, *The Politics of Agriculture in the European Community*, 1984.
52. In return, Hendriks notes that the farm lobby got fiscal concessions, improved social measures, investment subventions, and full compensation for the reduction of incomes as a result of the price alignment to the value of the about DM 1.1 billion in incentives—all as part of side-payments for the ongoing change. This is a real testament to the power of the farm lobby in this period; Gisela Hendriks, "The Politics of Food—The Case of Germany," *Food Policy*, February 1987, vol. 12, no. 1, pp. 35–45.
53. Tracy, *Agriculture in Western Europe*, 1982, pp. 16–38.
54. By this time, the German government was compensating its farmers annually by some DM 1.7 billion. The challenge of the MCA systems was really the establishment of artificial stability in the market; See Hendriks, 1989, p. 81; For a more detailed survey of problems with the coordination of Germany's agricultural policy in the Common Agricultural Program, see Stephen George, *Politics and Policy in the European Community*, 1991, pp. 145–156; See also Harold Priebe, "German Agricultural Policy and the European Community," from Basevi, 1980, pp. 139–150.
55. See S. Harris, A. Swinbank, and G. Wilkinson, *The Food and Farm Policies of the European Community*, 1983.
56. This plan was originally floated by the EC and announced as a method for reform of agricultural policy and a new financing of EC projects such as this on July 28, 1983; See *General Report on the Activities of the European Communities: 1984,* Brussels: European Community Information Service, 1985; It also became apparent during this period that issues relating to sectoral interests and EC cooperation were also directly related to issues of

German federalism. Because of the strong relationship between the Christian Socialist Union leadership and the farm lobby, the Bavarian state government evolved into another lobbying organization with the federal government on agricultural price issues. In an effort to interject in the debate over CAP reform, the agriculture minister for Bavaria was actively involved in trumping up federal government positions on sectoral reform in the EC; See Katzenstein, 1989, pp. 60–108; Katzenstein, "Problem of Model? West Germany in the 1980s," *World Politics*, July 1980, no. 32, no. 4; See also *Bayern Kurier*, "Erfolg fur Bayerns Bauern," December 15, 1984, p. 1.

57. Denton, 1987, p. 137; See also Josef Ertls, *Agrarpolitik ohne Illusionen*, Frankfurt, 1985, p. 35; See also Neville-Rolfe, 1984.
58. *Der Spiegel*, "Bauern: Dick und Dünn," February 4, 1985, no. 6, p. 28.
59. But at these meetings, *Bauernverband* spokesmen spoke little about one of the most serious problems with EC agricultural policies—overproduction. The result of this overproduction was that the EC, as a whole, produced around 50 percent more wheat than could be used or sold by the member states. In storage units around the continent lay about ten million tons of excess cereals products. By the summer of 1984, the press had latched on to this problem, and there was a great deal of public controversy about EC food reserves—the "butter mountains" and "wine lakes" created by the process and politics; See *Der Spiegel*, February 4, 1985, p. 32.
60. In fact, this proposal was originally approved by the Agricultural Council on March 11, 1984. The proposal was clearly defined and included a call for the elimination of MCAs. There was no outright opposition either "because the states felt that the proposed package represented an acceptable basis for further Council work or at least did not reject the Commission's approach outright."
61. Kiechle, "Bericht über die Tagung des Rates (Agrar)," March 20, 1985.
62. *Bulletin*, no.75, s.657, Bonn, den 28. Juni, 1985, "Zielsetzungen der Europapolitik der Bundesregierung," speech of the Chancellor before the German *Bundestag* on the June 27, 1985 debate over European policy and in favor of the June 28 summit in Milan for the European Council, pp. 657–662.
63. *Der Spiegel*, February 4, 1985, no. 6, p. 17.
64. Kiechle, January 17, 1985, *Bulletin*, January 22, 1985, no. 7, p. 57.
65. *Stuttgarter Zeitung*, "CDU kritisiert EG-Agrarpolitik," January 29, 1985, p. 2.
66. See Kiechle, *Und Grün Bleibt Unsere Zukunft*, 1985; Kiechle, 1985, p. 111 [author's translation]; See also *Süddeutsche Zeitung*, "Kiechle gegen Agrarpreis-Senkungen aller Art," February 8, 1985, p. 3.
67. In a March 1985 background briefing by Kohl for German journalists at the Brussels summit, Kohl appeared to support Kiechele and a hard-line stance on proposed price cuts; see *Die Zeit*, April 12, 1985.
68. *Die Zeit*, April 12, 1985, p. 1.
69. Kiechle, "Bericht über die Tagung des Rates (Agrar)," March 20, 1985; See also Agriculture Ministry Press Release, March 20, 1985; The ideas presented by German leaders were generally considered unacceptable by other Community leaders because of their base inequity. In particular, setting any type of quality standard for production was seen as a program that would give most German farm products an edge.

70. *Stuttgarter Zeitung*, "Kiechle will bei Agrarpreisen hart bleiben," March 29, 1985, p. 1; See also Peter Schmalz, "Die Gratwanderung von Kiechle zwischen Brüssel und München," *Die Welt*, March 23, 1985, p. 5.
71. *Frankfurter Allgemeine Zeitung*, "Unterstutzung für Kiechle in Fraktionen," March 29, 1985.
72. One particularly revealing interview with Kiechle that helped define his policy positions was a discussion with a reporter from the *Bonner Rundschau* on April 19, 1985. Kiechle argued that he would not rule out the use of the right of member governments of the EC to use a veto. He also argued that it was primarily his own reponsibility to represent the farm sector as his consituency. While saying that he was willing to compromise and that Germany did not "oppose every effort in the EC," he argued that any type of small reduction in prices would not affect the underlying problem of overproduction. As with other efforts, Kiechle stressed that the quality of the product should become a major issue of concern; *Bonner Rundschau*, "Veto-Recht nicht abschaffen," April 19, 1985, p. 5.
73. *FBIS-Western Europe*, transcript of article from *The Times,* May 15, 1985, p. B1.
74. See Kiechle, 1985, pp. 71–135; See also Hans-Jürgen Mahnke, Gefragt: Ignaz Kiechle, Dagmar Zirngibl-Verlag, 1985, pp. 1–89 [author's translation].
75. *Bayern Kurier*, "Den Bauern helfen," May 18, 1985, p. 1.
76. Based on the author's review of *Der Spiegel* and the *Frankfurter Allgemeine Zeitung*, January–June 1985.
77. See Gisela Hendriks, *Germany and European Integration: The Common Agricultural Policy—An Area of Conflict*, 1991, p. 146.
78. *Bayern Kurier*, "Den Bauern helfen," May 18, 1985, p. 1.
79. Hendriks, Winter 1988/89, p. 89; See also Forschungsgruppe Wahlen, *Political Barometer—Election Study 1986/87*, Mannheim, 1987; More data derived from Cerny, 1990, Appendix A: Percent of Party List Vote and the Distribution of Seats during Bundestag Elections, 1949–1987, from the Federal Office of Statistics, Wiesbaden, Federal Office Publications; See also W. Kohlhammer, ed., 1990, p. 277; See also Suzanne Schüttemeyer, "Die Ergebnisse der Landtagswahlen, 1946–1990," *Zeitschrift für Parlamentsfragen*, vol. 3, October 1990, pp. 464–473.
80. See *Der Spiegel*, "Genscher: "Kohl tut mir leid," 1985, no. 23, p. 22; This position hardened after the May 12 Nordrhein-Westfal electoral losses, See *Financial Times*, May 14, 1985, p. 13; See also "Koalition: Submissest Erinnert," *Der Spiegel*, June 9, 1985, no. 23, pp. 21–26.
81. *Financial Times*, May 14, 1985, p. 13.
82. *Der Spiegel*, June 9, 1985, no. 23, p. 23.
83. *Informationen Der Sozialdemokratischen Bundestagsfraktion*: Tagesdienst, Ausgabe 1249, June 24, 1985 [author's translation].
84. *Der Spiegel*, "Koalition: Das Wasser im Keller steigt," no. 26, June 21, 1985, p. 17.
85. *Der Spiegel*, "Im Herbst kommt es zum Schwur," no. 24, June 7, 1985, p. 31.
86. Exit polling was conducted by the Allensbacher Institut on May 12, 1985, in Nordrhein-Westfal, and was recorded in *Der Spiegel*, May 24, 1985, no. 23, p. 34.
87. *Frankfurter Allgemeine Zeitung*, May 8, 1985, pp. 2 and 4; *Der Spiegel*, "Koalition: Das Wasser im Keller steigt," no. 26, 1985, p. 20 (which means "the water in the cellar is rising"); A similar *Institut für Demoskopie* survey found in early 1985

that 60 percent of German reponsdents were unhappy with Kohl's performance, as reported in *Die Zeit*, "Kiechles sinnloser Kampf," June 21, 1985, p. 4.

88. *Der Spiegel*, "Koalition: Das Wasser im Keller steigt," 1985, no. 26, p. 17; See also *Die Welt*, "SPD fordert nationale Spielräume," February 2, 1985, p. 1.
89. See *General Report on the Activities of the European Communities: 1984*, Brussels: European Community Information Service, 1985.
90. Ignaz Kiechle, "Ergebnisse der Brusseler Agrarverhandlungen," Policy Declaration in the form of a telegram, May 17, 1985; See also *Pressemitteilung*, Press Release from the German Press and Information Office, dated May 31, 1985.
91. *Deutsche Presse Agentur*, "Bonner Veto Stosst auf kritik," June 13, 1985; Hendriks, Winter 1988/89, p. 86; See also *Frankfurter Allgemeine Zeitung*, "Harter Kampf der Agrarminister um den Getreidepreis," June 11, 1985, p. 2.
92. This veto right originated from France's "empty chair strategy" during 1965, which resulted in the Luxembourg compromise of 1966. This formal agreement was not ever incorporated into the Treaty of Rome, but it did represent a normative agreement in the organization. This allowed that when a member state feels that its personal interests are affected by negotiations, it can, within a set period, oppose a declaration and declare some acts null and void in accordance with national law.
93. See a report of Kiechle's actions in *Agence Europe*, June 14, 1985, p. 6.
94. *Die Welt*, "Kiechle legt in Luxemburg Veto ein," June 13, 1985, p. 1.
95. *Deutsche Presse Agentur*, June 13, 1985.
96. *Süddeutsche Zeitung*, "Warum der Getreidepreis kein Eckwet mehr ist," June 14, 1985; see also *Bayern Kurier*, "Konsequent und glaubwürdig," June 22, 1985, p. 6.
97. *Frankfurter Rundschau*, "Veto Statt Visionen," June 14, 1985, p. 9; See also *BPA: Nachrichtenabteiling from WDF*, June 15, 1985.
98. *Frankfurter Allgemeine Zeitung*, "Kiechle: Dieser Schritt ist mir nicht leicht gefallen," June 13, 1985, p. 1.
99. "Zielsetzungen der Europapolitik der Bundesregierung," speech of the Chancellor before the German *Bundestag* on the June 27, 1985 debate over European policy and in favor of the June 28 summit in Milan for the European Council; *Bulletin*, no. 75, June 28, 1985, p. 657.
100. *Deutsche Presse Agentur*, "Veto Zwei und Schluss," June 13, 1985.
101. Tutone: Informations Dienst of the SPD, "Genscher gegen-Kiechle für Veto," June 25, 1985.
102. *Deutsche Presse Agentur*, "Andriessen fordert mehr Exekutivvollmachten für die Kommission," June 21, 1985.
103. *Bulletin*, June 28, 1985, 149th session, June 27, 1985, p. 657.
104. *Frankfurter Rundschau*, "EG-Kommission diskutiert Agrarreform," July 3, 1985, p. 1.
105. "Aktuelle Fragen der Agrarpolitik," speech from Kiechle to the German Farmers Day in Ludwigshafen, July 5, reprinted in *Bulletin*, July 9, 1985, no. 81, p. 707.
106. *Süddeutsche Zeitung*, "Bangemann: Agrarpreise müssen gesenkt werden," November 26, 1985, p. 1.

5 NEW DIRECTIONS, 1986–1989

COOPERATION: THE SINGLE EUROPEAN ACT, 1985

The completion of the Single European Act (SEA) in December 1985 represents one of the most significant recent developments in the history of the EC. The SEA was an omnibus package of procedural and substantive reforms for the Community. Procedural reforms included initiatives designed to streamline the decision-making process in the organization, such as the agreement to expand the use of "qualified majority voting" in the Council of Ministers instead of the unanimous consent rule.[1] Substantive reforms in the SEA included the plan to finalize the internal market by December 31, 1992, thus facilitating the movement of goods, persons, services, and capital throughout Europe.[2]

As noted in chapter 4, German leaders like Chancellor Kohl and Foreign Minister Genscher strongly supported the SEA during the mid-1980s. Kohl described the program as "a major accomplishment and an expression of the commitment to fulfill Monnet's vision of a European Community," and the German government coordinated a special government conference where details of the reform plan were finalized in the fall of 1985.[3] However, German leaders were conscious of concerns in the domestic political arena about the specifics of the complex initiative. The history of leaders' efforts to develop and maintain support for such a dramatic restructuring of the EC in spite of these concerns is examined in this case study.[4]

Elite Decision Authority

The decision to support the SEA was taken in September 1985 by the same leaders who decided to defect from EC agricultural policy reform plans that June. Key leaders included: Chancellor Helmut Kohl (CDU), Finance Minister Gerhard Stoltenberg (CDU), Foreign Minister Hans-Dietrich Genscher (FDP), and Economics Minister Martin Bangemann (FDP). In addition, economic policy factions in the major party in government were represented by moderates including Kohl and Stoltenberg, who believed that cooperation through the EC was essential to promote German economic and political interests; and conservatives including CSU leader Lothar Späth and Bayern Minister-President Franz-Josef Strauss, who opposed any major reform of German–EC relations.

Historical Background of the Single European Act

The SEA was an extension of earlier achievements in the Community. In the early 1970s, leaders recognized that many of the main objectives laid out by the Treaty of Rome had been achieved, and they were concerned about charges that the Community faced "institutional stagnation" in the wake of its successes. This prompted some important soul-searching about continuing problems in the EC, and leaders targeted economic disparities and the EC policy-making process for further reform.[5]

German government representatives were actively involved in EC debates about the future of the Community. Chancellor Schmidt and Foreign Minister Genscher were very concerned about the long-term economic health of the organization and recognized that the EC had to make some procedural and substantive changes in order to progress. Specifically, some German leaders were concerned that any member of the organization could effectively block important policy initiatives in the Council of Ministers by veto—as France had done repeatedly in the late 1960s and early 1970s.[6]

Several developments in the late 1970s and early 1980s helped spur on new progress toward EC reform. First, in 1978, European leaders established the European Monetary System, a major program to coordinate monetary policy and currency exchange. The initiative breathed new life into ideas like a single European currency and a European central bank. Second, European leaders began to restructure the EC institutional decision-making process by scheduling the first open elections for the European Parliament for 1984. Third, leadership changes in powerful member states in the Community helped to spur on reform of the EC institutions in the 1980s. Chancellor Kohl and French President Mitterand were very active supporters of the EC and institutional reform, and they appeared ready to tackle difficult policy areas in the EC with new energy, perspective, and a willingness to cooperate.

EC Reforms in the Early 1980s

In the 1980s, EC leaders attempted to focus calls for a "treaty of renewal" toward a specific set of policy goals. The first step in this process was the 1981 European Council decision to create a special commission to study the completion of the European internal market that was led by Foreign Ministers Genscher of Germany and Columbo of Italy.[7] The Genscher–Columbo Commission Report called for reforms in the EC in the wake of global recession and institutional problems in the EC. This report highlighted needed reforms in five policy areas: the decision-making process, development funds, agricultural policy, internal market liberalization, and the question of the second enlargement of the EC, which was the entry of Spain and Portugal. Finally, the report expressed hope that all of these issues could be resolved as a package at the upcoming summit of Community leaders to be held later in 1981.

EC leaders in Brussels responded favorably to the report. Commission officials established several working groups to explore the possibilities for institutional reform raised in the Genscher–Columbo report. Working groups met throughout 1982 and 1983, focusing on the five areas of proposed substantive reform. Chancellor Schmidt supported the efforts of these groups and, given the chill in East–West relations in this period, was more than happy to support efforts of the working groups toward stronger European cooperation. Some specific issues that were being debated by the working groups were, however, controversial in Bonn—including the idea of giving up the right to veto EC initiatives that might counter German national interests.

The Stuttgart Summit

The Genscher–Columbo commission report and the working group studies paved the way for debates about reform at major Community meetings. Serious and open discussions about EC reform were held at the European Council summit in Stuttgart in June 1983, and the new German chancellor, Helmut Kohl, Foreign Minister Genscher, and Economics Minister Bangemann all participated in these discussions. Encouraged by recent national election success, German leaders agreed with others that the problems highlighted by the Genscher–Columbo report should be addressed through EC policy reforms.[8] They issued a joint summit communiqúe at the end of the summit titled "The Solemn Declaration of European Union," which stated their desire to reinforce and develop economic and security cooperation. The communiqúe called for states to "voluntarily abstain" from voting on measures they opposed in the European Council, rather than vetoing a measure. The comminiqúe supported the idea from the Genscher–Columbo report to "link together four outstanding issues in the Community: an increase in European development funds, agricultural reform, internal market liberalization, and the entry of Spain and Portugal," in hopes that they would be resolved soon. Finally, leaders agreed to hold regular conferences of government representatives to discuss EC reforms.[9]

The Solemn Declaration was received in very different ways across Europe. In the German press, it was hailed as the first "formal declaration of intent" to reform the EC. Kohl, Genscher, and Bangemann returned to Bonn and offered repeated, strong statements of support for the ideas embodied in the Stuttgart communiqúe.[10] However, other European leaders clearly had different perspectives on the Stuttgart summit and its implications for change in the EC. French leaders including President Mitterand expressed concern about losing the right to veto an initiative that countered French vital national interests, and British leaders demanded that the EC budget process be reformed first. In fact, almost every European government expressed specific concerns or reservations about the declaration. It seemed that the Stuttgart Declaration had opened a Pandora's box of new, short-term problems that had to be resolved.[11]

Government representatives participated in regular conferences on EC reform to iron out these differences throughout 1983 and 1984. Mid-level German government representatives from the

Foreign, Economics, and Finance Ministries participated in these conferences with full backing from the coalition leadership in Bonn. By 1984, these conferences had produced an Interim Report on EC reform, which became the blueprint for the SEA. The report stated a number of goals, including 1) an enhancement of the powers of the European Parliament; 2) reform of the voting procedures in the Council of Ministers so that qualified majority votes could be used to pass substantive policy programs; and 3) substantive reforms that would include changes in the monetary system and trade regulations.[12] A major focus of the plan was to reduce the veto to a more symbolic role than it previously held in the Community, which, after a blueprint was circulated to European capitals, was adopted by the European Council in a unanimous vote.[13]

The Fontainebleau Summit, 1984

Most German leaders were ready to support the completion of a full, comprehensive European Act in 1984. Chancellor Kohl publicly championed the work that had gone into the initiative, including the Genscher–Columbo report, the Stuttgart Solemn Declaration, and the Interim Report.[14] Kohl worked to consolidate support for the SEA inside his own government, especially from Finance Minister Gerhard Stoltenberg. FDP leaders, including Foreign Minister Genscher and Economics Minister Bangemann, offered strong support for the SEA during this period.[15]

The June 1984 Fontainebleau summit of EC leaders represented the next important forum for high-level talks on completion of the SEA. By June, it appeared that many European leaders favored some reform of the EC institutional structure and progress toward the completion of the internal market. In fact, past reservation and lingering resentment about the SEA seemed to give way to a general consensus in support of such reforms in time for the Fontainebleau summit. British Prime Minister Thatcher even expressed support for many reforms in the Community, and the past French government resistance to discussing procedural reforms in the Community gave way to honest consideration. While scholars have since explained this new willingness to cooperate with EC reforms as partly a reflection of increased East–West tensions and the need to develop and maintain a coherent Europe policy, it nevertheless produced immediate, concrete results. EC government leaders agreed to a "basic outline of the Single European Act." They unanimously supported the use of qualified majority voting in the Council of Ministers. They also agreed to generalize the principle of rebates into the EC budget, where "no member state should be required to sustain a budgetary burden which is excessive in relation to its relative prosperity."[16]

Two committees were created to formulate a final version of the SEA. They were the Ad Hoc Committee on People's Europe (tasked to address citizen issues and societal relations), and the Ad Hoc Committee for Institutional Affairs (mandated to consider institutional, political, and economic reform).[17] This second committee, later known as the Dooge Committee (named for its Irish chairman), was given several tough assignments. The first task was to design a new policy formulation process that would allow for interaction between the Council of Ministers and the European Parliament. The second task was to explore how the role of the European Parliament might be strengthened in the system, and this was related to progress in budgeting and other expected policy reforms. Third, the Dooge Committee was to reevaluate the relationship between the Parliament and other branches of the EC regarding the goal of streamlining the EC policy-making process. Even though the committee met many times and had high-level support from member governments, participants could not resolve key differences. Specific initiatives related to political cooperation, monetary policy, and defense policy coordination were subjects of intense debates.[18] In addition, committee members could not agree on the details of a reform plan for decision making in the EC. While the German leaders were able to convince the French government to support the increased use of majority voting, British, Greek, and Danish government representatives ultimately demanded that states have the veto right when "very important national interests were at stake." These representatives only wanted to accept the voluntary, informal steps to encourage majority voting already acknowledged in the Stuttgart Declaration. In late 1984, the only area of reforms on which almost everyone could agree was the call for internal market liberalization, which would eventually form the backbone of the SEA.[19]

Support Builds for the Single European Act

Deadlock in Dooge Committee sessions did not mean the end of consideration of the SEA. In fact, the open debate atmosphere of the committee served as an example for leaders who worried that the reform plan might further divide the Community. Some European leaders saw the experiences of the committee as lessons that the EC member states could work together to achieve substantive reforms. These lessons filtered throughout the EC system and through member states' polities. By early 1985 there was a noticeable buildup of support in Brussels and Bonn for formalizing and implementing EC reforms.[20]

The new European Commission president, Jacques Delors, saw great promise in the Dooge Committee discussions, and he sought to play an important leadership role in pushing EC reform. Even before taking office in January 1985, Delors traveled to a number of European capitals with French Foreign Minister Dumas to investigate the possibilities for institutional reforms, meeting with government, interest group, and business leaders. Delors had very productive discussions with German leaders on the prospects for the SEA, and they supported both procedural and substantive reforms.[21] In these discussions, Delors found broad political support for a return to the principles of the Treaty of Rome and the consolidation of a common market, but many state leaders were reluctant to commit to a wide-ranging SEA any time soon. Instead, most favored reform in one or two areas of policy, and often these did not overlap with other countries' interests. States like France preferred a reform of the internal market and decision-making mechanisms, while others like Britain and Greece wanted to first see dramatic progress on economic and social policy coordination.[22]

Commission officials set about restructuring a reform package for the Community based on the results of Delors' investigation. Delors pushed for reform that would represent a significant improvement in the workings of the organization—but also one that would garner enough political support. The Commission released a white paper entitled "Completing the Internal Market" in March 1985 that defined substantive reforms that could garner widespread support, outlined a clear path for the removal of all EC nontariff barriers to trade, and gave a specific timetable for the adoption of these items as part of a general reform package.[23]

Trudging to the Milan Summit, June 1985

Germany's Europe policy was not without its problems in early 1985.[24] The governing coalition was slowly losing public support in 1985 because of continuing economic problems, unemployment, and general discouragement about government policies. Public opinion surveys showed a loss of 5 percent of support for the Union party between November 1984 and May/June 1985. This manifested itself in results of the May *Landtag* election in Nordrhein-Westfal in which the Union party lost 6.7 percent of its popular support.[25] This loss of public support was also related to a face-off between Germany and the EC over agricultural policy reforms (see chapter 4). In January 1985, the European Commission proposed a significant cut in cereals price subsidies, and German farmers mobilized to fight the government's initial promise to cooperate with the cut. In the spring, Germany's Agriculture Minister Kiechle pushed the coalition to allow him to veto a Commission proposal to cut cereals price subsidies in Europe. When Kiechle vetoed the plan in mid-June, it created real uncertainty about Germany's ability to uphold agreements on many other issues in the Community.

Kohl and Genscher worked hard, however, to convince other EC members that the cereals veto was an isolated incident. The chancellor made an important speech on SEA reforms to the *Bundestag* on June 26, 1985—one day before the Milan summit opened. He called on his fellow German politicians to recognize the importance of the EC and its contribution to German growth and political development. Kohl stated that his government was "ready to accept the Treaty of Rome in all formalities, with a widening of institutions and rules." Kohl accounted for the German veto on agricultural price reforms in early June by suggesting that it was "sometimes necessary for states to invoke the Luxembourg compromise."[26] Foreign Minister Genscher also spoke out on behalf of the German government before the summit, proposing majority voting rules on internal market issues and an informal agreement to abstain from invoking the veto.

At the summit, Chancellor Kohl and French President Mitterand issued a joint call for a special government conference that would finalize SEA once and for all. Representatives of Greece, Britain, and Denmark, however, held back support for the special conference and sought concessions in the SEA program.[27] British government leaders continued to oppose the elimination of the veto right in the Council of Ministers and some measures to complete the internal market. Instead, British leaders preferred only an informal agreement on the veto right. At the other end of the development spectrum, Greek government opposition to the SEA was part of a political strategy to get concessions from large states on agricultural and development issues. After a series of backchannel negotiations, German and French government leaders were able to convince the Council members to convene a special government conference on EC reform.[28]

The decisions reached at Milan also had important implications for the European political arena. For many leaders, the Milan summit signaled the beginning of a period of intensive public consideration of the SEA. The initiative received the greatest public attention during the unprecedented special government conference in early September 1985. Top representatives of all twelve member states were in attendance. German representatives included the same leaders that had guided the SEA through to this point—Foreign Minister Genscher, Finance Minister Stoltenberg, and Economics Minister Bangemann. Even though British, Danish, and Greek leaders had opposed the special conference, they sent representatives to this meeting who became actively involved in debates.[29]

Within the first few weeks of the conference meetings, a full draft of the SEA was written. By early October, representatives of all twelve member states were in general agreement on the plan, and the document continued to gain support as it was refined and honed to incorporate the "vital national interests" of all member states. When EC foreign ministers met in October to review the progress of the special government conference and to plan for the Luxembourg summit of European leaders, they also agreed that the EC was ready for a final vote on the SEA December.[30]

Post-Commitment Political Conditions

The SEA did not prompt much public attention in EC member states before 1985, and the initiative was never considered a deeply divisive issue for the German polity. Generally, Germany experienced less partisan infighting over the SEA than did many other EC member states for at least three reasons. First, many party leaders in Germany were of the opinion that their country would gain from the SEA initiative in the long run. Both the CDU and the opposition Social Democratic leaders in the *Bundestag* favored EC reforms and eventual European union.[31] Second, there was strong coalition consensus in support of the SEA. Key FDP leaders like Genscher and Bangemann were involved in formulating the initiative every step of the way. Third, the German public and most interest groups saw the SEA as an important reform package, and they supported any improvement in the Community decision-making process.

Most Union party leaders supported the SEA in the fall 1985, even though Kohl had faced a struggle for control of the Union party in the spring related to continuing economic problems and concerns about the party's standings in regional elections.[32] While these differences were generally unrelated to the SEA and appeared to be resolved by the fall, the chancellor continued to face minor, post-hoc opposition to the SEA from regional Conservative leaders including Bayern Minister-President Strauss and Bayern State Secretary Edmund Stoiber. These leaders were interested in using the SEA debate to gain more influence in the elite decision authority and to enhance the regional governments' say in Europe policy. In 1986, Länder leaders raised some technical concerns about the SEA and general criticisms of the federal government's handling of issues that would impact the regions.[33] Stoiber warned that unless the Länder were granted some say in Europe policy, ratification of the SEA might be jeopardized by political deadlock in the *Bundesrat*.[34] Leaders from Bayern and Nordrhein-Westfal, which were predominantly farming regions, were particularly concerned that the federal government would sacrifice the veto right in the Council of Ministers.[35] Agricultural Minister Kiechle and regional leaders had just completed a fight over the right to veto EC initiatives, and these leaders were wary of losing control of policy to the Community.[36]

In spite of this internal squabble, the coalition leadership was in complete agreement on the SEA, and Kohl said in June that the government would "speak as one entity" at the Milan summit. Kohl's assessment of interparty relations in the period before the final decision on the SEA was borne out by the actions and statements of the FDP leadership. Foreign Minister Genscher argued that political integration and an enhancement of the decision-making process would be a "vital complement to *Ostpolitik*." He stated his support for an improved European Parliament as a step toward political union. Any differences between the parties in government that had arisen in the spring were apparently resolved.[37]

Consensus in support of the SEA inside the government, however, did not immediately translate into broad public support for government policies. The Union party was still reeling from its 6.7 percent loss in May elections in Nordrhein-Westfal during the struggle over proposed EC agricultural policy reforms.[38] Also, the net change in support for the Union party was a loss of 1 percent in the year leading up to the final decision. But public support for the Union party was on the rebound in the summer and fall months of 1985. A survey conducted by the *Forschungsgruppe Wahlen* showed a marked improvement in public support in the period from June to November 1985. Leaders seem to have adopted an attitude of cautious optimism with regard to public support, and the net loss of support did not seem to sidetrack those interested in implementing the SEA that fall. Figure 5.1 summarizes Germany's domestic political conditions in the SEA case.

Germany Supports the SEA

EC leaders agreed that the SEA program would be ready for review at the December European Council summit in Luxembourg. Accordingly, Kohl held several meetings with political leaders in the months leading up to the summit in an effort to shore up support for the SEA.[39] Land leaders of Bavaria and SPD-dominated regions like the Saarland and Bremen, including CSU leader Strauss, privately expressed concerns that the SEA would mean a loss of control over certain trade controls and development policy to federal and even supranational institutions. With help from the FDP leadership, Kohl and other federal government officials worked out a

Conditions	Case Study Analysis Questions	Coding
Major Party Unity	A. No Different Statements B. No Different Positions C. No Disputes	Consensus
Coalition Consensus	A. No Different Statements B. No Different Positions C. No Disputes	Consensus
Symmetry of Effects	A. Symmetrical B. Some Impact C. Some Sectors	Symmetrical
Election Results	A. Influenced by Elections B. Very Negative Impact C. Elections Offer Little Support	Influential
Popular Support	A. Yes, Upcoming Elections B. Negative Polls C. Polls Offer Little Support	Little Support

Figure 5.1 Summary of domestic political conditions in the SEA case.

deal to overcome these differences by promising "regular consultations" and a legal clarification of the rights of the federal government versus the regional government. Regional representatives were also granted permission to attend and participate in EC discussions of major EC programs like the SEA.

This compromise paved the way for a final decision on the SEA. The German cabinet met on November 10, 1985, and unanimously agreed to introduce an initiative on SEA to the *Bundestag* in advance of the Luxembourg summit.[40] On November 26, the legislature debated the initiative, and there were strong statements of support for the plan from government leaders. Genscher, Kohl, Bangemann, and Stoltenberg, and other leaders all spoke in favor of the SEA. Social Democrats criticized the "heavy-handed government foreign policy approach," but Genscher spoke out strongly about coalition unity in support of SEA. He accused the SPD and Greens of simply wanting to exacerbate latent tensions in the government and create further instability by claiming there was dissensus.[41]

On December 2–3, 1985, Chancellor Kohl, Bangemann, Stoltenberg, Genscher, and other leaders represented West Germany at the Luxembourg Summit.[42] Decisions were reached to allow the formal entry of Spain and Portugal into the Community on January 1, 1986, and several procedural issues were addressed.[43] But the negotiations over the SEA at the Luxembourg summit were not problem-free. They were described by Kohl afterwards as "thirty hours of laborious negotiation" during which there "were several phases when leaders feared the possible collapse of the conference." In these debates, German and French leaders argued in favor of the whole SEA package, with baskets of both substantive and procedural reforms. Meanwhile, British, Danish, and Greek government representatives continued to raise concerns about sacrificing too much authority to the EC and over technical issues associated with development funds. As before, supporters of the SEA made a few final concessions on technical matters and wording, and opponents of the plan put aside their differences.[44]

The final SEA plan included packages of substantive and procedural reforms for the EC. The plan included 279 substantive initiatives designed to enhance trade and exchange within the Community. These included changes in agricultural regulations, tariff reductions, monetary policy, environmental regulations, and trade laws designed to make the attainment of organizational goals and membership interests more possible.[45] The act also included elements of social policy, with improvements in standards of health and safety, research, and technological development. All of these changes would facilitate the formal adoption of the internal market as an objective to be achieved by December 31, 1992.[46]

The other section of the SEA included a call for procedural reforms, including an attempt to improve the decision-making process in the organization. The primary focus of this reform was on the Council of Ministers, which in the past had operated using rules of unanimous consent. The SEA expanded the use of qualified majority voting in the Council of Ministers, although only on matters pertaining to the internal market. The SEA did not explicitly say anything about eliminating the Luxembourg Compromise.[47] Finally, the role of the European Parliament would be expanded to influence substantive questions of enlargement and EC–Third World relations.

The SEA was approved by all Community members and the European Parliament.[48] The ratification of the SEA Treaty by seven member parliaments represented an important final stage in the saga of the treaty and required almost another full year of debate. In West Germany, a final series of discussions on the SEA were held in mid-November 1986, but by then there was very little serious debate over the initiative. Finally, on December 17, 1986, a majority in the German *Bundesrat* voted in favor of the SEA, and the act went into effect for the whole Community in January 1987.

DEFECTION: NATO SHORT-RANGE NUCLEAR FORCE MODERNIZATION

The decision taken by West German leaders in April 1989 to support an arms control initiative instead of a NATO modernization plan for short-range nuclear forces (SNF) represented a very significant defection from previous commitments. In 1983, NATO members had voted in favor of a decision to modernize short-range systems within six years, and the German government had authorized the deployment of modernized, intermediate-range nuclear missiles (INF) a few weeks later.[49] In 1987, the completion of the INF Treaty and the elimination of several classes of intermediate-range nuclear weapons from the theater reopened the short-range modernization question.[50] But in spite of Western pressure to cooperate with NATO plans, German leaders ultimately decided in April 1989 not to uphold the Montebello commitment. This case study explores the domestic political conditions that brought Chancellor Kohl to challenge the NATO alliance on SNF modernization.

Elite Decision Authority

The German leaders who decided not to support NATO plans for modernization of short-range nuclear systems in 1989 included many of the same officials who had supported INF modernization in 1983. Chancellor Helmut Kohl, Foreign Minister Hans-Dietrich Genscher, and Defense Minister Gerhard Stoltenberg (CDU)—after Rupert Scholz was removed from this office on April 21, 1989—all played important roles. In addition, security policy factions in the major party in government were represented by conservative Gaullists, led by Alfred Dregger (CSU); Arms Controller moderates such as Volker Rühe (CDU, Union party spokesperson) and cabinet member Heinrich Geissler (CDU, Party General Secretary); and "Atlanticists" Kohl and Stoltenberg.[51] It should be noted that both defense ministers played particularly important roles in security policy formulation in this period. Stoltenberg, an old political ally of Helmut Kohl and an experienced Conservative party operator, took a moderate position on the SNF issue and acted to turn the political tide in April 1989. Rupert Scholz, the outgoing secretary of defense, took a much stronger stand on German security policy and saw SNF modernization as crucial in spite of systemic changes.

History of the SNF Debate

As noted in chapter 4, NATO nuclear strategy in the 1980s was profoundly affected by the Dual Track decision of December 1979 and the ensuing debate over intermediate-range nuclear force modernization. The INF debate overshadowed many other alliance developments including the NATO decision taken at a summit in Montebello, Quebec in October 1983 to modernize short-range nuclear systems within six years. But the completion of the INF Treaty allowed NATO leaders, military strategists, and scholars to direct their attention to these other issues.[52]

One key concern was the charge by some critics that NATO had sacrificed an important element of its European defense strategy and lost some of the most advanced and accurate systems in the INF Treaty. They noted that the complete implementation of the treaty would leave NATO with 3,700 nuclear weapons in Europe—including about 1,400 nuclear tipped bombs, 88 Lance missile launchers, 700 Lance warheads, and at least 1,400 artillery munitions. As the sole remaining missile system, the Lance's 120-kilometer range only threatened Warsaw Pact troops in the German Democratic Republic.[53] Meanwhile, the Soviets were expected to retain some 1,365 *Frog*, *Scud*, and SS-21 short-range missile systems in theater, as well as 1,000 nuclear-capable artillery with at least 8,000 nuclear shells. This Soviet theater nuclear superiority was coupled with numerical superiority in Warsaw Pact manpower, tank forces, and armored vehicles.[54]

In 1988, British Prime Minister Margaret Thatcher, German Defense Minister Rupert Scholz, and French Foreign Minister Roland Dumas decided to bring these theater force imbalances to the public agenda.[55] They each made appeals for action at NATO planning meetings, and subsequent consultations produced a series of possible modernization options for consideration in 1988. Options at that time included the following:

1. The transfer of 100 U.S. Navy sea-based nuclear weapons to allied command
2. A focus on the modernization and deployment of tactical air-to-surface missiles (TASM)
3. The deployment of new nuclear-capable artillery
4. The modernization of the Lance missiles on the ground in Germany, or their replacement with similarly tasked systems.

While German Defense Minister Scholz supported this list of choices, all of these options had serious political and military implications.

U.S. and British leaders seized on the January agreement on modernization options as a sign of progress toward a preferred outcome. President Reagan went on the record in support of the Lance program because it pointed to the most "logical and justified enhancement of NATO nuclear capability." Ground-based systems were viewed as important in both their political symbolism and in their utility in overall European flexible response strategy.[56] Accordingly, British Prime Minister Thatcher and government officials argued publicly that:

1. SNF systems were due to become obsolete by 1995.
2. The SNF systems that existed were not considered a viable deterrent.

3. The ultimate outcome of INF had shown that the West could gain victories in arms control.
4. The Soviets under Gorbachev seemed willing to accept a new interpretation of the European security environment—an environment in which there could be real changes and progress toward arms control.

By the spring of 1988, high-level, backchannel negotiations on SNF modernization were underway.[57]

This movement on the SNF question must also be viewed in the context of international system changes in 1987 and 1988. By this time, some Europeans were beginning to see tangible effects of Soviet domestic and foreign policy reforms. The completion of the INF Treaty was an important step toward revitalizing East–West relations. Subsequently, some European leaders were more willing than the Anglo–U.S. leadership to accept that Soviet leader Gorbachev was sincere about reform initiatives. The changing political environment was to have important ramifications for Western leaders' perceptions of the need for SNF modernization.

SNF Modernization and the German Polity

As early as 1987, German leaders began to express their opinions on new NATO defense plans and SNF modernization. Chancellor Kohl stated that Germany supported its commitment to uphold all elements of NATO defense strategy—including the program for the modernization of short-range nuclear forces in Europe—in a highly publicized September 1987 government policy declaration to the *Bundestag*.[58] On several occasions in the months to follow, Defense Minister Scholz also spoke out in parliament demonstrating strong support for cooperation with the 1983 Montebello decision. But other members of the Union party voiced some dissent on the question of SNF modernization very early in the debate. For example, Volker Rühe, the *Fraktion* spokesman for the Union party, stated in several interviews in early 1988 that he favored cuts in short-range nuclear forces over any type of modernization plan and suggested that there were serious disagreements in the Union party ranks over this question. Other leaders of the elite decision authority, including conservative Dregger, argued that short-range systems should be reduced in the theater.[59]

This division in the Union party actually increased as the debate wore on—a reflection of latent differences on security policy that had evolved over many years. In fact, SNF modernization was only the latest issue in larger debates over German security policy during this period. Leaders of each of the key factions on security policy within the Union party declared their different positions. Gaullists Dregger and Jürgen Todenhöfer worked to support more conservative, European responses to the SNF modernization debate. Atlanticists like Chancellor Kohl, Defense Minister Rupert Scholz, and Finance Minister Gerhard Stoltenberg pushed for upholding the commitments made at Montebello for SNF modernization. A third group favored arms control negotiations above all, and included Heinrich Geissler, CDU parliamentary backbenchers, and most of the CDU Länder leaders. These different stands on German security policy, in general, and SNF modernization, in particular, were a product of different perceptions of the security environment and political commitments.[60]

At the level of interparty coalition politics, statements by Foreign Minister Genscher in 1988 suggested that the FDP leadership may have been opposed to a complete implementation of the Montebello decision. As part of his "foreign policy of responsibility," Genscher favored providing support for the improvement of East–West relations.[61] Specifically, FDP leaders addressed the "Follow on to the Lance" (FOTL) question early on by arguing that it favored the immediate opening of negotiations over the reduction of Lance, parallel to talks on conventional force reductions occurring in Geneva. Only reluctantly, the party made clear, would it support the eventual deployment of new systems—and only if the negotiations for these systems failed in the process. Also, the FDP leaders supported the postponement of a final decision about Lance modernization until 1992.[62]

Concerns About Public Support

These statements suggested that Kohl and Scholz, key Union party leaders and supporters of the Montebello decision, faced a rising tide of resistance to SNF modernization from leaders inside the elite decision authority. At the same time, leaders also had to contend with changing public attitudes about cooperation with NATO and their own party programs. Public opinion on cooperation in the alliance was mixed, and it remains unclear to what extent it impacted on

German foreign policy in the late 1980s. By 1987–1988, the wave of peace activism from the early 1980s had passed, and the German–American relationship remained in many ways unchanged. In a study of this period in German history, Mueller and Risse-Kappen found that "Germans in general were not increasingly hostile to NATO, nor to German cooperation with the United States . . . basic attitudes remained favorable and stable over the years; large majorities still favored cooperation with the United States." Leaders also appear to have interpreted public mood in 1988 and 1989 as generally supportive of continued cooperation with the NATO alliance.[63]

But there were also signs of growing opposition to the SNF modernization plan and Union party programs in general. Public opinion polls taken in early 1988 showed 68 percent of all West Germans rejected nuclear modernization ideas, with 79 percent calling for the removal of all nuclear weapons from West German soil.[64] Clearly, the INF debate had marked the Germans indelibly, but concerns about the Strategic Defense Initiative (SDI) and the aftereffects of the Chernobyl disaster also contributed to changes in German attitudes about nuclear issues across the board. At the same time, public support for the Union party (measured in weekly surveys) was declining.[65] This suggested a gradual disaffection from Conservative party programs because of continued economic problems and slower regional development.

Progress Toward Modernization

In spite of the specific opposition from party elites and diffuse opposition from the public, the German chancellor and defense minister continued to support the development of a NATO plan to modernize short-range nuclear forces. In the fall of 1988 and early 1989, NATO planning meetings were held, in which concrete discussions of SNF modernization occurred.[66] In November 1988, a very important, high-level meeting between Helmut Kohl, President Reagan, and President-elect George Bush occurred in Washington. Leaders discussed the question of German support for SNF modernization directly. Kohl stated publicly that he would support a decision to modernize short-range nuclear forces, and he anticipated that this would take place in time for NATO's fortieth birthday celebration at the Brussels Summit in late May 1989. At the EC conference in Rhodes in December 1988, Kohl made a similar statement to the press.[67]

Chancellor Kohl's statements of support for SNF modernization suggested that he and other Union party leaders believed they could overcome internal division and cabinet differences and implement the Montebello decision. This belief was echoed in statements by the defense minister. In January, Defense Minister Scholz reiterated that Germany was "openly supporting the need to retain short-range land-based missiles to maintain the credibility of flexible response."[68] Scholz argued that there should be some sort of comprehensive package formulated in Brussels to include the reductions of artillery shells and a restructuring of European defense strategy in light of the coming SNF modernization plan. This also meant that Scholz and the conservatives could not support a plan to remove or negotiate away all nuclear systems from the European continent. Carefully, Scholz never suggested that there should be a postponement of the decision to modernize SNF.

In the wake of these German statements, British and U.S. leaders again turned up the heat on their European allies to cooperate with the SNF modernization plan in the spring 1989. Newly elected President Bush argued that maintaining a NATO short-range nuclear posture was an important goal in alliance security policy and called on the alliance to settle the issue of SNF modernization in time for the upcoming fortieth anniversary summit of the NATO alliance.[69] To facilitate German cooperation, the president also announced that he would send his secretary of state, James Baker, to European capitals to "discuss security concerns" in February 1989. Soon thereafter, the U.S. government announced that it would begin the production of modernized Lance missiles in late February, so as to facilitate deployment "at the appropriate time" in the future. In the fiscal year 1991 defense budget, the president requested some $150 million for research and development of a new short-range system. U.S. leaders did offer a concession to the Germans on the issue, however, by stating that the new Lance systems were to have a 280-mile range, designed "to fall outside of German territory."[70]

Changes in the International Security Environment

The impact of U.S. and British pressure on the German government was mediated in 1988–89 by changes in the Soviet threat and East–West relations in general. In fact, this push for alliance solidarity on the question of SNF modernization occurred at roughly the same time that the Soviet leadership began making direct appeals to

Western European governments for arms control and cooperation. The best example of these appeals came in Mikhael Gorbachev's speech to the United Nations General Assembly on December 7, 1988. Gorbachev made a strong appeal for disarmament and peace in Europe, and he announced a withdrawal of a significant number of conventional troops and weaponry from Eastern Europe.[71]

The Kohl government was buffeted by these changes in the international security environment and by a series of new domestic political challenges to German support for SNF modernization. The Union party experienced a significant defeat in the Berlin *Landtag* elections, which Kohl reportedly took as a personal challenge to his leadership. Media sources attributed this defeat as a further reflection of economic problems and a loss of confidence in Union party leadership. A few weeks later, the Social Democratic leadership issued a direct challenge to the government's stated support for SNF modernization in the SPD party conference's Munster Declaration.[72]

By February 1989, members of all major political parties were publicly arguing that a new consensus was emerging *against* SNF modernization. SPD leader Egon Bahr said the idea had lost any credibility it had in the SPD, and even conservatives were expressing doubts. Volker Rühe suggested that there should be significant reductions in nuclear forces in Europe before there would be any consideration of SNF modernization.[73] And Foreign Minister Genscher also made it clear in early 1989 that he could not support a "heavy-handed approach" toward the East on the issue of SNF simply because of some NATO concerns. Genscher used the initiatives presented by Gorbachev to bolster his own argument about nuclear and conventional policy. Genscher and FDP party leaders were clearly arguing that the Soviets should be given a chance to let their proposed reforms take root in early 1989.[74]

Given this factionalism among the elite decision authority, Kohl created a special working group to deal with SNF issues and to develop an acceptable security policy stance for Germany in February 1989. This was a bipartisan, high-level working group consisting of the key political figures from the Union parties and the Free Democrats, including Wolfgang Schäuble; Defense Minister Rupert Scholz; Foreign Minister Genscher; FDP Party Chair Otto Lambsdorff; and CSU Party Chairman Theo Waigel. This group was designed to include the chiefs of all three major parties to resolve what had become a difficult and politicized issue.[75]

After two preliminary meetings of this working group, it appears that Kohl began to reevaluate his position on rapid SNF modernization. On February 10, 1989, Kohl said in an interview with the *London Times* that "Lance would remain in place until 1995," and that "the alliance really did not have to reach a decision on whether or not to modernize short-range, land-based missiles until a period after the West German elections." He said, "It doesn't interest me at all if others see this as a sort of litmus test. I have to represent German interests, and I am a reliable partner." Kohl's press spokesman said that the German government would still try to "keep options open."[76]

The Final Round of International Pressure

The February 14, 1989, visit of U.S. Secretary of State James Baker to Bonn to discuss preparations for the NATO Brussels summit was overshadowed by the news that the German leadership was now unwilling to commit its support for the Montebello agreement. In fact, the German announcement took the Americans by surprise, and it set the tone for the months of negotiations to come. During the meetings, Kohl reportedly stated to Baker, "I have not changed my position . . . I have no doubt that the commitment made in the 1988 NATO final communiqúe should stand." While he reiterated the position of the government that any real decision about force modernization could not occur until 1991 or 1992, he stated a general commitment to seek a compromise with British and U.S. leadership.[77] Another report of the meeting quoted Genscher as telling Baker, "the momentum which now has been achieved in the disarmament process in Europe, in particular by the unilateral steps taken by Gorbachev, would not be stopped by a false signal to modernize the Lance, that could be interpreted as a rearmament instead of disarmament."[78] Further, Genscher made clear his party's position that the SNF should not be some type of test case of alliance solidarity.[79]

In the end, Baker stated that he expected the situation to be cleared up by the May summit and that there really were no major differences between the United States and Germany that could not be resolved quickly. A few days later, Kohl publicly responded that "all options needed to be kept open" on the issue—even a third zero option had to be considered.[80] By March 1989, Kohl was facing a new round of very heavy external pressure to accede to modernization including the visits of Baker and Margaret Thatcher and cables from other alliance leaders.

Post-Commitment Political Conditions

Chancellor Kohl was buffeted by contending alliance, domestic, and international pressures. Struggles for leadership and different interpretations of the international security environment created challenges for Kohl inside the Union party. In fact,German political analysts suggested that top political leaders at the time believed Kohl was gradually losing power and his appeal as chancellor.[81] Public opinion surveys also showed that support for the Union party was declining steadily in the year leading up to the final modernization decision.[82] Union party leaders interpreted these losses and poor regional election returns as serious concerns, and some quietly adopted the position that if there was no victory for the CDU in June *Landtag* and European Parliament elections, the party would jettison Kohl as leader. All indicators suggest that Kohl was in his most vulnerable political position ever in the first three months of 1989.[83]

The struggles within the party for control of security policy soon devolved into a series of public debates in the media between Defense Minister Scholz, Foreign Minister Genscher, and Chancellor Kohl on SNF modernization. For example, in an interview with *Deutschland-Rundfunk*, Scholz said that Kohl and the majority had made it clear that peace through NATO depends on further atomic weapons development. He was also quoted as saying at this time that the government had agreed there could be no "third zero" plan for the complete elimination of short-range and chemical weapons in the theater. Scholz believed that there was strong consensus in the government about SNF modernization.[84] The next day, however, CDU General Secretary Heiner Geissler argued that a third zero had "not been ruled out" by the government. He reiterated a different factional position on the question, suggesting that the potential for SNF modernization should be directly linked to the progress in conventional force talks going on in Geneva.[85] Essentially, Geissler argued the position that Genscher had adopted—that NATO should simply consider leaving the SNF question "open" until a later date. Geissler made a side reference that he had spoken with Genscher during this period, and he said that Genscher was in support of this approach to the SNF issue within the context of upcoming NATO meetings.[86]

In response to these developments, Kohl and his close supporters began to consider restructuring the Conservative–Liberal coalition. The route which Kohl chose was not an uncommon practice in

Germany or in other parliamentary democracies: a cabinet reshuffle or a change in top leadership. This move would allow Kohl to fight off personal leadership challenges mounted by Lothar Späth and Heiner Geissler and to rebuild the waning support of the Bavarians in the Union party by moving Theo Waigel into the cabinet. Finally, this would also offer a way to challenge the rise of the *Republikaner* party and the right conservative movement.[87]

On April 12, Kohl announced cabinet ministerial changes in a press conference. He stated that both political and policy considerations were at the root of the reshuffle. By reshuffling his cabinet, he was implicitly admitting stagnation in the leadership and rescinding a number of failed initiatives. At the press conference, Kohl stated that he was concerned about a growing lack of authority in the government. He named several new ministers, including, Gerhard Stoltenberg as the minister of defense, Theo Waigel (the leader of the CSU arm of the Union party) as finance minister, and Wolfgang Schäuble as minister of the interior.[88] Kohl also made it clear that the new cabinet assignments would be coupled with a formal declaration of the government's policy intentions on April 27 in the *Bundestag*. The formal swearing-in ceremony for the new ministers would be held on April 21, and the old ministers were to hold their posts until then.[89]

Policy considerations were also very important in this reshuffle. The chancellor made it clear that he wanted new and fresh ideas from the incoming ministers. Moving Rupert Scholz out of the Defense Ministry seems to have been intended to reduce the influence of the conservative leader on defense policy. Subsequently, some experts have suggested that this cabinet reshuffle marked the point of policy change for the German leadership on SNF modernization. Gerhard Stoltenberg took over the ministry, giving Kohl's personal friend and trusted confidant a much stronger voice in government decisions.[90] Figure 5.2 summarizes Germany's domestic conditions in the SNF modernization case.

The SNF Debate Heats Up

April 1989 was the month in which leaders resolved to settle the SNF modernization question. Kohl was forced to carefully consider German security policy as part of an effort to prepare a formal declaration of intentions of the German government for a speech that was scheduled for April 27 in the *Bundestag* in the wake of the

Conditions	Case Study Analysis Questions	Coding
Major Party Unity	A. Repeated Different Statements B. Many Different Positions C. Very Serious Disputes	Intense Dissensus
Coalition Consensus	A. Repeated Different Statements B. Many Different Positions C. Very Serious Disputes	Intense Dissensus
Symmetry of Effects	A. Intensely Symmetrical B. Direct Public Impact C. Many Sectors	Symmetrical
Election Results	A. Highly Influenced by Elections B. Results Have Negative Impact C. Elections Offer No Support	Influential
Popular Support	A. Yes, Upcoming Elections B. Very Negative Polls C. Polls Offer No Support	Very Negative

Figure 5.2 Summary of domestic political conditions in the SNF modernization case.

reshuffle. In addition, several important NATO consultation sessions were to be held in April to firm up an agenda for the May Brussels summit, and it was important that the German leadership establish a firm position on SNF modernization soon. April was also a crucial month because it represented a time of transition for a number of key ministries.[91]

Soon after the announcement of the cabinet reshuffle, Kohl expressed some new ideas on SNF in an interview on *Zweite Deutsche Fernsehen* (a German television station). He said, "we are working now to prepare for the May NATO Conference where we will come up with a unified concept for dealing with the issue." Kohl also stressed that NATO must consider the possibility of beginning negotiations on the SNF forces sometime very soon—taking the form of START negotiations—and in conjunction with conventional force reductions. This was important because it marked the first public statement in which the chancellor leaned heavily toward the position on SNF held by Genscher and the Free Democrats.[92]

Kohl and Genscher initiated an important meeting of top security policy officials on Tuesday evening, April 18, with the expressed purpose of formalizing coalition policy on short-range nuclear force modernization. The meeting also served to debate and formalize government policy on the SNF issue in preparation for the NATO Nuclear Planning Group session, which began the next day. The meeting was held in the *Kanzleramt*, and it was a closed-door session of top coalition leaders including Kohl, Genscher, incoming Defense Minister Stoltenberg, *Kanzleramt* Minister Schäuble, FDP party chief Lambsdorff, conservatives Dregger and Geissler, and several state secretaries. Most notable, perhaps, was that the outgoing defense minister, Rupert Scholz, was not invited to the meeting—an indication of his waning role in German security policy. This is particularly interesting in light of the fact that Scholz was to go to Brussels the next day to represent Germany in the NPG meetings.[93]

The Tuesday meeting at the *Kanzleramt* lasted well into the night. Indications were that there were some hints of growing consensus between the CDU and FDP on German security policies. At the culmination of the meeting, Schäuble and Genscher were tasked to draw up a paper on the issues and resolutions raised at the meeting. Indirect reports from this meeting also suggested that Genscher had begun to take more control in the debate over security policy with the removal of Scholz from office.[94] One concern that was expressed in the session was that CDU leaders feared that the upcoming June 18 regional elections would turn into another *Raketenwahlkampf*, as in the 1983 national elections during the INF debate. According to several reports, the actual text of the Schäuble–Genscher paper called for the coalition to support "rapid" negotiations on the SNF, but only after a successful conclusion of the Mutual Balanced Force Reduction (MBFR) talks in Geneva.[95]

A special meeting of the NATO Nuclear Planning Group was held in Brussels on April 19 to prepare alliance policy programs and reach common ground in preparation for the NATO fortieth anniversary in late May. The official German government stance on SNF modernization there was to push NATO allies to agree to postponing a final decision on SNF until at least 1991.[96] During the meeting, German Defense Minister Rupert Scholz reached a compromise with U.S. leaders that Germany would not ask for speedy negotiations on SNF—in exchange for an agreement from the United States and Britain not to press Bonn to decide on Lance deployment until after the German 1990 national elections.[97] U.S. Defense Secretary Cheney reiterated at the meeting that he was opposed to direct negotiations with the Soviets on all nuclear systems with ranges of less than 300 miles.

This final settlement was declared in the "NATO Nuclear Planning Group Final Communiqúe" issued on the morning of Thursday April 20. The communiqúe stated that the allies unanimously "reaffirmed the continuing validity of NATO's strategy and noted with satisfaction that in the forty years since NATO was formed, peace and freedom has been preserved for all members of the alliance." Further, the communiqúe stated the Allied "determination to ensure that NATO possesses diversified, survivable and operationally flexibly nuclear forces across the entire spectrum. These forces must be kept up-to-date where necessary." This included "continued support for the efforts of member countries to meet requirements stemming from Montebello to maintain a credible nuclear deterrent posture."[98]

Thus, according to U.S. representatives at the session, Defense Minister Scholz had really committed the German government to uphold the tenets of the Montebello decision.[99] He argued that the only real change in German security policy had been the wish to postpone SNF modernization for several years based on domestic political concerns. After the conference, Scholz was actually quoted as saying that development of the new nuclear missiles was agreed to be in the "long-term interest of the alliance."[100] But Scholz's own political position was actually in question at the time. He was a lame-duck defense minister who was set to leave his ministerial post 48 hours after the NPG meeting. Also, because he was absent for the special meeting in the *Kanzleramt*, Scholz was out-of-touch with the new German stance on SNF modernization that had been debated on the 18th. Scholz negotiated a compromise with the NATO allies, but his status as a real representative of the German government was in question.[101]

German Leaders Pass on SNF Modernization

On Thursday, April 20, Scholz returned to Bonn and reported on what had transpired in Brussels. In the meantime, members of the elite decision authority who had met on April 18 to discuss security policy had already scheduled another meeting for the evening of April 20. Participants in the Thursday night meeting included Kohl, Genscher, incoming Defense Minister Stoltenberg, FDP leader Lambsdorff, Chief of Staff Schäuble, Traffic Minister Zimmerman, CSU leader Waigel, and Interior Minister Jurgen Möllemann. The Union party *Fraktion* leader Volker Rühe and foreign policy speaker

Michaela Geiger also took part. Notably, Defense Minister Scholz was again not invited to attend the meeting.[102]

The meeting began with the announcement by Kohl, Lambsdorff, and Theo Waigel that they would absent themselves from this session. The intent of this move was to demonstrate that the debate over SNF should not be oriented around political divisions. Several reports also suggested that Kohl did not believe that anything would be accomplished at this session.[103] The debate that occurred at the meeting was based on the Genscher–Schäuble paper that had been drafted two days earlier. But different leaders had established positions on the aspects of the SNF modernization question. Geissler and Rühe represented the Atlanticists in the Union party and wanted to simply establish a postponement of the decision on SNF modernization until well after the 1990 national elections. Conservatives in the Union party, represented by Zimmerman and Schäuble, supported the postponement argument, and they also wanted a formal affirmation that there would be no third zero permitted in Europe. They vehemently opposed any type of arms control initiative that would leave the Germans with no short-range nuclear, chemical, or biological defenses facing massive Warsaw Pact conventional superiority in the theater. Meanwhile, the Liberal leadership wanted the German government to call for immediate arms control negotiations parallel to the MBFR talks.[104]

The meeting lasted most of the night, and reports about the session have suggested that the debate was quite heated. Nevertheless, leaders emerged from the meeting early Friday with a compromise plan. Subsequent diplomatic and published reports suggest that the leaders decided to: 1) Postpone the decision on SNF modernization until 1992, based on an assessment of Warsaw Pact threats, with possible deployment to occur no sooner than 1996; 2) Make no firm commitment to alliance partners about its consideration;[105] and 3) Call on the United States to seek "speedy" talks with the Soviet Union about the elimination of the Lance systems and nuclear artillery from Europe. This third part of the decision was a clear challenge to the United States' government position on SNF modernization.[106] Finally, the question of the third zero was settled in the declaration of support for the presence of land-, sea-, and air-based nuclear and conventional weapons as part of the overall NATO deterrent strategy under "current circumstances"—leaving open the possibility that a third zero might become a viable option if the security environment changed by 1992. The results of the April 20 all-night meeting were considered a success for Genscher's plan for West German security and a radical reversal of German position on SNF.[107]

Aftermath of the Decision

When Chancellor Kohl was informed of the decision early on April 21, he was very surprised that a resolution had been reached.[108] After several hours of emergency meetings on German strategy with close advisers, Kohl telephoned President Bush and informed him of the official change in German security policy. Reports of the 30-minute conversation indicate that Bush was not pleased with this news, and he expressed his concern that this was a reversal in German policy on the SNF question. Accordingly, Kohl asked Bush to receive two senior German cabinet officials, the new defense minister, Gerhard Stoltenberg, and Foreign Minister Genscher, to further explain the policy change.

The harsh U.S. and British government reactions to the German call for "speedy negotiations" were in part due to their perceptions that the compromise reached in Brussels only days earlier had been violated. Diplomats had come away from the NPG meetings at Brussels under the impression that a compromise with Germany had been reached. Thus, the German decision was perceived as a "pocketing" of the compromise and a "slap in the face of the U.S. leadership." In U.S. newspapers, an anonymous administration official was quoted as saying, "what we have here is grandstanding by a panic-stricken government. . . . The Kohl government needed something that would give it the image of being in control on a major issue." Specifically, the U.S. leadership believed that the German leadership made this change in order to benefit the CDU in regional and all-European elections that had been scheduled for June 18, 1989.[109]

Genscher and Stoltenberg arrived in Washington a few days after the German decision and met with U.S. Secretary of Defense Cheney and Secretary of State Baker to outline their new security policy stance.[110] Reports of the meetings said that they were "confrontational," and diplomatic sources said that Baker was "livid" with the envoys. The Americans told the German representatives that they felt Germany had gone back on its word, violated the trust of key allies, and reneged on its Brussels agreements.[111] The Germans offered no signs, however, that they were willing to change their minds, and the chancellor stuck to his guns at a declaration of government policy on April 27 in which he justified Germany's new position on SNF.[112]

The Brussels Summit and a Final Compromise

In the weeks leading up to NATO's fortieth anniversary summit in Brussels in late May, there was a great deal of public and backchannel communication flowing between NATO members on the question of SNF modernization. U.S. and British diplomats tried to get the West Germans to agree to support a set of negotiations on short-range nuclear forces that would be held only after there was some agreement on conventional forces. But according to German press reports, Genscher saw the latest proposals as a "mockery" to Germany and spent time trying to convince Kohl (who was still undecided) that "to let the summit end in open dissension was better for the Germans than to crawl on their knees." In the same period, German officials were insisting that Bonn's position on this issue was shared within NATO by Italy, Norway, Denmark, Greece, Spain, and Belgium.[113]

Nevertheless, continued pressure did have an effect on the ultimate German position. On a visit to Italy in early May, Kohl said that West Germany was willing to modify its proposal for SNF negotiations by linking them with progress on the Conventional Forces in Europe talks. Accordingly, President Bush responded by stating his intention not to completely rule out negotiations, rather that the United States would agree to delay holding superpower talks on SNF for a "substantial period of years."[114] The final German position adopted before the Brussels summit was coordinated by Kohl, Genscher, and Stoltenberg—stating that SNF negotiations should begin but their starting point could be tied to progress on CFE.[115]

On May 29 and 30, 1989, leaders of NATO member states—including Thatcher, Bush, and Kohl—attended the NATO Brussels summit. In the course of negotiations, there was some initial disagreement over the proper course for SNF modernization. But leaders ultimately agreed to a broad compromise that included the following elements:

1. The United States agreed, in principle, to carry out negotiations with the Soviets on SNF.
2. There would be the consideration of the partial elimination of short-range nuclear systems from Europe.
3. The leadership pledged its commitment to keep the Lance missiles "up to date."
4. The NATO leaders agreed to consider negotiations on nuclear-capable aircraft in the European theater.

5. The leaders, with guidance by Bush, proposed major new conventional force levels for negotiations.
6. NATO leaders reached an understanding that SNF negotiations would be tied to progress in the CFE talks.[116]

Bush added a surprise proposal on May 28, calling on the superpowers to adhere to a mutual ceiling of 275,000 troops in the theater as part of an effort to help boost the CFE negotiation process. At the close of the conference, the group formally issued a communiqúe on major issues discussed and resolved at the conference which outlined the progress on SNF as well as a number of additional key issues.[117]

While the agreement was billed as a grand compromise, the results were most compatible with Germany's preconference goals. The final product was pleasing to Kohl because he had invested a great deal of political capital into the maneuver on the SNF question, and NATO acceptance of what had once been a largely untenable position gave Kohl greater authority.[118] The final agreement met Bonn's insistence on SNF negotiations, but certainly did not go all the way to accommodate the German government. The compromise hinged upon a U.S. commitment to enter into negotiations to achieve a *partial* reduction in land-based nuclear missiles—or no third zero. Generally, German and American leaders were pleased because of their ability to gain support for progress in Vienna and a joint alliance declaration of support for U.S. negotiating positions.[119]

In summary, the same German leadership that committed to SNF modernization at Montebello in 1983 chose to renege on this commitment in 1989. Clearly, a number of domestic political factors were involved in the leaders' calculations about this policy including a commitment on the part of Kohl and the Atlanticist faction of the Union party to support NATO plans, disagreements in the ruling party, squabbles in the coalition, and concerns about public support. But the chancellor was able to maneuver successfully between serious elite opposition and strong international pressure to formulate a compromise on the SNF question. In fact, Kohl emerged from the May 1989 Brussels summit with more political strength and public support than ever before.

NOTES

1. Andrew Moravcsik, "Negotiating the Single European Act," in Robert O. Keohane and Stanley Hoffman, eds., *The New European Community: Decision-Making and Institutional Change*, 1991, p. 47.

2. Werner Weidenfeld, "Basic Questions of European Integration Seen From a German Point of View," from Paul Michael Lützeler, *Western Europe in Transition: West Germany's Role in the European Community*, 1986, p. 278.
3. Helmut Kohl, "Die Europaische Gemeinschaft—Bilanz und Perspektive," speech included in edited collection, *Europa—Unsere Zukunft: ein Traum wird Wirklichkeit*, 1991 p. 33.
4. "Conclusion of the Milan Summit," Text from *Europa-Archiv* Documents, vol. 40, 1985, pp. 456–460; See also "Schlußfolgerungen des Ratspräsidenten zue den Arbeiten der Konferenz der Regierungsvertreter der EG-Mitgliedstaaten über die Einheitliche Europaische Akte in Luxemburg am 2. und 3. Dezember 1985," *Europa Archiv: Zeitschrift für Internationale Politik*, Dokumente 1989, p. D157.
5. Many of the proposals for reform in this period focused on enhancing the power of the European Parliament in EC decision making. It was believed this type of parliamentary authority could legitimate reforms in EC budgetting and steps toward EC political cooperation; See Weidenfeld, 1986, p. 14; See also Werner Ungerer, "German Interest in the European Community and Interests Within It," *Aussenpolitik*, February 1986, p. 212.
6. The French government threatened on more than one occasion to leave the EC if some effort was made to override its national interests in the body. Other member states followed suit. In 1965, French government officials absented themselves from several key EC debates as a protest against certain policy initiatives. Ultimately, it was agreed at a high-level summit of EC leaders in Luxembourg in 1966 that one state could effectively block EC initiatives by laying a veto [the "Luxembourg Compromise"]; For a brief history of the struggle over the veto right, see Peter Ludlow, *Beyond 1992: Europe and Its Western Partners*, Brussels, 1989; See also Wolfgang Wessels, "Die Einheitliche Eurpäische Akete-Zementierung des Status Quo oder Einstieg in die Europäische Union?" *Integration*, 1986, vol. 2, p. 68.
7. *Perspektiven für die Europäische Zusammenarbeit*: Bericht der Colombo-Kommission an den Europarat, European Commission Report, Brussels, 1981, p. D535.
8. For details on the Stuttgart package, see *Bulletin*, German Press and Information Office, June 23, 1983, pp. 2415–2476.
9. *Jahrbuch der Europäischen Integration 1983*, Bonn 1984, pp. 417–424; The actual text of the call stated that "Within the Council every possible means of faciliating the decision-making process will be used, including, in cases where unanimity is required, the possibility of abstaining from voting."
10. Reference by Helmut Kohl in "Die Europaische Gemeinschaft-Bilanz und Perspektive," 1987; See also Karl von Wogau, *Binnenmarkt 1992—die Idealle Vision*, 1989; See also "Kommunique der Stuttgarter Summit" and follow-up statements of government leaders, *Europa-Archiv, Berichte und Dokumente*, 1983.
11. Moravcsik, 1991, p. 661.
12. *Jahrbuch der Europäische Integration 1984*, Bonn 1985, Chapter 6.
13. Another important development in the progress toward the Single European Act was the Brussels Conference of EC leaders held in March 1984. The Brussels conference was an important forum for the European leaders to debate what had become a serious reform package for the Community. Major

issues that were debated there included subsidization plans for sectors hurt by reform, efforts toward better coordination of monetary policy, and plans to further institute European monetary reforms. The actual meeting was contentious because the German leadership expressed its concern that the Community was demanding too much and receiving too little from the group. There were also concerns raised that the British government would remove itself from certain initiatives. Shortly after the Brussels meeting, Chancellor Kohl again tried to take the lead on EC reform by announcing that "decisive conditions had been created" to move toward completion of the European market and majority voting in the Council.

14. Kohl's support was later recorded in FBIS-Western Europe, "Cologne Westdeutsche Rundfunk speech broadcast," Address to the *Bundestag*, Reprinted December 6, 1985, p. J1.
15. FBIS-Western Europe, Interview with Foreign Minister Hans-Dietrich Genscher, from Cologne Westdeutscher Rundfunk, December 2, 1985, p. 1.
16. On details of the Fontainbleau summit agreement, see Geoffrey Denton, "Restructuring the EC Budget: Implications of the Fontainbleau Agreement," *Journal of Common Market Studies*, 1986, vol. 23, no. 2.
17. Andrew Moravcsik, "Negotiating the Single European Act." In *The New European Community: Decision-Making and Institutional Change,* eds. Robert O. Keohane and Stanley Hoffman, 1991, p. 58.
18. This included support for reforms of the decision-making process such as elevating the power of the European Parliament and allowing for qualified majority votes in the Council of Ministers; See Claus-Dieter Ehlermann, The Institutional Development of the EC Under the Single European Act," *Aussenpolitik,* vol. 22, November 1990, p. 138.
19. Claus-Dieter Ehlermann, "The Institutional Development of the EC Under the Single European Act," *Aussenpolitik*, November 1990, p. 135; See also Wayne Sandholtz and John Zysman, "1992: Recasting the European Bargain," *World Politics*, vol. 42, October 1989, no. 1.
20. For a good summary of the negotiations leading up to the SEA formalization, see Roy Pryce, ed, *The Dynamics of European Union*, 1987.
21. See Moravcsik, 1992, pp. 44–51; See also A. M. El-Agraa, *The Economics of the European Community*, 1990.
22. Pryce, ed., 1987, p. 149.
23. The German leadership took different positions on major issues of EC policy coordination. German leaders were opposed to monetary coordination unless capital flows could be liberalized. Germany was opposed to political and defense cooperation until existing programs of collaboration were formalized. Leaders supported the reform of the decision-making process in the EC, including a revision of the treaty to give more power to the European Parliament. But, German leaders would not easily forego the Luxembourg Compromise concept of a veto. Also, German leaders came out in general support for a reform to the EC internal market program; See Moravcsik, 1991, p. 53.
24. "Die Ergebnisse des Bonner Weltwirtschafts-Gipfeltreffens im Mail 1985," from *Europa-Archiv*, Folge 11, 1985.
25. *Politbarometer—Election Study 1986/1987*, Forschungsgruppe Wahlen, Mannheim, 1987.

26. Kohl speech to the *Bundestag*, *Bulletin*, Bonn, June 28, 1985, 149th session, pp. 657–662 [author's translation].
27. "Zielsetzungen der Europapolitik der Bundesregierung," speech to the *Bundestag*, *Bulletin*, Bonn, June 28, 1985, 149th session, pp. 657–662; Later, President von Weizsäcker declared his support for further integration in a statement to the European Parliament on Oct.23, 1985.
28. Conclusion of the Milan Summit, Text from *Europa-Archiv Documents*, vol. 40, 1985, pp. 456–460.
29. *Europa Archiv—Zeitschrift fur Internationale Politik*, 1989.
30. Reinhold Gemperle, *Neue Zürcher Zeitung*, "Die Europäische Union ante portas?" September 1, 1985, p. 1; See also *Frankfurter Allgemeine Zeitung*, "Mit der EG-Reform dommen die Außenminister nicht voran," October 23, 1985, p. 4.
31. *Flensburger Tageblatt*, "CDU- und SPD-Fraktion für Europäische Union," May 22, 1985, p. 1.
32. *Der Spiegel*, May 22, 1985, no. 23, pp. 24–25.
33. *Der Spiegel*, May 29, 1985, no. 24, p. 41.
34. *Deutsche Presse Agentur*, "Europa: CSU Hofft Bei Konflit um Europaische Akte auf gemeinsame Lösung," September 19, 1986
35. *Hamburg BILD*, June 10, 1985, p. 4.
36. Also, there was concern expressed by some interest groups in Germany about what the treaty would mean for German sectoral interests.
37. FBIS-European Communities, "Cologne Westdeutscher Rundfunk-Interview with Hans Dietrich Genscher," December 2, 1985, p. B1.
38. *Der Spiegel*, May 16, 1985, no. 23, p. 22.
39. *Der Spiegel*, August 17, 1985, no. 34, p. 30; *Süddeutsche Zeitung*, "Kabinett setzt Europäische Akte von der Tagesordnung ab," September 18, 1986, p. 2; For a good summary of the negotiations leading up to the SEA formalization, see Roy Pryce, ed, *The Dynamics of European Union*, 1987.
40. *Deutsche Presse Agentur*, "Bundestag empfindet EG-Reform nur als Zwischenschritt"; See also FBIS: European Communities, December 4, 1985, p. B1; Interview with Foreign Minister Genscher from Cologne Westdeutscher Rundfunk Newtork, December 2, 1985.
41. Based on a review of *Stenographische Bericht des Deutschen Bundestages*, 8 Sitzung, 10 Wahlperiod, November 26, 1985, pp. D1673–1714; See also DPA: "Bundestag empfindet EG-Reform nur als Zwischenschritt."
42. Jürgen Wahl, "In Luxemburg ist endlich eine Wende fällig," *Christ und Welt: Rheinischer Merkur*, November 30, 1985, p. 1.
43. "Colonge Westdeutsche Rundfunk, December 5, 1985—Address by Kohl to the *Bundestag* in Bonn-live transcript," reprinted in FBIS-Western Europe, December 6, 1985, p. J1.
44. FBIS: Press Comments on the Luxembourg EEC Summit, FBIS, December 6, 1985, p. J8; Analysis from from Cologne Dutschlandfunk Newtork in German, December 5, 1985; See also "Vorsichtiger Optimismus und skeptische Stimmen vor dem EG-Treffen in Luxemburg," *Frankfurter Allgemeine Zeitung*, December 2, 1985, p. 1; see also Antrag der Fraktionen der CDU/CSU and FDP, "Ergebnis des Europaisichen Rates in Luxemburg am 2. und 3. Dezember 1985, Deutscher Bundestag 10. Wahlperiode, Drucksache 10, 4474, December 5th.
45. Kohl, from FBIS-Western Europe, December 6, 1985, p. J1.

46. Werner Ungerer, "German Interest in the European Community and Interests Within It," *Aussenpolitik*, February 1986, pp. 31–37.
47. Through this move, the veto right was retained in weaker form in Article 100(4) of the revised treaty, which permits nations outvoted in the Council to invoke a safeguard clause to retain their domestic regulations for reasons of exigencies perceived as important to them. But the invocation of this clause was designed to require that governments inform the Commission and leave it up to this body to decide whether vital national interests were really at stake; See "Einheitlich Europäische Akte, unterzeichnet von den Außenministern der EG-Mitgliedstaaten in Luxemburg im February 1986," text of Act reprinted in *Europa-Archiv*, Folge 6, 1986, p. 163.
48. *Seite 2/1986, Einheitliche Europäische Akte*, text from the Luxembourg announcement, actual text wording of the SEA, from the *Bulletin der Europaischer Gemeinschaften*, Beilage 2, 1986.
49. *Communiqúe of the Nuclear Planning Group of NATO*; 34th Ministerial Meeting in Montebello, Issued October 28, 1983, Montebello, Quebec, Canada; published in the Press- und Informationsamt der Bundesregierung's *Bulletin*, November 3, 1983, no. 115, p. 1045; See also "Kommunique über die 34. Ministertagung der Nuklearen Plannungsgruppe der NATO in Montebello (Kanada) am 27. und 28. Oktober, 1983," and "Synopsis," *Europa Archiv*, Folge 5, 1984, pp. D124–128.
50. See Thomas L. Friedman, "U.S. Anger Rising Against Germans Over NATO Stand," *New York Times*, April 30, 1989, p. A1.
51. Clay Clemens, "Beyond INF: The Conservative Party and Arms Control," *International Affairs*, 1989, vol. 32, no. 4.
52. *Der Spiegel*, May 1, 1989, no. 18, p. 20.
53. The Lance was originally deployed in 1972, but it was classified as "poor" in the accuracy column by many security analysts; See Matthias Dembinski, ed., *Amerikanische Weltpolitik nach dem Ost–West Konflikt*, 1989.
54. *Friedensgutachten 1990*, Hessische Stiftung Friedens und Konfliktforschung, Herausgegeben von Gert Krell, Egon Bahr, und Johannes Schwerdtfeger, p. 11.
55. For a good review of the origins of the security debate in the early 1980s, see Thomas Risse-Kappen, *Die Krise der Sicherheitspolitik*, 1988.
56. Serge Schmemann, "Lance Modernization On Course," *New York Times*, December 3, 1988, p. A4.
57. Stephen F. Szabo, *The Changing Politics of German Security*, 1990, p. 109; See also *Bericht zur Rüstungskontrolle und Abrüstung 1989/90*, Presse- und Informationsamt der Bundesregierung through June 1990; text of all documents and reports on arms control and developments and intiatives from July 1989 to June 1990.
58. This statement of the government's intentions comes from the *Regierungserklarung von Bundeskanzler Dr. Helmut Kohl*, titled "Die Schöpfung bewahren-die Zukunt gewinnen"; from the Presse- und Informationsamt der Bundesregierung, Reihe Berichte und Dokumentation, 1987.
59. See a record of Volker Rühe's opposition from *Süddeutsche Zeitung*, January 21, 1988, "One should not underestimate the political consequences the remaining potential in Western Europe could have. . . . The formula 'the shorter the range, the more German the effect' does not only

apply to the remaining short-range Soviet systems. . . . It is much more a question of the potential political consequences NATO's remaining nuclear weapons could have for the FRG. This is a nuclear posture that, if its current structure and scope remain unchanged, would include only land-based systems that would only destroy German territory if they were to be used." from "Perspektiven zur Friedenssicherung in Europa," *Europa Archiv*, no. 23, 1987, p. 678; See also Rühe, interview from *Süddeutsche Zeitung*, January 21, 1988, p. 1; *Die Zeit*, February 15, 1988, p. 4; See also Rühe, *Die Welt*, March 15, 1988, p. 2.

60. Concern about reliance on the United States and an "automaticity" in alliance relations was addressed by Dregger in an interview in *Der Spiegel*, February 22, 1988, p. 20; Elizabeth Pond analyzed this position in "Sind Wir Verraten und Verkauft?" *Die Zeit*, July 1986, p. 3; Also see Jürgen Todenhofer, statement from Richard Cohen, "And the Germans," *The Washington Post*, January 10, 1989, p. A23.
61. Author's Interview with Hans-Dietrich Genscher, April 29, 1993; See also interview with Genscher from *Frankfurter Allgemeine Zeitung*, November 8, 1988, p. 4.
62. Interview with Genscher from *Frankfurter Allgemeine Zeitung*, November 8, 1988, p. 1; He even suggested that the FDP would consider rejoining a coalition with the Social Democrats earlier in the year; See his interview with editors of the same paper, *Frankfurter Allgemeine Zeitung*, January 6, 1988, p. 2; Regardless of the existence of some division within the party, the Social Democrat Special Party Congress in the fall of 1988 in Munster brought about the resolution of SPD stance on the issue. The SPD declared that it was unified against the modernization of SNF and against any type of compensation for the removal of SNF systems from Western Europe.
63. *Institut für Demoskopie* poll, quoted by Gebhard Schweigler, *Grundlagen der aussenpolitischen Orientierung der Bundesrepublik Deutschland*, 1985, p. 71; But there was broad public approval of cooperation with the United States. Rattinger also notes that, in his surveys, there was consistent general support for NATO from 1970–1990 based on a review of EMNID surveys of public opinion; Hans Rattinger, "Deutsche Einstellungen und ihre Auswirkungen auf die amerikanische Präsenz," in *Public Opinion and National Security in Western Europe: Consensus Lost?* 1989, p. 38.
64. Elisabeth Noelle-Neumann, "Demoskopie," *Frankfurter Allgemeine Zeitung*, July 22, 1988, p. 4; See also May 16, 1989, *Frankfurter Allgemeine Zeitung*, p. 3; See also Allensbach Institute Survey, recorded in Hans Rattinger and Gregory Flynn, eds., *The Public and Atlantic Defense*, 1985, pp. 47–54; See also Karl-Heinz Reuband, *Demoskopische Verwirrungen in der Nachrüstungsfrage: Was halten die Bundesbürger vom Nachrüstungsbeschluß?* November 1983, pp. 64–78.
65. "Parteien im April: Grüne auf Zehn Prozent," *Der Spiegel*, April 17, 1989, p. 67.
66. See Ronald D. Asmus, "West Germany Faces Nuclear Modernization," *Survival*, November/December 1988.
67. *Washington Post*, November 16, 1988, p. 1; "Erklärung von Bundeskanzler Helmut Kohl auf dem Gipfeltreffen der Staats- und Regierungschefs der NATO in Brussels, *Frankfurter Allgemeine Zeitung*, May 29, 1989, p. 13.

68. However, it is important to note that his power and influence "was increasingly undercut by Scholz's own political trouble." But Scholz was rapidly becoming a political liability for the chancellor.
69. George Bush, quoted in *New York Times*, January 26, 1989, p. A1.
70. *New York Times*, February 23, 1989, p. A3.
71. Ibid., December 9, 1988, p. A1.
72. *Der Spiegel*, January 27, 1989, no. 5, pp. 23–27; See also *Frankfurter Rundschau*, May 3, 1989, p. 2.
73. Rühe argued that there should be a change to "loosen the Gordian knot of nuclear modernization," *Die Zeit*, February 15, 1989, p. 1 [author's translation]; *Der Spiegel*, no. 4, January 25, 1989, pp. 16–18.
74. From interview in *Süddeutsche Zeitung*, April 18, 1987, p. 2; See also Genscher interview in *Frankfurter Rundschau*, May 3, 1989, p. 1.
75. Information from author's interview with former Foreign Minister Hans-Dietrich Genscher, April 29, 1993; See also analysis from *Washington Post*, February 10, 1989, p. 1.
76. *Financial Times*, February 10, 1989, p. 5 [*Times* translation]; See also *Washington Post*, February 10, 1989, p. 1.
77. *Süddeutsche Zeitung*, February 15, 1989, "Baker: Differenzen mit Bonn nicht ausgeräumt," p. 1.
78. *Washington Post*, February 14, 1989, p. 1.
79. *Süddeutsche Zeitung*, February 15, 1989, "Baker: Differenzen mit Bonn nicht ausgeräumt," p. 1.
80. *Die Welt*, February 20, 1989, "US–Außenminister Baker: Es gibt keinen Streit mit Bonn," p. 6; See also Kohl, as quoted in Aachen *Volkzeitung*, February 14, 1989, p. 1.
81. *Der Spiegel*, no. 18, May 1, 1989, p. 17.
82. *Der Spiegel*, "Parteien im April: Grüne auf Zehn Prozent," April 17, 1989, p. 67.
83. In fact, the German government had been experiencing a "crisis of leadership" for some time. Faced with a global recession, significant unemployment figures, and a sense on the part of the German public of detachment from the Conservative–Liberal coalition, the social context of support for the coalition had dwindled significantly in the latter half of the 1980s. In particular, the CDU was experiencing a challenge from the *Republikaner* party on the right, as well as losing some support in the realm of foreign policy to the Free Democrats. By March, after dismal results from the West Berlin and Hessen regional elections, Kohl was facing the worst political crisis for the Union party since he had come to power in 1982; Drawn from analysis in *Der Spiegel*, no. 18, May 1, 1989, p. 18 [author's translation].
84. Editorial, *Frankfurter Allgemeine Zeitung*, "Zeitpunkt der Modernisierungs-Entscheidung und das Gesamtkonzept sekundär," April 3, 1989; See also *Die Welt*, "Lance wird modernisiert," April 3, 1989, p. 1.
85. Eghard Mörbitz, "Geißler schließt dritte Null-Lösung nicht aus," *Frankfurter Rundschau*, April 4, 1989; See the positions of the "arms controllers" as enunciated in a series of public statements by leaders like Geißler and Rühe; See *Deutsches Monatsblatt*, June 1986, pp. 4–6; *Die Zeit*, May 18, 1987, p. 2; and *Deutsches Monatsblatt*, June 1987, pp. 4–6.

86. *Frankfurter Allgemeine Zeitung*, "CDU möchte über Raketen-Modernisierung erst später entscheiden," April 4, 1989, p. 2.
87. *Der Spiegel*, April 14, 1992, no. 16, 1989; See also "Noch Zwei Kugeln für Kohl," *Der Spiegel*, April 28, 1989, pp. 18–23.
88. See "Ich kann nicht anders," *Der Spiegel*, no. 16, 1989, p. 18–22; See also *Bulletin*, "Umbildung der Bundesregierung," *Bulletin*, no. 34, pp. 297–302; In his official statement to the press on the cabinet reshuffle, Kohl said the following: "I have undertaken a reshuffle of the cabinet. This is the right time to do it because the large reform efforts of the legislative period are complete: the tax reform plan and the health plan, also the rent and post reforms have been completed; See also "Ich kann nicht anders," *Der Spiegel*, no. 16, 1989, p. 18–22; See also *Bulletin*, "Umbildung der Bundesregierung," *Bulletin*, no. 34, pp. 297–302.
89. "Erklärung des Bundeskanzlers," *Bulletin*, April 28, 1989, no. 111, p. 2648.
90. Asmus, *The Politics of Modernizing Short-Range Nuclear Forces in West Germany*, September 1989, #R-3846-AF, p. 7; See also Kohl's speech reprinted in the *Bulletin*, no. 40, April 28, 1989, p. 1417.
91. *Frankfurter Allgemeine Zeitung*, April 3, 1989, pp. 2–4.
92. Interview with Kohl on April 14, 1989, from *Zweite Deutsche Fernsehen*, transcript from Deutsche Presse Agentur, April 15, 1989.
93. "Lance Wird Modernisiert," *Die Welt*, April 3, 1989, p. 1.
94. *Der Spiegel*, April 22, 1989, no. 17, p. 16.
95. Interview with Genscher, April 29, 1993; See also Genscher interview in *Frankfurter Rundschau*, May 3, 1989, p. 1; See "Koalition will Raketenstreit beenden," *Süddeutsche Zeitung*, April 19, 1989, p. 3.
96. "Bush Rejects Demand by Bonn on Missiles," *The Washington Post*, May 6, 1989, p. 1.
97. Winfried Münster, "Die NATO ist uber Bonn Verärgert," *Süddeutsche Zeitung*, April 20, 1989, p. 1.
98. NATO Nuclear Planning Group Final Communiqúe, Service of the NATO Press; Press Release M-NPG-1(89)12; Released April 20, 1989; Also, see a citation in Presse- und Informationsamt der Bundesregierung, *Bulletin*, no. 37, April 1989, p. 257; see also "Kommunique der Nuklearen Planungsgruppe der NATO"; 45. Ministerkonferenz am 19. und 20. April 1989 in Brüssel, from the *Bulletin*, April 25, 1989.
99. See *New York Times*, April 25, 1989, pp. 1 and 7.
100. Andrew Rosenthal, "Bonn Wins a Delay from Allies on the Missile Deployment Issue," *New York Times*, April 20, 1989, p. A1.
101. NATO Press Release, "NATO Nuclear Planning Group Final Communiqúe, after Brussels session on 19 and 20 April"; full text; for immediate release, April 20, 1989; Büro Willy Brandt.
102. *Deutsche Presse Agentur*, "Neue Raketen Runde in Kanzleramt-Genscherentwurf durchgesetzt?" news wire report April 21, 1989.
103. Asmus, September 1989, p. 27.
104. Report on *Deutsche Presse Agentur*, "Neue Rakenten Runde in Kanzleramt-Genscherentwurf durchgesetzt?" April 22, 1989.
105. "Bonner Beratungen über Kurzstreckenraketen," *Frankfurter Allgemeine Zeitung*, April 21, 1989, p. 2; Some reports indicated that Foreign Minister

Genscher threatened to topple the coalition over the SNF issue. But officials from the foreign office and the chancellory subsequently denied that Genscher had threatened to resign, noting that in cabinet discussions before the Stoltenberg trip, FDP minister Jurgen Moellemann had asked Stoltenberg the rhetorical question of whether he really wanted to go so far in seeking to reach a compromise with Washington that four FDP ministers would find resignation necessary; Author's interview with Genscher, April 29, 1993; See also *Frankfurter Allgemeine Zeitung*, May 27, 1989, p. 1.

106. Derived from the coalition's position paper, reprinted in the *Frankfurter Allgemeine Zeitung*, April 24, 1989, p. 1.

107. *Frankfurter Allgemeine Zeitung*, April 24, 1989, p. 2; See also Serge Schmemann, "Struggling Kohl Sending Two Aides to an Edgy U.S." *New York Times*, April 24, 1989, p. A1.

108. Kohl had not expected a solution to the problem to be formulated so quickly, and he was described as having felt "duped" by the decision group in one report. Kohl immediately called an emergency *Fraktion* meeting in Dregger's office to discuss the implications of the decision. The CDU leadership met for about two hours on strategy and the coalition settlement. The impromptu meeting of the CDU *Fraktion* was paralleled by talks early Friday morning by the CSU and FDP *Fraktion* groups; See "Die Koalition schwenkt offenbar auf Genschers Linie ein," *Frankfurter Allgemeine*, April 19, 1989, p. 1.

109. "Nach dem Bonner Formelkompromiss Sorgen in der NATO über die Zuverlässigkeit der Deutschen," *Frankfurter Allgemeine Zeitung*, April 24, 1989, p. 1; "Im Raketen-Streit will Bonn in Washington Hart Bleiben," *Die Welt*, April 25, 1989, p. 1; In fact, this was even considered more of a surprise because when SPD Chief Hans Jochen Vogel was in Washington the week before the German decision, he said that the decision to modernize the old Lance systems was "as good as decided already"; see "Eckige Klammern," *Der Spiegel*, no. 15, 1989, p. 61; See also *New York Times*, April 25, 1989, p. A5; *New York Times*, April 22, 1989, p. A1.

110. Serge Schmemann, "U.S. Spurns a Plea by Bonn to Open New Arms Talks," *New York Times*, April 25, 1989, p. A8.

111. Genscher and Stoltenberg knew that his visit to Washington would be confrontational, but they perceived this as a political opportunity to stand up to the English-speaking nuclear powers. Genscher promptly returned home and announced he would next take the idea of "speedy negotiations" to his European partners; See analysis in Serge Schmemann, "German Calls U.S. Talks Amicable," *New York Times*, April 26, 1989, p. A10.

112. Kohl said in his justification speech in the *Bundestag*, "Everyone will understand why the federal government is adopting this position. On account of the range of short-range systems, the Federal Republic of Germany is more strongly affected than the other members of the alliance. I therefore consider it a natural that our friends show the same understanding for our intersts as we have shown for their interests on many occasions." Reprinted in the *Bulletin*, no. 40, April 28, 1989, p. 1417.

113. Josef Joffe, "Bonn und Washington auf Kollisionskurs," *Süddeutsche Zeitung*, April 25, 1989, p. 1; See also James Markham, "Bonn's Dovish Nuclear Stand

Winning Support in NATO," *New York Times*, April 26, 1989, p. A1; See *Der Spiegel*, no.18, May 1, 1989, p. 23.

114. *New York Times*, May 21, 1989, p. A7.

115. See "Erklärung von Bundeskanzler Helmut Kohl auf dem Gipfeltreffen der Staats- und Regierungschefs der NATO in Brussels, *Bulletin*, May 29, p. 1279.

116. Statements from "Joint Communiqúe from the Fortieth Anniversary NATO Summit Meeting, Brussels, Belgium," from *New York Times*, May 31, 1989, p. A7; See also NATO Summit Communiqúe, "A Comprehensive Concept of Arms Control and Disarmament," *NATO Press Communique*, M-1 (89)20, May 30, 1989.

117. NATO Communiqúe, NATO Headquarters Release, English; "A Comprehensive Concept of Arms Control and Disarmament," A Report Adopted by the Heads of State and Government at the meeting of the North Atlantic Council in Brussels on 29 and 30 May 1989; from *Bulletin*, Presse- und Informationsamt der Bundesregierung, no. 53, p. 465.

118. James M. Markham, "NATO Chiefs Agree to a Compromise in Missile Dispute," *New York Times*, May 31, 1989, p. A1; See also R. W. Apple, Jr. "Bush in Europe: Looking to the Germans," *New York Times*, June 2, 1989, p. A4.

119. "Erklärung der Staats- und Regierungschefs im Rahmen der NATO-Gipfelkonferenz in Brussel vom 30 May 1989," *NATO Communique* M-1, released May 30, 1989 points 14–19, p. 19.

6 LESSONS FOR INTERNATIONAL COOPERATION

Each of the case studies examined here demonstrates how elite commitments to cooperate with international organizations are dependent upon domestic support in the post-commitment politics phase. This chapter analyzes data from the cases and presents some important conclusions about international cooperation and the practice of foreign policy analysis. Finally, lessons from this study are related to contemporary foreign policy issues using the example of German responses to the civil war in the former Yugoslavia (1991–1995).

RESULTS

Major Party Unity

The following hypothesis about elite unity and cooperation was put forward in chapter 1.

> Hypothesis 1: An initial commitment to cooperate with other states in the context of an international organization is less likely to be sustained in the post-commitment phase, *ceteris paribus*, when the leaders of the major party in government are divided over the issue.

This hypothesis was supported by evidence from seven of the eight case studies, and factionalism in the major party corresponded with defection in all four cases examined for this study. In 1975, serious disagreements in the major party about support for the "watering can" principle contributed to the defection from the European Regional Development Fund. Later, the 1982 decision not to support NATO sanctions on Poland and the Soviet Union was related to differences of opinion between Schmidt, his defense minister, and other SPD leaders, and the 1985 decision to veto EC cereals price subsidy cuts was a function of serious disagreements in the Union party between Kohl, Agriculture Minister Kiechle, and other Conservative leaders. Finally, the Conservative leadership was so divided over the question of whether to support SNF modernization in 1989 that Chancellor Kohl even reshuffled his cabinet to correct the policy direction of his more conservative defense minister.

Conversely, consensus inside the major party in government corresponded with cooperation in three of the four cases examined. Chancellor Schmidt was in a particularly strong position inside his party when he committed his support for the creation of the European Monetary System, and SPD leaders remained unified throughout the ratification phase. Similarly, Kohl enjoyed strong support inside the Union party in the fall of 1983, and intraparty consensus helped him to overcome serious public opposition to cooperate with NATO plans to modernize INF systems. He was also able to garner strong support inside the Conservative party for the Single European Act in late 1985.

As illustrated in Figure 6.1, only the 1979 decision to cooperate with the NATO Dual Track plan was taken in spite of intense factionalism inside the Social Democratic party. Chancellor Schmidt faced challenges to his continued leadership in the party, but he was able to build support for the Dual Track plan by articulating the strategic imperative of INF modernization, by forging a strong alliance with the Free Democrats and, by drawing on his base of popular support. The special nature of this case study is examined in more detail in another section of this chapter.

In sum, seven of the eight case studies support the hypothesis that factionalism in the major party corresponds with defections and that consensus is related to international cooperation. Cases show that dissensus sharply curtailed government leaders' room to maneuver on foreign policy. Disagreements threatened the power base of the government leaders and weakened the extent to which chancellors

	Cooperation	Defection
Major Party Unity	**3** 1978 EMS 1983 INF 1985 SEA	
Major Party Split	**1** 1979 INF	**4** 1989 SNF 1982 Pipe 1985 Cereal 1975 ERDF

Figure 6.1 Major party unity and cooperation.

were willing to take risks to support EC or NATO programs. On the other hand, while major party unity in the post-commitment phase did not guarantee that leaders would sustain international commitments, it appeared to be quite valuable in these cases.

Ruling Coalition Consensus

The second hypothesis advanced in this book was that decisions about foreign policy cooperation with an international organization could be affected by post-commitment coalition dynamics.

> Hypothesis 2: An initial commitment to cooperate with other states in the context of an international organization is less likely to be sustained in the post-commitment phase, *ceteris paribus*, when leaders of different parties in the coalition government are divided over the issue.

Ruling coalition consensus in the post-commitment phase had a profound effect on the ability of the leadership to uphold plans to cooperate in seven of the eight case studies examined. Interparty coalition differences were present in all four case studies of defection: in the 1975 struggle over plans for a European Regional Development Fund; in 1985, when Foreign Minister Genscher and other FDP leaders opposed the plan to veto proposed EC cereals price subsidy cuts; in the 1982 decision not to support NATO sanctions and to build the Siberian pipeline; and finally, when Chancellor Kohl faced serious opposition from the junior party leadership on the question of SNF modernization in 1989.

Conversely, consensus among leaders of the ruling coalition in the post-commitment phase corresponded with cooperation in three of four cases. Coalition consensus allowed leaders the necessary policy-making latitude to support the NATO Dual Track plan in December 1979. Second, Foreign Minister Genscher and other leaders were in agreement with Chancellor Kohl that the deployment of modernized INF systems was in Germany's best interest in the fall of 1983. Finally, the decision for the Single European Act was also facilitated by consensus inside the ruling coalition throughout 1985.

As illustrated in Figure 6.2, only the case of the 1978 European Monetary System decision did not match expectations—showing that cooperation can sometimes occur in spite of interparty coalition dissensus. Specifically, this decision was taken over the objections of FDP Economics Minister Lambsdorff, who believed that the monetary system was a potential drag on the German economy. But Lambsdorff's challenge came at the height of Schmidt's political popularity. The chancellor was determined to see the program

	Cooperation	Defection
Coalition Consensus	**3** 1979 INF 1983 INF 1985 SEA	
Coalition Dissensus	1978 EMS	**4** 1989 SNF 1982 Pipe 1985 Cereal 1975 ERDF

Figure 6.2 Ruling coalition consensus and cooperation.

through and was able to build a coalition of support for EMS that included Social Democratic leaders, interest groups, and the public.

Seven of the eight case studies support the hypothesis that ruling coalition dissensus corresponds with defections and that consensus improves the chances for international cooperation. Differences of opinion between coalition leaders seriously constrained the government leader's room to maneuver. Conversely, coalition consensus in the post-commitment appeared to bolster leaders' efforts to sustain international commitments.

Symmetry of Domestic Effects

The argument that decision makers must consider the satisfaction of domestic interest groups in the post-commitment politics phase was based on an extension of the comparative foreign policy literature using symmetry as a measure of the impact of issue area on cooperation. In this context, scholars assume that economic/developmental issues involve tangible and asymmetrical potential costs or benefits, and they argue that the struggle of many different groups for influence over policy may make stable cooperation with international organizations less likely. Accordingly, they believe that military/security issues have more of a symmetrical potential impact on the populace and do not tend to generate as much competition over resource distribution. To review, the following hypothesis about domestic interests was introduced in chapter 1,

> Hypothesis 3: An initial commitment to cooperate with other states in the context of an international organization is less likely to be sustained in the post-commitment phase, *ceteris paribus*, when it involves economic/developmental issues rather than military/security issues.

Cases were selected for this study in relation to issue area and other key variables. Figure 6.3 illustrates that the statement of the third hypothesis does not capture the depth of the exploration related to symmetry noted in the introduction, where I made the case for a shift of focus to the expected symmetry of effects of cooperation as a modification of the issue area argument in the comparative foreign policy literature. By focusing on the symmetry of cooperation, I sought to explore the proposition that both military/security and economic/developmental issues stir public and government debates in the post-commitment politics phase.

	Cooperation	Defection
Military/ Security	**2** 1979 INF 1983 INF	**2** 1982 Pipe 1989 SNF
Economic/ Development	**2** 1978 EMS 1985 SEA	**2** 1975 ERDF 1985 Cereal

Figure 6.3 Issue area and cooperation.

In contrast, this study has shown that the symmetry of effects corresponded with international cooperation *regardless of issue area*. In 1978, Chancellor Schmidt, the *Bundesbank*, and other leaders viewed the EMS as a program that would have some public impact and have a relatively symmetrical effect on the German polity. The 1979 decision to support the NATO Dual Track plan was also viewed as intensely symmetrical. A third case, the 1983 decision to support INF modernization, was also viewed as intensely symmetrical. Finally, the 1985 decision regarding the Single European Act was viewed as having a relatively symmetrical distribution of costs and benefits for the German polity.

Conversely, asymmetry corresponded with two of the four cases of defection. The 1982 decision not to support NATO sanctions and to build the Siberian pipeline was taken with the knowledge that the German steel and manufacturing sectors would be hurt by cooperation with NATO. Later, the 1985 decision by the German leadership to veto EC cereals price subsidy cuts represented a situation were costs were perceived to be asymmetrical in the post-commitment phase. German cereal and rape seed oil farmers, represented by the powerful *Bauernverband*, made it clear to leaders that they would be hurt by cooperation with the EC.

	Cooperation	Defection
Symmetry of Effects	**4** 1978 EMS 1979 INF 1983 INF 1985 SEA	**2** 1975 ERDF 1989 SNF
Asymmetry of Effects		**2** 1982 Pipe 1985 Cereal

Figure 6.4 Symmetry and cooperation.

The results of this study support the argument that cooperation is somewhat more likely where the costs and benefits of a foreign policy decision are perceived as symmetrical, and less likely when they are perceived as asymmetrical. Policymakers are more likely to agree with, and to provide long-term support for, international organization programs that benefit the polity relatively equally. They are somewhat more likely to defect if they are asymmetrical, although the relationship in the eight cases is far from perfect. Ultimately, the relationship between issue area and symmetry is not clear-cut, and a comparison of the results presented in Figures 6.3 and 6.4 illustrates this difference. While all four case studies of military/security issues were categorized as having symmetrical effects, two cases of economic/developmental issues were also relatively symmetrical. These results challenge key assumptions of the comparative foreign policy literature and are discussed in more detail in another section of this chapter.

The Impact of Elections

Another domestic political condition examined in the conceptual framework was past election performance, and the following hypothesis about election impact was put forward.

> Hypothesis 4: An initial commitment to cooperate with other states in the context of an international organization is less likely to be sustained in the post-commitment phase, *ceteris paribus*, when the major party loses support in national or regional elections.

This hypothesis was supported by six of the eight case studies examined in this project. Each case of defection from a major international commitment was preceded by regional or national election losses, and leaders often made some reference to these results as catalysts for policy change. For example, the 1975 defection from the European Regional Development Fund followed a series of *Landtag* election losses in Rheinland-Pfalz, Schleswig-Holstein, Nordrhein-Westfal, and the Saarland. The 1982 decision not to support NATO sanctions was also affected by very negative results in regional elections in Berlin. Third, the 1985 decision to veto EC cereals price subsidy cuts came after the Union party suffered regional election losses in Berlin and in Nordrhein-Westfal, which cast doubt on the ability of the Union party leadership to maintain the support of German farmers. Finally, the Union party leadership took serious losses in two regional elections in Hessen and Berlin during the period leading up to the April 1989 decision not to support SNF modernization.

Conversely, election gains in the post-commitment phase were associated with decisions to cooperate in two of the four cases examined. The Social Democrats experienced strong election gains in the period leading up to the 1978 decision to support the European Monetary System. Later, the Union party leadership solidified its position with gains in regional and national elections in early 1983, several months before a final decision on INF modernization. However, the decisions to support the NATO Dual Track plan and the Single European Act were both preceded by regional elections losses, but leaders proceeded with plans to support the initiatives anyway.

This book offers some support for the hypothesis that election losses correspond with decisions to defect from commitments and that gains correspond with international cooperation. Election losses in the post-commitment phase contributed to defections from major international organization programs, but gains did not always improve chances for cooperation. The results suggest an important, but often unrecognized relationship between election results and foreign policy behavior.

Public Support

A final domestic political condition examined in this book was public support for the major party in the post-commitment phase. This was expected to be important because leaders in parliamentary systems with rotational election schedules should always be sensitive to their party's prospects for upcoming elections. Thus, a leader's ability to uphold international agreements could be affected by gains or declines in public support in the post-commitment phase.

> Hypothesis 5: An initial commitment to cooperate with other states in the context of an international organization is less likely to be sustained in the post-commitment phase, *ceteris paribus*, when the major party loses support in public opinion polls.

This hypothesis was not convincingly supported by the case studies examined. Declining public opinion did correspond to three of the four cases of defection examined for this study: in 1982, when the Schmidt government was forced to respond to a steady decline in popular support in the period leading up to the decision about NATO sanctions; in 1985 when there was a steep decline in public

	Cooperation	Defection
Prior Election Gains	**2** 1978 EMS 1983 INF	
Prior Election Losses	**2** 1979 INF 1985 SEA	**4** 1989 SNF 1982 Pipe 1985 Cereal 1975 ERDF

Figure 6.5 Election results and cooperation.

support for the Union party before the decision to veto the EC cereals price cut initiative was taken; and in the period leading up to the April 1989 decision not to support SNF modernization. However, one case of defection actually occurred in spite of increasing public support in the post-commitment phase: the decision to defect from the EC's European Regional Development Fund plan in 1975.

Conversely, there were two instances where the German government upheld major commitments in spite of losses of public support. Earlier, in November 1983, Union party leaders authorized the modernization of intermediate-range nuclear systems in spite of a steep drop in public support in the post-commitment phase. And in November 1985, leaders supported the Single European Act even though they lost public support in the year leading up to the decision. These results are illustrated in Figure 6.6.

In sum, only five of the eight case studies fit the expected pattern of relationships between popular support and cooperation and defection. While three cases of defection were preceded by declining public support, cooperation also occurred in spite of lower public approval ratings. Overall, these results were less robust than those for more proximate variables and tell little about the nature of domestic political constraints on foreign policy decisions that may emerge in the post-commitment politics phase.

	Cooperation	Defection
Gains in Popular Support	**2** 1978 EMS 1979 INF	**1** 1975 ERDF
Loss of Popular Support	**2** 1983 INF 1985 SEA	**3** 1989 SNF 1982 Pipe 1985 Cereal

Figure 6.6 Public support and cooperation.

Summary of Results

A summary of the results is presented in Figure 6.7. These data allow the comparison of relationships between the different domestic political conditions and outcomes. This summary includes an analysis of the discriminatory power of the intervening variables, the fit of the cases and the variables to the expected outcomes, the importance of issue areas for international cooperation, and the role of political proximity.

Discriminatory Power of the Variables

One important measure of the utility of the intervening variables in the conceptual framework is their discriminatory power, which can be measured in terms of the fit of variables to the expected outcome. Together, the leadership variables examined in this study (intra- and interparty relations) account for all cases of cooperation and defection. The level of consensus among leaders

		Major Party Unity	Coalition Consensus	Symmetry of Effects	Election Gains	Public Support Gains
Cooperation	1978 EMS	Y	N	Y	Y	Y
	1979 Dual Track	N	Y	Y	N	Y
	1983 INF	Y	Y	Y	Y	N
	1985 SEA	Y	Y	Y	N	N
Defection	1975 ERDF	Y	Y	N	Y	N
	1982 Pipeline	Y	Y	Y	Y	Y
	1985 Cereals	Y	Y	Y	Y	Y
	1989 SNF	Y	Y	N	Y	Y

Y = Yes, Results Support Hypotheses
N = No, Results Do Not Support Hypotheses

Figure 6.7 Summary of results.

in the major party in government corresponded with seven of the eight foreign policy decisions about international agreements. Following a similar pattern, the level of interparty coalition agreement was related to foreign policy behavior in seven of the eight cases. In tandem, these variables offer real discriminatory power for explaining cooperation and defection in the post-commitment phase. It can be argued that with unity in the major party in government and consensus among elites in the coalition, the predominant leader could uphold an international commitment regardless of other domestic opposition. At the same time, elite dissensus could override leaders' promises to uphold international commitments, sharply curtailing foreign policy latitude and threatening their personal power base in the post-commitment phase. Further, results support arguments from the comparative politics literature that party politics play a prominent role in the ratification process.

Results also show that cooperation could be related to the symmetry of the foreign policy decision. In all four cases of cooperation, the effects of a decision were viewed as symmetrical. Symmetry also correctly accounts for cooperation and defection in the two cases missed by the two earlier variables but incorrectly estimates two others. Thus, symmetry of effects offers less discriminatory power for understanding why cooperation or defection may occur in the post-commitment phase.

Finally, regional and national election results and popular support offer even less discriminatory power. Election results appear to have affected foreign policy behavior in six of the eight case studies examined for this project. But the relationship between changes in public opinion and international cooperation is not so clear-cut. Overall, results for these variables do not match expectations for four of the eight case studies in the book, and the whole dimension of public support captured by these variables offers less discriminatory power.

Case Fit to Predicted Outcomes

Expectations about the effects of domestic political conditions can also be compared with outcomes on a case-by-case basis. Some support for hypotheses advanced in chapter 1 can be found by looking at the data in the rows of Figure 6.7, which demonstrate outcomes for all variables across each case. Cases where expectations match the outcome for all five conditions provide strong confirmation for my arguments. Cases where four of the five conditions match expectations could be considered to provide some confirmation of these relationships.

Two cases of defection provide strong confirmation for my framework. Expectations about the relationships between domestic political conditions and cooperation and defection were fully confirmed in my study of the 1982 rejection of NATO sanctions on Poland and the Soviet Union and the 1985 veto of EC cereals price subsidy cuts. The NATO sanctions case was preceded by dissensus in the Social Democratic party, differences with the FDP leadership, the perception that the agreement would have asymmetrical costs and little benefit, declining election results, and losses of public support. Likewise, conditions preceding the 1985 decision to veto EC cereals price subsidy cuts matched expectations: dissensus in the major party, differences between the SPD and FDP leaders, a perception of asymmetry of the agreement, election losses, and declining public support.

The exact match between expectations and outcomes in these two cases suggests that they are of a special nature. Drawing on the contextual information presented in these cases, there is a sense that these decisions to defect were both taken in the context of uncertainty and instability in the domestic political arena. In 1981, Schmidt debated the proper response to calls for NATO sanctions with his close allies in the Social Democratic party, with Foreign Minister Genscher and other FDP leaders, and even with corporate leaders who would be hurt by cooperation with NATO. But the chancellor was tied down by many smaller concerns and issues, and unable to establish real political control and overcome domestic political opposition in the post-commitment phase.

In 1985, a different constellation of leaders faced similar domestic political unrest on the question of support for proposed EC cereals price subsidy cuts. Leaders inside the Union party and in the ruling coalition could not agree on the proper response to the European Commission plans. Agriculture Minister Kiechle wanted support for a German veto, but Chancellor Kohl and Foreign Minister Genscher both feared that a veto would derail their plans for reform of institutional arrangements in the EC. Meanwhile, German leaders faced opposition to cereals price subsidy cuts from German cereals farmers and declining public and electorate support.

Overall there appear to be two common denominators behind these decisions to defect, operating both together and separately. First, both decisions were taken when the predominant leaders faced internal challenges to their own political positions. Schmidt was rapidly losing party support and public confidence, and he lost his position as chancellor less than a year later. Kohl also faced serious political challenges in 1985. German periodicals carried numerous accounts of rumors of his political demise in this period, and many critics compared him to Ludwig Erhard, who was washed out of office due to a lack of Union party support in the late 1960s. Thus, both leaders were insecure and troubled by declining public support before making these decisions to defect.

Second, these cases represent the only two in the study where cooperation with an international organization program would have a substantial asymmetrical distribution of costs and benefits for the German polity. Leaders knew that cooperation would hurt specific sectors of the German economy, and many corporate leaders and government ministry officials lobbied the chancellor not to sustain initial commitments to cooperate. In 1981, executives from the German firm Mannesman and from General Electric's division offices in Germany lobbied Chancellor Schmidt not to cooperate with NATO sanctions. Specifically, they feared that COCOM and NATO plans would cancel the planned Siberian natural gas pipeline project—on which they depended for fiscal survival. In 1985 it was the German farm lobby and sympathetic Agriculture Ministry officials that pushed for a veto of the proposed EC cereals price cuts. In similar ways, vocal and organized lobbies worked to derail plans for cooperation with international programs that would hurt their own interests.

Finally, these two domestic political factors also worked in conjunction to produce defection. Both Chancellors Schmidt and Kohl were under fire and faced serious political challenges at the same time they were considering whether to sustain international commitments. Both chancellors were also being lobbied heavily by those interests who feared being sacrificed for the larger goal of international cooperation. Thus the need to avoid alienating significant groups domestically became a greater consideration when the leader, his party, and the coalition were already weak and divided. In that context, leaders defected from commitments to show their loyalty to domestic interests and, it was hoped, to reinforce their own leadership roles in foreign and domestic policy making.

Interestingly enough, this maneuver only resulted in long-term political success for Chancellor Kohl. His 1985 decision to allow Kiechle to veto the EC price cut plan actually enhanced his support within the Union party and in the eyes of the powerful German *Bauernverband*, and it produced a concomitant upswing in popular support. For Schmidt, the decision to allow the construction of the Siberian pipeline only forestalled his own political demise. Within months of this decision, Schmidt was again fighting pitched battles for control within his own party and the coalition. In October 1982, legislators in the *Bundestag* voted Schmidt out of office.

Issue Area Revisited

A comparison of the effects of the different domestic political conditions on cooperation and defection across issue areas yields very interesting results. The data in Figure 6.7 reveal a very significant conclusion: there was no real distinction in the results across issue area. A brief comparison of the conditions behind the 1979 Dual Track decision (military/security issue) and the 1985 cereals veto (an economic/developmental issue) illustrates this point. In the case of cooperation with NATO in 1979, leaders in the Social Democratic party were divided and there was a perceived symmetry of effects, prior election losses, and prior public opinion gains. In the case of the veto of the EC cereals price cut proposal, there was dissensus in the major party and in the ruling coalition; there was perceived asymmetry; and there were election and public opinion losses. In general, there were no notable differences between the results of these cases or the examined variables, and no particular variable stands out in terms of presence or absence in the framework. This pattern holds for a comparison of all other cases by issue area.

The inconclusive nature of this result is important and supports a key point about issue area distinctions in the study of foreign policy. Most traditional studies of issue area have at least implied that different levels of actors and interests are engaged by different issue areas. As noted in chapter 1, Brecher made such a distinction in his early work and Baldwin supported this in his study of economic statecraft.[1] Domestic structuralists like Gourevitch and Katzenstein have employed the issue area distinction as a way to better understand and predict foreign policy behavior.[2] Even one editor of the *Double-Edged Diplomacy* project, Evans, argued that "systemic arguments have greater relevance in security cases, [while] constituency-driven arguments better explain economic issues."[3]

However, this study shows that both economic/developmental and military/security issues stir public and government debates in the post-commitment politics phase. In all cases, initial elite commitments to cooperate placed issues on the public agenda and led to the mobilization of domestic interest groups and the public. Thus, my conclusions support recent interpretations of the questionable importance of issue areas in the comparative study of foreign policy. They parallel conclusions of scholars like Evangelista and Risse-Kappen, who have emphasized that factors like the domestic structure and the sociopolitical environment play more important roles than issue area in foreign policy decision making.[4] In fact, a mix of domestic political actors and conditions are important for foreign policy decisions relative to international commitments, regardless of the issue area. Alternative approaches like the focus on symmetry are a step in the right direction toward measurement of the relationship between domestic interests and foreign policy decision-making.[5]

The Role of Political Proximity

This book has also provided some support for the political proximity argument. Generally, the results suggest that the more proximate conditions may be the most influential, but they are inconclusive as to whether dissensus in the major party or between parties in the coalition government is more responsible for defections from international commitments. Thus, while leaders may begin to construct consensus in support of international commitments within their own party organization, they must also incorporate junior party interests.[6] Overall, this study has shown that post-commitment elite political maneuvering clearly represented (to some extent) what Risse-Kappen has termed "an institutionalized policy consensus" with a primary role in foreign policy decision-making.[7]

The existence of factionalism inside the major party in government coupled with ruling coalition dissensus may serve as an important opening for less-proximate conditions to become influential in the post-commitment phase. And beyond the window of opportunity created by dissensus at the major party level, intensity appears to have been the key factor affecting the relative influence of other factors on foreign policy decision-making. For example, domestic interest groups really only became serious actors in the process when specific groups with intensely held beliefs lobbied the government to undertake a certain foreign policy decision, when there were splits in the major party on the issue, and where leaders were looking for alternative solutions to the foreign policy problem. In the same way, polls and election results were interpreted as signs of trouble for the major party only when the party leadership was already divided and showed their concerns in public. In sum, intensity and proximity appear to be key catalysts in the foreign policy-making process relative to international commitments.

TWO-LEVEL GAME THEORY REVISITED

Overall, this book has demonstrated the importance of modifying Putnam's work to account for the sequential process of international cooperation, the importance of the post-commitment politics phase, and the relationship between domestic constraints and defections. Further, this study has uncovered some interesting ideas about political proximity and the role of third variables in the foreign policy process relative to international commitments.

Constraints can emerge in the post-commitment politics phase that may derail leaders' plans for international cooperation. Put simply, this book has shown that cooperation is not guaranteed by elite agreements at the international negotiating table. Rather, new and important political maneuvering actually begins back at home for leaders as soon as they commit to support a new program in an international organization. This emphasis on the domestic politics behind international cooperation supports arguments by scholars like Eckart Kehr about the *Primat der Innenpolitik* and relates to comparative politics, international relations, and historical scholarship.[8]

Specifically, this study modifies Putnam's work by highlighting the importance of three factors involved in international cooperation: time, leadership, and complexity in the domestic political arena.[9]

Time

Focusing on post-commitment politics clearly means extending Putnam's two-level game construct. While Putnam suggested that leaders formulate international commitments and establish domestic political consensus "simultaneously," this study has shown that any kind of alignment of domestic and international interests is affected by time and sometimes unanticipated change.[10]

After the leader makes an initial commitment and places an issue on the agenda, some time passes before domestic actors and conditions become mobilized to support an agreement, pressure the government to modify its plans, or to oppose an agreement outright. It is this post-commitment phase when domestic conditions can intervene between a leader's policy preferences and his or her ability to implement those preferences through a final foreign policy decision on cooperation. Editors of *Double-Edged Diplomacy* implied that time was important in Evans' statement, "the relative autonomy of international leaders decreases continuously and substantially over the course of most negotiations."[11]

Time becomes a factor in international cooperation in at least two ways. First, leaders sometimes miscalculate the time required to ratify an international commitment. For example, Chancellor Kohl led the charge in the EC for the Single European Act in 1985, and Union party leaders believed that the SEA would provide an important step forward for European integration. However, confirmation for the SEA in Germany was slowed by a series of concerns voiced by the *Bundesbank*, and *Länder* leaders delayed ratification of the SEA for six months in an effort to attain a greater say in Europe policy.

Second, and perhaps more important, leaders sometimes miscalculate the scope and intensity of domestic political opposition that can arise over time to an international commitment. A good example of this phenomenon can be seen in an examination of what occurred after Chancellor Schmidt's initial commitment of German support for the NATO Dual Track plan at the Brussels summit in December 1979. After the summit, Schmidt had to return home and begin a complex process of building and maintaining legitimacy for German support for INF modernization. In the post-commitment phase, Schmidt had to contend with growing public opposition, emerging peace movements, and an increased number of opponents to modernization inside his own party organization. When his support waned, Schmidt was forced out of office and became a victim of his own political commitments. Of course, this represents somewhat of an extreme case where post-commitment domestic political opposition overrode the leader's support for an international agreement. Evans hinted that "the very act of putting new issues on the international agenda, COGs [Chiefs of Governments] and their negotiators cannot help but awaken and mobilize constituencies with the potential of undercutting the attempted agreement."[12] This project has picked up where Putnam and his supporters left off by showing how and why this is the case—rounding out the scholarly picture of the origins of international cooperation and defection.

Leadership

This study has demonstrated the importance of leadership in the post-commitment politics phase. As representatives of the people and of the government in parliamentary democracies, party leaders serve as a nexus between government and public responsibility. International cooperation should be seen as a function of leaders' efforts to manage multiple domestic political constraints in the post-commitment phase: confirming commitments by forming elite consensus on the issue, building legitimating coalitions, and properly calculating public support.

An emphasis on post-commitment consensus and coalition building has important theoretical implications. Instead of simply managing two-level games simultaneously, as Putnam suggests, government leaders interact with leaders and conditions at multiple levels inside the state. They must also work to form coalitions with certain domestic political actors or groups in order to formulate foreign policy relative to an international commitment. In other words, leaders may use their connections with particular constituencies to legitimate particular foreign policy programs—what Putnam termed "domestic resonance."

The importance of elite consensus, and coalition building in the post-commitment phase, was illustrated by the case studies of defection. In each of these cases, leaders of the German government were unable to uphold a commitment to a major program in NATO or the EC because of multilevel, domestic political constraints. For example, in the case of the 1985 cereals veto decision, Agriculture Minister Kiechle worked to develop a German response to EC plans to reform agricultural policies and prices. Kiechle and other Conservative leaders were very concerned about maintaining the support of the German farmers, and these concerns led to fights within the Union party and between coalition partners. Faced with a series of regional election losses, government leaders were unable to develop consensus in support of the EC plan inside the major party, in the ruling coalition, in relation to the Agricultural Ministry, and with the German *Bauernverband*. Multiple-level domestic constraints drove Chancellor Kohl and Minister Kiechle to defect from a commitment to reform EC agricultural policy.

In short, this literature informs Putnam's model of international cooperation by emphasizing the importance of elite leadership. A committed leader can often work to bring about international cooperation, but he or she must build coalitions of support for commitments inside the party and among leaders of the coalition government. Widening the focus of Putnam's framework to capture these actors at work in the commitment and post-commitment phase of politics should enhance future research.

Complexity

Finally, this book has highlighted the complexity of the post-commitment ratification process. Putnam originally discussed the idea of ratification of international agreements, but he emphasized strategies for leaders to achieve "negotiated win-sets." Putnam also supported efforts to catalog the key domestic political actors involved in international cooperation, but these ultimately produced only ad hoc lists of domestic factors.

This book demonstrates the complexities of the ratification process in the post-commitment phase and identifies key domestic actors and conditions that can be related to cooperation and defection. While the ratification process often begins inside the major party in government, it also extends to incorporate the interests of other actors, and to recognize other domestic political conditions. Specifically, the project identified leaders' attempts to build consensus on at least five levels inside the state in the post-commitment phase. Major party unity and ruling coalition consensus were shown to be associated with defections from international commitments. The symmetry of effects, elections, and public opinion also contributed to the domestic political context behind key foreign policy decisions. Of course, this does not rule out the possibility that other actors and conditions of domestic politics could also influence foreign policy making.

An example of the complexity of domestic political constraints on cooperation can be seen in the case of the 1989 debate about SNF modernization. In the spring 1989, Chancellor Kohl was concerned about intraparty factionalism and threats from the Free Democrats to leave the coalition if Germany supported modernization of short-range systems. Serious election defeats in Hessen and Berlin also seem to have convinced Kohl to reconsider the German commitment. Generally, domestic political constraints arose at multiple levels in the post-commitment stage of politics that overrode systemic pressures.

Finally, another aspect of complexity in the post-commitment politics phase is the importance of factional leaders in foreign policy decision-making. I have shown that an informed study of leadership and cooperation should examine: cabinet leaders relevant to the issue who are typically vested with decision-making authority (i.e., the chancellor, minister of defense, minister of finance, foreign minister, and so on); and factional leaders of parties in the government itself, including the Party General Secretary and the leader of the *Bundestag* party *Fraktion*. Each group of leaders can pose serious constraints on the decision-making latitude of the predominant leader.

Even after promising to cooperate with others, state leaders must work very hard to sustain cooperation inside their own domestic arena. While this may not be such a mystery to legislators in the *Bundestag* or on Capitol Hill, it is a complex and important concept to capture in the social sciences. To the extent that this project has defined post-commitment politics (including its longitudinal nature and key domestic political conditions that affect leaders' policy-making latitude), it has made an important contribution to the discipline.

LESSONS FOR INTERNATIONAL COOPERATION

Factionalism in the major party and the ruling coalition, the symmetry of effects of cooperation, and election losses clearly affected German policy toward international organizations in the 1970s and 1980s. But are these results significant for understanding contemporary problems with international cooperation? In fact, there are many examples in post–Cold War era politics that reaffirm the importance of key domestic political conditions for international cooperation. One such case is the record of German responses to the civil war in Yugoslavia, which formally began when the republics of Croatia and Slovenia declared their independence on June 25, 1991.

In the first year of the crisis, Germany experienced a massive influx of refugees seeking asylum, and many Western leaders were concerned about the potential spillover of the Balkan conflict into other areas. Accordingly, Chancellor Kohl enjoyed intraparty, interparty, and popular support for foreign policy initiatives designed to respond to the conflict. German leaders worked to guarantee the participation of Croatia and Slovenia in the EC's first peace conference at the Hague on September 7, 1991. When the cease-fire brokered at the September conference fell through, German leaders pushed EC diplomats to impose economic sanctions against all republics of Yugoslavia in November 1991. Later, domestic political support enabled Kohl and Genscher to push for an even tougher trade embargo against Serbia.[13]

But this strong domestic pressure for German action also prompted a very significant post-commitment defection from an EC initiative. On December 10, 1991, German leaders expressed their support for the EC Maastricht Treaty on European Union, which included a set of preconditions for the multilateral recognition of new states. However, Chancellor Kohl announced on December 15 that Germany would unilaterally recognize the Republics of Croatia and Slovenia *without any preconditions*.[14] European leaders were outraged and demanded that Germany withdraw its offer of recognition, but the leaders' hands were tied by domestic political conditions that had reached a boiling point in the days after the Maastricht summit. German leaders had perceived strong domestic pressure for this kind of action from the roughly 400,000 Croats who already lived in Germany during 1991 (many in Bavaria, which had strong ties with Catholic Croatia), from the regional party organizations, and from the general public. Essentially, this tide of popular pressure supplanted the commitment German leaders had made in the Maastricht agreement only days earlier.[15]

Serious domestic disagreements about the proper course of German foreign policy toward the crisis that emerged in 1992 constrained any further activism. After a July decision by the cabinet leadership to send German ships and aircraft to the Adriatic Sea to support the NATO monitoring mission of Serbia and Montenegro, domestic support for activism began to wane.[16] In spite of Kohl's support for cooperation, disagreements resurfaced inside the Union party and in the coalition about the proper course for German foreign policy responses to the crisis. To further complicate matters, the Social Democrats launched a formal challenge to the decision in the German Constitutional Court and forced the convening of a special session of the *Bundestag*. Even though the government received a favorable ruling from the Court and won a vote of support for the deployment in the legislature, this challenge created a rift between the foreign and defense ministries on Balkan policy. Overall, this experience contributed to factionalism inside the coalition and reduced the Conservatives' room to maneuver on security policy matters.[17]

In early 1993, Chancellor Kohl made another promise to NATO allies that almost collapsed in the post-commitment phase. He pledged to support the deployment of AWACs aircraft over Bosnia to enforce the no-fly zone even though about 30 percent of the military personnel would be German officers. When they learned of this pledge, FDP leaders were so outraged that they sponsored a challenge to the Conservative initiative in the German Constitutional Court. While judges ultimately ruled in favor of the Conservatives, the court challenge demonstrated the loss of support for German activism inside the coalition. Finally, real political deadlock emerged when key regional election losses allowed the SPD to gain control of a majority in the *Bundesrat*. As a result, the coalition could no longer muster a two-thirds majority to support constitutional changes that might legalize any such deployments in the future, and many Union party leaders blamed Kohl for this predicament.

Germany remained on the sidelines of the conflict throughout most of 1993 and 1994, but the logjam was finally broken when the Conservatives received a favorable Constitutional Court ruling in July 1994. The Court ruled that German troops could be deployed in peacekeeping missions out of the NATO area as long as the initiative had a simple majority of support in the *Bundestag*. In fact, this legal development—coupled with the national election victories for the Conservatives in October 1994—laid the foundation for a major sea change in German security policy and reenergized elite consensus in the cabinet

With this newfound sense of stability and latitude, Chancellor Kohl and Foreign Minister Kinkel announced a plan in June 1995 to contribute 1,000 German soldiers and eight Tornado fighter planes to a new NATO Rapid Reaction force for the Balkans. On June 30, the cabinet plan received an oversized majority of support in the *Bundestag* (386–258). On September 1, 1995, German pilots even participated in air strikes on Bosnian Serb military positions as part of a NATO Rapid Reaction Force operation. Finally, the German cabinet voted to deploy 4,000 *Bundeswehr* soldiers in the former Yugoslavia in December 1995 to support the NATO Implementation Force peace operation mandated by the Dayton Peace Accord. Domestic political support enabled the coalition leadership to fashion an entirely new German security policy construct—one that permitted out-of-area operations and even allowed soldiers to engage in combat within collective security arrangements.

CONCLUSION

This book has shown that international cooperation is not simply a function of a one-time alignment of state interests, and it has provided conceptual alternatives to the two-level game construct. Elite influence on foreign policy cooperation is clearly bounded by a series of domestic political constraints that often emerge in the post-commitment phase. The theoretical discussion and case studies presented here raise many important issues for further study, including the often hidden role of intraparty factionalism in policy making, the utility of the issue area distinction, and the quiet influence of regional elections on foreign policy making. Ultimately, the example of German responses to the crisis in the Balkans in the 1990s illustrates that leaders in parliamentary democracies must carefully design foreign policy initiatives relative to expected, long-term domestic political support.

NOTES

1. David Baldwin, *Economic Statecraft*, 1985; See also Michael Brecher, Blema Steinberg, and Janice Stein, "A Framework for Research on Foreign Policy Behavior," *Journal of Conflict Resolution*, vol. 13, 1969; Brecher et al., *The Foreign Policy System of Israel: Setting, Images, Process*, 1972.
2. See Katzenstein, "The Third West German Republic: Continuity in Change," *Journal of International Affairs*, Summer 1988, vol. 41, no. 2; See also Gourevitch, 1986.
3. Peter B. Evans, Harold K. Jacobson, and Robert D. Putnam, eds., *Double-Edged Diplomacy: International Bargaining and Domestic Politics,* 1993, p. 404.
4. Matthew Evangelista, "Issue Area and Foreign Policy Revisited," *International Organizations*, Winter 1989, vol. 46; See also Risse-Kappen, 1994, p. 257; See also Risse-Kappen, "Public Opinion, Domestic Structure, and Foreign Policy in Liberal Democracies," *World Politics*, July 1991, no. 4.
5. In chapter 1, I argued that because economic/developmental issues often involve tangible potential costs or benefits, the struggle of many different groups for influence over policy makes stable cooperation with international organizations less likely. On the other hand, military/security issues have more of a symmetrical potential impact on the populace, some scholars argue, and will not tend to attract a divisive debate about potential policy resource distribution. In the end, the data suggest that symmetry could be associated with cases of cooperation, but the relationship between asymmetry and defection is unclear.
6. It is important to note that the importance of the junior party in German foreign policy in the 1970s and 1980s may have been a function of the special leadership of Hans-Dietrich Genscher as the FDP Foreign Minister. Genscher served as the leader of the junior party in both coalition governments and played an important role in all of the foreign policy decisions

about international commitments examined for this project; See Moravcsik, "Introduction: Integrating International and Domestic Theories of International Bargaining," in *Double-Edged Diplomacy: International Bargaining and Domestic Politics*, Peter B. Evans, Harold K. Jacobson, and Robert D. Putnam, eds., 1993, p. 30.

7. Risse-Kappen, July 1991, pp. 485–491.
8. See Eckart Kehr, "Englandhass und Weltpolitik: Eine Studie über die innenpolitischen und sozialen Grundlagen der deutschen Aussenpolitik um die Jahr hundertwende," *Der Primate der Innenpolitik*, vol. 19, 1965, p. 149.
9. For a related critique, see Jeffrey W. Knopf, "Beyond Two-Level Games: Domestic-International Interaction in the Intermediate-Range Nuclear Forces Negotiations," *International Organization*, vol. 47, no. 4, Autumn 1993.
10. Putnam, "Diplomacy and Domestic Politics: the Logic of Two-Level Games," *International Organization*, Summer 1988, vol. 42, no. 3, Summer 1988.
11. Evans, in Evans, et al., 1993, p. 400.
12. Ibid., 1993, p. 405.
13. Cabinet leaders also authorized an airlift of relief supplies for Bosnia that began in July 1992; *Deutschland Nachrichten*, May 29, 1992, p. 1; See also *Deutschland Nachrichten,* June 6, 1992, p. 1.
14. *Deutschland Nachrichten*, "EC and Bonn Cabinet Confirm Recognition of Slovenia and Croatia," December 20, 1991, p. 1.
15. Also, German politicians were driven to action because the crisis in Yugolsavia was an intrastate conflict for which the structures of the EC, NATO, and the United Nations were ill-prepared to handle. There is general fear that if this type of conflict could erupt in Yugoslavia, there is also potential for spillover of ethnic crises in other regions of Eastern Europe and the former Soviet republics; See William Drozdiak, "Pressure Rising in Europe for Action on Balkan War," *Washington Post,* June 25, 1991, p. A33.
16. David Binder, "UN Fights Bonn's Embrace of Croatia," *New York Times*, December 14, 1991, p. 3; See also *This Week in Germany*, "EC and Bonn Cabinet Confirm Recognition of Slovenia and Croatia," December 20, 1991, p. 1.
17. From Deutscher Bundestag, *Stenographischer Bericht*, 101st Sitzung, Bonn, Wednesday, July 22, 1992, pp. 8608–8660; See also "Bundestag Billigt Adria-Einsatz der Marine Kluft zwischen Koalition und SPD," *Süddeutsche Zeitung*, July 23, 1992, p. 1; Additional information is taken from direct observation of *Bundestag* debate and the author's notes.

SELECT BIBLIOGRAPHY

ARCHIVES

Arbeitstelle Friedenforschung, Bad Godesberg
Deutsche Gesellschaft für Auswärtige Politik, Bonn
Europäische Institut, Bonn
Friedrich Ebert Stiftung, Bonn
Friedrich Naumann Stiftung, Bonn
Konrad Adenauer Stiftung, Sankt Augustin
Presse- und Informationsamt der Bundesregierung, Bonn
Universität Bibliothek Bek, Bonn

MAJOR NEWSPAPER AND NEWS MAGAZINE SOURCES

Aachen Volkzeitung
Bayern Kurier
Christian Science Monitor
Deutsches Monatsblatt
Economist
Financial Times
Flensburger Tageblatt
Frankfurter Rundschau
Frankfurter Allgemeine Zeitung
Kölner Stadt-Anzeiger
New York Times
Rheinischer Merkur

Der Spiegel
Stuttgarter Zeitung
Süddeutsche Zeitung
United Nations Chronicle
Wall Street Journal
Washington Post
Die Welt
Die Zeit

NEWS AGENCY DISPATCHES—WIRE SERVICES

Agence Europe
Associated Press
Bulletin, Federal Republic of Germany Press and Information Office
Bundespresse-Agentur
Deutsche-Press Agentur
Foreign Broadcast Information Service Daily Reports
Reuters

SPECIALIST JOURNALS

American Political Science Review
Armed Forces and Society
Aussenpolitik
Bulletin der Europäischen Gemeinschaften
Comparative Politics
Diplomacy and Statecraft
Europa Archiv
Europa Archiv: Dokumente und Berichte
Foreign Affairs
Foreign Policy
German Politics
German Politics and Society
International Affairs
International Organization
International Security
Jahrbuch der Europäischen Integration
Journal of Common Market Studies
NATO Review
OECD Main Economic Indicators
Official Journal of the European Communities
Orbis
Survival
World Politics
Zeitschrift für Parlamentsfragen

INTERVIEWS

Genscher, Hans-Dietrich. Foreign Minister of Germany from 1974–1992. Columbus, Ohio. April 29, 1993.

Smyser, William R. Distinguished Foreign Service Officer and former Charge D'Affairs in the U.S. Embassy, Bonn. Washington, D.C. September 2, 1992.

UNPUBLISHED MATERIALS

Clemens, Clayton M. 1986. "The CDU–CSU and West German Ostpolitik, 1969–1982." Ph.D. Dissertation. Fletcher School of Law and Diplomacy. Tufts University.

Crawford, Beverly. 1993. "German Foreign Policy After the Cold War: The Decision to Recognize Croatia." Center for German and European Studies, Working Paper 2.21. August.

Driscoll, Robert F. 1983. "West German Nuclear Politics: A Study of International Cooperative Behavior." Ph.D. Dissertation. The American University.

Hermann, Charles F. 1987. "Political Opposition as Potential Agents of Foreign Policy Change: Developing a Theory," Paper presented at the 28th Annual Meeting of the International Studies Asssociation, Washington, D.C., April.

Mastanduno, Michael. 1985. "Between Economics and National Security: The Western Politics of East–West Trade." Ph.D. Dissertation. Princeton University.

Schwartz, David. 1980. "U.S. Policy and NATO's Strategic Dilemma." Ph.D. Dissertation. The Massachusetts Institute of Technology.

DOCUMENTS

Bundesminister der Verteidigung. *Weißbuch 1979: Zur Sicherheit der Bundesrepublik Deutschland und zur Entwicklung der Bundeswehr*. Bonn.

______. *Weißbuch 1984–1985*. Bonn.

______. June 1988. *Dokumente: Vertrag Zwischen den Vereinigten Staaten von Amerika und der Union der Sozialistischen Sowjetrepubliken über die Beseitigung ihrer Flugkörper mittlerer und kürzerer Reichweite*, from *Der Abbau der Mittelstreckenflugkörper*, Stand. Informations- und Pressestab, Referat Öffentlichkeitsarbeit.

Christian Demokratische Union Documentation Series. 1983. "Rechtspositionen in der Diskussion um den NATO- Doppelbeschluss." No. 36, November 10.

Commission of the European Communities. 1984. "Eurobarometer: Public Opinion in the European Community." No. 22. December.

______. 1975. "European Regional Development Fund." First Annual Report. *Bulletin of the European Economic Communities*, Supplement 7/76. Brussels.

______. 1973. "Proposals for a Community Regional Policy." *Official Journal of the European Communities*, OJ C86 and OJ C106.

______. 1973. "Report on the Regional Problems of the Enlarged Community." COM (73) 550. "The Thomson Report." Brussels.

______. 1970. "Economic and Monetary Union in the Community." The Werner Report. *Bulletin of the European Communities*, Supplement 11/70.

"East–West Commerical Policy: A Congressional Dialogue with the Reagan Administration." February 16, 1982. Study prepared for the Joint Economic Committee of Congress.

Europa Archiv: Zeitschrift für Internationale Politik, Dokumente 1989. p. D157, "Schlußfolgerungen des Ratspräsidenten zur den Arbeiten der Konferenz der Regierungsvertreter der EG-Mitgliedstaaten über die Einheitliche Europaische Akte in Luxemburg am 2. und 3. Dezember 1985."

Europa Archiv: Zeitschrift für Internationale Politik. 1986. Beitrage und Berichte. Bonn: Deutsche Gesellschaft für Auswärtige Politik.

Europa Archiv: Zeitschrift für Internationale Politik: Beitrage und Berichte. 1972. Selected Volumes, 1972–1992. Bonn: Deutsche Gesellschaft für Auswärtige Politik.

European Commission Report. 1981. *Perspektiven für die Europäische Zusammenarbeit.* Bericht der Colombo Kommission an den Europerat. Brussels. D535.

European Community Committee for the Study of Economic and Monetary Union. 1989. *Report on Economic and Monetary Union in the European Community, the "Delors Report."* Luxembourg: Office for Official Publications of the European Community.

European Community Information Service. 1984–1985. *General Report on the Activities of the European Community.*

Forschungsgruppe Wahlen. 1987. *Political Barometer-Elections Study 1986/87.* Mannheim.

Hardt, John, and Kate Tomlinson. 1982. "Soviet Gas Pipeline: U.S. Options." Congressional Research Service, Government Printing Office: Washington, D.C.

Herausgegeben von Gert Krell, Egon Bahr, und Johannes Schwertfeger. 1990. *Friedensgutachten 1990.* Bonn: Hessische Stiftung Friedens und Konfliktforschung.

International Monetary Fund. *International Financial Statistics*, Washington, D.C.: International Monetary Fund Publishing. Various Issues.

Jahrbuch der Europäischen Integration. 1972. Brussels.

Kiechle, Ignaz. March 20, 1985. "Bericht über die Tagung des Rates (Agrar)." Agricultural Ministry Press Release. Bonn.

NATO Information Service. 1981. *NATO Facts and Figures.* Brussels.

______. 1976. *NATO Final Communiqúes.* 1949–1974. Brussels.

Nerlich, Uwe. 1976. "The Modernization of NATO's Theater Nuclear Forces: Some European Policy Constraints." London.

Presse- und Informationsamt der Bundesregierung. 1992. *Reden: Zu Fragen der Sozial Marktwirtschaft.* Reihe: Berichte und Dokumentationen.

______. 1990. *Bericht zur Rüstungskontrolle und Abrüstung 1989/90.* Reihe: Berichte und Dokumentationen. Bonn.

Reden zu Fragen der Sozialen Marktwirtschaft. 1989. Bundeskanzler Helmut Kohl, Presse- und Informationsamt der Bundesregierung, Reihe Berichte und Dokumentationen.

"Resolution of the European Council of 5 December 1978 on the Establishment of the European Monetary System (EMS) and Related Matters." 1978–1979. Reprinted in *Journal of Common Market Studies* 17 (4): 298–313.

"SALT and the NATO Allies." 1979. U.S. Senate Committee on Foreign Relations, Subcommittee on European Affairs Report. Washington, D.C.: U.S. Government Printing Office.

Schmidt, Helmut. January 15, 1982. "Erklärung der Bundesregierung zur Entwicklung in Polen und den Gesprächen in Washington and Paris." Speech to *Bundestag*, 76 Sitzung on January 14. Reprinted in *Bulletin* no. 5, p. 29.

Sloan, Stanley. 1983. "NATO Nuclear Forces: Modernization and Arms Control." Congressional Research Service. Brief Number #1B8 1128. Washington, D.C. August 2.

Social Democratic Party *Fraktion*. October 6, 1979. "Materialen: Sicherheitspolitik im Rahmen der Friedenspolitik." *Leitantrag des Parteivorstands für den Parteitag in Berlin*. Bonn: Vorstand der SPD, Abteilung Presse und Information.

Stenographischer Bericht des Deutschen Bundestages, Deutscher Bundestag. Selected Volumes, Bonn. 1979–1992.

Stiftung Wissenschaft und Politik: Forschungsinstitute fur Internationale Politik und Sicherheit. May, 1991. *Die Reform der NATO-Strategie unter Bedingungen Strategischer Entflechtung in Europa*, Ebenhausen.

Subcommittee on Europe and the Middle East. 1980. "The Modernization of NATO's Long-Range Theater Nuclear Forces." Report prepared for the U.S. House Committee on Foreign Affairs. Washington, D.C.: U.S. Government Printing Office.

U.S. Department of State, Bureau of Public Affairs. October, 1981. *Soviet–Western European Natural Gas Pipeline.* Current Policy, no.331.

U.S. Department of State. 1987. *Documents on Germany, 1944–1985.* Public Document #9446.

MAJOR BOOKS AND ARTICLES

Aberbach, Joel D., Robert D. Putnam, and Bert A. Rockman, eds. 1981. *Bureaucrats and Politicians in Western Democracies*. Cambridge, Mass.: Harvard University Press.

Adler, Emanuel, and Beverly Crawford. 1991. *Progress in Postwar International Relations*. New York: Columbia University Press.

Adler, Emanuel, and Peter M. Haas. 1992. "Conclusion: Epistemic Communities, World Order, and the Creation of a Reflective Research Program." *International Organization* 46 (1): 367–390.

Alderman, R. K., and J. A. Cross. 1987. "The Timing of Cabinet ReShuffles." *Parliamentary Affairs* 40 (1): 1–19.

Alger, Chadwick F. 1984. "Bridging the Micro and the Macro in International Relations Research." *Alternatives* 24: 319–344.

______. 1977. "Analytical Approaches: Functionalism and Integration." *International Social Science Journal* 29 (1): 73–93.

Allen, Polly A. 1989. "The ECU and Monetary Management in Europe." In *The ECU and European Monetary Integration*, edited by Paul de Grauwe and Theo Peters. London: Macmillan.

Allison, Graham. 1971. *The Essence of Decision: Explaining the Cuban Missile Crisis*. Boston: Little, Brown.

Almond, Gabriel A. 1950. *The American People and Foreign Policy.* New York: Praeger Publishers.

Armstrong, H.W., and J. Taylor. 1978. *Regional Economic Policy and Its Analysis.* Oxford: Philip Allen.

Art, Robert. 1973. "Bureaucratic Politics and American Foreign Policy: A Critique." *Policy Sciences* 4 (4): 467–490.

Asmus, Ronald D. 1989. *The Politics of Modernizing Short-Range Nuclear Forces in West Germany.* Santa Monica, Calif.: RAND Corporation.

Averyt, W. F. 1977. *Agropolitics in the European Community*. New York: Praeger.

Axelrod, Robert. 1984. *The Evolution of Cooperation.* New York: Basic Books.

Axelrod, Robert, and Robert O. Keohane. 1985. "Achieving Cooperation Under Anarchy: Strategy and Institutions." *World Politics* 38 (1): 226–254.

Baldwin, David A. 1985. *Economic Statecraft.* Princeton, N.J.: Princeton University Press.

Barnes, Samuel, and Max Kaase. 1979. *Political Action: Mass Participation in Five Western Democracies.* London: Sage Publishers.

Barnett, Michael. 1990. "High Politics Is Low Politics: The Domestic and Systemic Sources of Israeli Security Policy, 1967–1977." *World Politics* 42: 529–562.

Bennett, S. E. 1972. "Attitude Structures and Foreign Policy Opinions." *Social Science Quarterly* 55: 732–742.

Berger, Suzanne D., ed. 1985. *Organizing Interests in Western Europe: Pluralism, Corporatism, and the Transformation of Politics.* Cambridge, England: Cambridge University Press.

Bertsch, Gary K. 1983. *East–West Strategic Trade, CoCom and the Atlantic Alliance.* New York: Basic Books.

Binder, David. 1975. *The Other German: Willy Brandt's Life and Times.* Washington, D.C.: New Republic.

Blechman, Barry, and Cathleen Fisher, eds. 1988. *The Silent Partner: West Germany and Arms Control.* Cambridge, Mass.: Ballinger.

Blondel, Jean, and Jean-Louis Thiebault. 1988. The Study of Western European Cabinets. *European Journal of Political Research* 16: 115–123.

Bluth, Christoph. 1992. "Germany: Towards a New Security Format." *The World Today* 48 (11): 196–198.

Bofinger, Peter. 1988. "Das Europäische Währungssystem und die geld-politische Kooperation in Europa." *Kredit und Kapital* 21: 317–345.

Bogdanor, Vernon, ed. 1983. *Coalition Government in Western Europe.* New York: Heinemann Educational Books.

Boutwell, Jeffrey. 1990. *The German Nuclear Dilemma.* Ithaca, N.Y.: Cornell University Press.

______. 1983. "Politics and the Peace Movement in West Germany." *International Security* 7 (4): 72–92.

Boyd, Gavin, and Gerald W. Hopple. 1987. *Political Change and Foreign Policies.* London: Frances Pinter.

Brass, Paul R. 1987. "Faction and Party in Indian Politics." *Annals of the American Academy of Political and Social Sciences* 491 (17): 3–5.

Brauch, Hans Gunter. 1982. *Die Raketen kommen, Vom NATO-Doppelbeschluss bis zur Stationierung.* Köln: Bund Verlag.

Braunthal, Gerard. 1965. *The Federation of German Industry in Politics.* Ithaca, N.Y.: Cornell University Press.

Brecher, Michael, Belma Steinberg, and Janice Stein. 1972. *The Foreign Policy System of Israel: Setting, Images, Process.* New Haven, Conn.: Yale University Press.

______. 1969. "A Framework for Research on Foreign Policy Behavior." *Journal of Conflict Resolution* 13 (1): 75–101.

Brunberg, Isabelle. 1990. "Exploring the Myth of Hegemonic Stability." *International Organization* 57: 126.

Bulmer, Simon. 1984. "The Federal Republic of Germany." In *Direct Elections to the European Parliament 1984*, edited by J. Lodge. New York: St. Martin's Press.

______. 1987. *The Domestic Structure of European Policy-Making in West Germany.* London: Macmillan.

Bulmer, Simon, and William Paterson. 1987. *The Federal Republic of Germany and the European Community.* London: Allen and Unwin.

Caldwell, Dan. 1991. *The Dynamics of Domestic Politics and Arms Control.* Columbia: University of South Carolina Press.

Calingaert, Michael. 1988. *The 1992 Challenge from Europe: Development of the European Community's Internal Market.* Washington, D.C.: National Planning Association.

Callahan, Patrick, Linda Brady, and Margaret Hermann, eds. 1982. *Describing Foreign Policy Behavior.* Beverly Hills, CA: Sage Publications.

Calleo, David. 1978. *The German Problem Reconsidered.* Cambridge, England: Cambridge University Press.

Carr, E. H. 1954. *The Twenty Years Crisis, 1919–1939: An Introduction to the Study of International Politics.* London: Macmillan.

Cerny, Karl H., ed. 1990. *Germany at the Polls.* Durham, N.C.: Duke University Press.

______. 1978. *Germany at the Polls: The Bundestag Election of 1976.* Washington, D.C.: American Enterprise Institute for Public Policy Research.

Cervenka, Zdenek, and Barbara Rogers. 1978. *The Nuclear Axis.* New York: Times Books.

Cheng, Peter P. 1990. "Japanese Interest Group Politics: An Institutional Framework." *Asian Survey* 30: 251–265.

Clemens, Clay. 1989. "Beyond INF: West Germany's Center-Right Party and Arms Control in the 1990s." *International Affairs* 65 (1): 55–74.

______. 1989. *Reluctant Realists: The Christian Democrats and West German Ostpolitik.* Durham, N.C.: Duke University Press.

Coate, Roger A. 1982. *Global Issue Regimes.* New York: Praeger Publishers.

Cooney, James A., Gordon Craig, and Hans Peter Schwarz, eds. 1984. *The Federal Republic of Germany and the United States: Changing Political, Social and Economic Relations.* Boulder, Colo.: Westview.

Cottam, Richard W. 1977. *Foreign Policy Motivations.* Pittsburgh, PA: University of Pittsburgh Press.

Cowhey, Peter. 1990. "The International Telecommunications Regime: The Political Roots of Regimes for High Technology." *International Organization* 44: 169–199.

Craig, Gordon A. 1984. *Deutschland und der Westen: Vorträge und Diskussionsbeitrage des Symposions zu Ehren von Gordon A. Craig.* Veranstaltet von der Freien Universitat Berlin, vom Dezember 1–3, 1983.

Crawford, Beverly. 1988. "Western Control of East–West Trade Finance: The Role of U.S. Power and the International Regime." In *Controlling East–West Trade and TechnologyTransfer: Power, Politics and Policies*, edited by Gary K. Bertsch. Durham, N.C.: Duke University Press.

Czempiel, Ernst-Otto. 1969. *Die Anachronistische Souveränität: ZumVerhältnis von Innen- und Außenpolitik.* Kohl: Opladen Verlag.

Dahl, Robert A., ed. 1973. *Regimes and Oppositions.* New Haven, Conn.: Yale University Press.

DeHaven, Mark J. 1991. "Internal and External Determinants of Foreign Policy: West Germany and Great Britain During the Two-Track Missile Controversy." *International Studies Quarterly* 35: 87–108.

Delors, Jacques. 1989. Committee for the Study of Economic and Monetary Union. *Report on Economic and Monetary Union in the European Community.* Luxembourg: Office for Official Publications of the EC.

Dembinski, Matthias, ed. 1989. *Amerikanische Weltpolitik nach dem Ost-West Konflikt.* Baden-Baden: Nomos.

Denton, Geoffrey. 1981. "Regional Divergence and Policy in the Community, with Special Reference to Enlargement." In *Economic Divergence in the European Community*, edited by M. Hodges, and W. Wallace. New York: Allen and Unwin.

______. 1986. "Restructuring the EC Budget: Implications of the Fontainbleau Agreement." *Journal of Common Market Studies* 23 (2): 117–140.

Deutsch, Karl W. 1957. *Political Community and the North Atlantic Area: International Organization in the Light of Historical Experience.* Princeton, N.J.: Princeton University Press.

______. 1954. *Political Community at the International Level.* Garden City, N.Y.: Doubleday and Company.

Diskin, Abraham, and Itzhak Galnoor. December 1990. "Political Distances Between Knesset Members and Coalition Behavior: The Peace Agreements with Egypt." *Political Studies* 38: 710–717.

Dodd, Lawrence C. 1976. *Coalitions in Parliamentary Government.* Princeton, N.J.: Princeton University Press.

Döring, Herbert, and Gordon Smith, eds. 1982. *Party Government and Political Culture in Western Germany.* New York: St. Martin's Press.

Downs, George W., David M. Rocke, and Randolph Siverson. 1986. "Arms Races and Cooperation." In *Cooperation Under Anarchy,* edited by Kenneth Oye. Princeton, N.J.: Princeton University Press.

DuVerger, Maurice. 1969. *Political Parties.* Paris: A Colin.

Dyson, Kenneth H. F. 1977. *Party, State, and Bureaucracy in Western Germany.* Beverly Hills, Calif.: Sage Publications.

East, Maurice A., Stephen A. Salmore, and Charles F. Hermann, eds. 1978. *Why Nations Act.* Beverly Hills, Calif.: Sage Publications.

Eckstein, Harry. 1975. "Case Study and Theory in Political Science." In *Handbook of Political Science*, edited by Fred Greenstein, and Nelson W. Polsby. Reading, Mass.: Addison-Wesley.

Edinger, Lewis J. 1986. *West German Politics*. Basingstoke, N.Y.: Columbia University Press.

Ehlermann, Claus-Dieter. November 1990. "The Institutional Development of the EC Under the Single European Act."*Aussenpolitik* 22: 134–157.

Eichenberg, Richard C. 1989. *Public Opinion and National Security in Western Europe*. New York: Macmillan Publishers.

Eichenberg, Richard, ed. 1986. *Drifting Together or Apart?* Cambridge, Mass.: Center for International Affairs, Harvard University.

Eisfeld, Rainer. 1983. "The West German Elections: Economic Fears and the Deployment Debate." *Government and Opposition* 18 (3): 291–303.

El-Agraa, A. M. 1990. *The Economics of the European Community*, 3d ed. London: Macmillan.

Eusebio, Mujal-Leon. 1988. "The West German Social Democratic Party and the Politics of Internationalism in Central America." *Journal of Interamerican Studies and World Affairs* 29: 89–123.

Evangelista, Matthew. 1989. "Issue Area and Foreign Policy Revisited." *International Organization* 43 (1): 147–171.

______. 1988. *Innovation and the Arms Race*. Ithaca, N.Y.: Cornell University Press.

Evans, Peter B., Harold K. Jacobson, and Robert D. Putnam, eds. 1993. *Double-Edged Diplomacy: International Bargaining and Domestic Politics*. Berkeley, Calif.: University of California Press.

Fennell, Rosemary. 1975. "Reform of the CAP: Shadow or Substance?" *Journal of Common Market Studies* 26 (4): 1282.

Flynn, Gregory, and Hans Rattinger, eds. 1985. *The Public and Atlantic Defense*. London: Croom Helm.

Forndran, Erhard. 1987. "Abrüstung und Rüstungskontrolle Chancen und Risiken nach dem Vertrag über die Mittelstreckenraketen." In *Abrustung und Rustungskontrolle*, edited by E. Forndran. Cologne: Nomos Verlaggesellschaft.

Frankland, Gene E. 1988. "The Role of the Greens in West German Parliamentary Politics, 1980–1987." *The Review of Politics* 50: 99–120.

Fratianni, Michele, and Jürgen von Hagen. 1992. *The European Monetary System and European Monetary Union*. Boulder, Colo.: Westview Press.

Fratiani, Michele, and Theo Peeters, eds. 1978. *One Money for Europe*. Boulder, Colo.: Westview Press.

Frost, Ellen L., and Angela E. Stent. 1983. "NATO's Troubles with East–West Trade." *International Security* 8: 179–200.

Fukui, Haruhito. 1970. *Party in Power*. Berkeley: University of California Press.

Gallarotti, Giulio. 1991. "The Limits of International Organization: Systematic Failure in the Management of International Relations." *International Organization* 45: 183–220.

Garrett, Geoffrey. Spring 1992. "International Cooperation and Institutional Choice: The European Community's Internal Market." *International Organization* 46 (2): 530–561.

Gatzke, Hans W. 1980. *Germany and the United States: A Special Relationship?* Cambridge, Mass.: Harvard University Press.

Genscher, Hans-Dietrich. 1982. "Toward an Overall Western Strategy." *Foreign Affairs* 61 (1): 17–26.

George, Alexander. 1982. "Case Studies and Theory Development." Paper presented to the Second Annual Symposium on Information Processing in Organizations, Carnegie-Mellon University.

______. 1980. *Presidential Decisionmaking in Foreign Policy: The Effective Use of Information and Advice.* Boulder, Colo.: Westview Press.

______. "Case Studies and Theory Development: The Method of Structured, Focused Comparison." In *Diplomacy: New Approaches in History, Theory, and Policy*, edited by Paul G. Lauren. New York: Free Press.

George, Alexander L., and Richard Smoke. 1974. *Deterrence in American Foreign Policy: Theory and Practice.* New York: Columbia University Press.

George, Aurelia. 1992. "The Politics of Interest Representation in the Japanese Diet: The Case of Agriculture." *Pacific Affairs* 64: 506–528.

George, Stephen. 1991. *Politics and Policy in the European Community*. London: Pinter Publishers.

______. 1989. "Nationalism, Liberalism and the National Interest: Britain, France, and the European Community." *Strathclyde Papers on Government and Politics*. no. 67. Glasgow: Department of Government, University of Strathclyde.

______. 1983. "Regional Policy." In *Institutions and Policies of the European Community*, edited by J. Lodge. London: Frances Pinter.

Giavazzi, Francesco, and Micossi Pagano. June 1988. "The Advantage of Tying One's Hand: EMS Discipline and Central Bank Credibility." *European Economic Review* 32: 1055–1075.

Giavazzi, Francesco, Stefano Micossi, and Marcus Miller, eds. 1988. *The European Monetary System.* Cambridge, England: Cambridge University Press.

Gilpin, Robert. 1983. *War and Change in World Politics.* New York: Cambridge University Press.

Ginsberg, Benjamin. 1986. *The Captive Public: How Mass Opinion Promotes State Power.* New York: Basic Books.

Goldman, Marshall I. 1980. *The Enigma of Soviet Petroleum.* London: George Allen and Unwin.

______. 1975. *Detente and Dollars.* New York: Basic Books.

Goldstein, Judith. 1988. "Ideas, Institutions, and American Trade Policy." *International Organization* 42 (1): 179–217.

Goldthorpe, John H., ed. 1984. *Order and Conflict in Contemporary Capitalism.* Oxford: Clarendon Press.

Gourevitch, Peter. 1986. *Politics in Hard Times.* Ithaca, N.Y.: Cornell University Press.

______. 1978. "The Second Image Reversed: The International Sources of Domestic Politics." *International Organization* 32 (4): 881–911.

Graber, N. A. 1983. "Public Opinion and Foreign Policy: A Pragmatic View." In *Interaction: Foreign Policy and Public Policy*, edited by D. C. Piper and R. J. Terchek. Washington, D.C.: American Enterprise Institute.

Graham, Thomas. 1989. *American Public Opinion on NATO, Extended Deterrence, and the Use of Nuclear Weapons.* Cambridge, Mass.: Center for Science and International Affairs, Harvard University.

Grieco, Joseph M. 1990. *Cooperation Among Nations: Europe, America, and Non-Tariff Barriers to Trade.* Ithaca, N.Y.: Cornell University Press.

______. 1988. "Anarchy and the Limits of Cooperation: A Realist Critique of the Newest Liberal Institutionalism." *International Organization* 42: 485–507.

Griffith, William E. 1978. *The Ostpolitik of the Federal Republic of Germany.* Cambridge, Mass.: MIT Press.

Haas, Ernst B. 1990. *When Knowledge Is Power: Three Models of Change in International Organization.* Berkeley: University of California Press.

______. 1980. "Why Collaborate? Issue Linkage and International Regime." *World Politics* 1: 357–405.

______. 1976. "Turbulent Fields and the Theory of Regional Integration." *International Organization* 30 (2): 147–174.

______. 1964. *Beyond the Nation-State: Functionalism and International Organization.* Stanford, Calif.: Stanford University Press.

______. 1958. *The Uniting of Europe: Political, Economic, Social and Economic Forces, 1950–1957.* Stanford, Calif.: Stanford University Press.

Haas, Peter M. 1992. "Introduction: Epistemic Communities and International Policy Coordination." *International Organization* 46 (1): 1–35.

______. 1989. "Do Regimes Matter? Epistemic Communities and Mediterranean Pollution Control." *International Organization* 43 (3): 377–403.

Hacke, Christian. 1988. *Weltmacht Wider Willen: Die Außenpolitik der Bundesrepublik Deutschland.* Stuttgart: Ernst Klett-Cotta Verlage.

Haftendorn, Helga. 1988. "Transatlantische Dissonanzen: Der Bericht uber Selective Abschreckung und die Strategiediskussion in den USA." *Europa Archiv* 8: 213–222.

______. Sicherheit und Stabilität: Aussenbezihungen der Bundesrepublisk zwischen Ölkrise und NATO Doppelbeschluss, Deutscher Taschenbuch Verlag, München.

______. 1983. *Sicherheit und Entspannung: Zur Aussenpolitik der Bundesrepublick Deutschland, 1955–1982.* Baden-Baden: Nomos Verlaggesellschaft.

______. 1980. *Sicherheit und Stabilität: Aussenbeziehungen der Bundestrepublik zwischen Ölkrise und NATO Doppelbeschluss.* Berlin: Deutscher Tagenbuch Verlag.

______. "West Germany and the Management of Security Relations." In *The Foreign Policy of West Germany*, edited by Ekkehart Krippendorff and Volker Rittberger. Baden-Baden: Nomos Verlaggesellschaft.

______. 1974. *Abrustungs- und Entspannungspolitik zwischen Sicherheitsbefriedigung und Friedenssicherung: Zur Aussenpolitik der BRD 1955–1973.* Düsseldorf: Bertelsmann Universitätsverlag.

Haftendorn, Helga, Wolf-Dieter Karl, Joachim Krause, and Lothar Wilker, eds. 1978. *Verwaltete Aussenpolitik: Sicherheits- und entspannungspolitische Entscheidungs-prozesse in Bonn.* Cologne: Nottbeck Verlag.

Hagan, Joe D. 1993. *Political Opposition and Foreign Policy in Comparative Perspective.* Boulder, Colo.: Lynne Rienner.

______. 1989. "Linking Multiple Autonomous Actors to Foreign Policy Decision Outcomes: A Theoretical Overview." Prepared for Conference on How Decision Units Shape Foreign Policy. Jackson Hole, Wyoming.

______. 1989. "Domestic Political Regime Changes and Foreign Policy Restructuring in Western Europe: A Conceptual Framework and Initial Empirical Analysis." *Cooperation and Conflict* 24: 141–162.

______. 1987. "Regimes, Political Oppositions, and the Comparative Analysis of Foreign Policy." In *New Directions in the Study of Foreign Policy*, edited by Charles F. Hermann, Charles Kegley, and James Rosenau. Boston: Allen and Unwin.

Haggard, Stephan. 1990. *Pathways from the Periphery.* Ithaca, N.Y.: Cornell University Press.

Haggard, Stephan, and Beth Simmons. 1987. "Theories of International Regimes." *International Organization* 41 (3): 491–517.

Hall, Peter A., ed. 1989. *The Political Power of Economic Ideas: Keynesianism Across Nations.* Princeton, N.J.: Princeton University Press.

Halperin, Morton H. 1974. *Bureaucratic Politics and Foreign Policy* Washington, D.C.: The Brookings Institution.

Hanmer, Stephen. 1980. "NATO's Long-Range Theater Nuclear Forces: Modernization in Parallel with Arms Control." *NATO Review* 28: 357–374.

Hanrieder, Wolfram. 1989. *Germany, America and Europe: Forty Years of German Foreign Policy*. New Haven, Conn.: Yale University Press.

______. 1967. "Compatibility and Consensus: A Proposal for the Conceptual Linkage of External and Internal Dimensions of Foreign Policy." *American Political Science Review* 61: 971–982.

Hanrieder, Wolfram, ed. 1980. *West German Foreign Policy 1949–1979.* Boulder, Colo.: Westview Press.

Harrison, Reginald J. 1980. *Pluralism and Corporatism: The Political Evolution of Modern Democracies.* London: George Allen and Unwin.

Heinze, Rolf G. 1981. *Verbändepolitik und Neokorporatismus*. Cologne: Opladen.

Hendriks, Gisela. 1991. *Germany and European Integration: The Common Agricultural Policy—An Area of Conflict.* Dulles, Va., Berg Publishers.

______. 1987. "The Politics of Food—The Case of Germany," *Food Policy*, February, 12 (1): 35–45.

Henkin, Louis. 1968. *How Nations Behave: Law and Foreign Policy.* New York: Praeger Publishers.

Hennings, K. H. 1982. "West Germany." In *The European Economy: Growth and Crisis*, edited by A. Boltho. Oxford: Oxford University Press.

Herf, Jeffrey. 1991. *War By Other Means: Soviet Power, West German Resistance, and the Battle of the Euromissiles.* New York: Macmillan Publishers.

______. 1986. "War, Peace, and the Intellectuals: The West German Peace Movement." *International Security* 31: 172–200.

Hermann, Charles F. 1989. "Changing Course: When Governments Choose to Redirect Foreign Policy." *International Studies Quarterly* 34: 3–22.

______. 1983. "Foreign Policy." In *Encyclopedia of Policy Studies*, edited by Stuart Nagel. New York: Dekker Publishing.

______. 1969. *Crises in Foreign Policy.* Indianapolis: Bobbs-Merrill Company.

Hermann, Charles F., Charles W. Kegley Jr., and James N. Rosenau, eds. 1987. *New Directions in the Study of Foreign Policy.* Boston: Unwin Hyman.

Hermann, Charles F., Margaret G. Hermann, and Joe D. Hagan. 1987. "How Decision Units Make Foreign Policy: Development of a Model." In *New*

Directions in the Study of Foreign Policy, edited by Charles F. Hermann, Charles W. Kegley, and James N. Rosenau. Boston: Allen and Unwin.

Heumann, Hans-Dieter. February 17, 1989. Aus *Politik und Zeitgeschichte: Beilage zur Wochenzeitung Das Parlament"* Nationale Interessen und Sicherheit in Europa." Version 8/89.

Hofferbert, R. J., and H. D. Klingemann. 1983. "The Policy Impact of Party Programmes and Government Declarations in the Federal Republic of Germany." *European Journal of Political Research* 18: 277–304.

Holsti, Ole R. 1992. "Public Opinion and Foreign Policy: Challenges to the Almond-Lippmann Consensus." *International Studies Quarterly* 36: 439–466.

Holsti, Ole R., and James N. Rosenau. 1988. "The Domestic and Foreign Policy Beliefs of American Leaders." *Journal of Conflict Resolution* 32: 248–294.

Hrbek, Rudolf, and Thomas Läufer. 1986. "Die Einheitliche Europäische Akte: Das Luxemburger Reformpaket: Eine Neue Etappe Integrationsprozeß." *Europa-Archiv* 6: 173–185.

Hudson, Valerie M., and David Skidmore. eds. 1993. *The Limits of State Autonomy: Societal Groups and Foreign Policy Formulation.* Boulder, Colo.: Westview Press.

Hudson, Valerie M., and Eric Singer. 1992. *Political Psychology and Foreign Policy.* Boulder, Colo.: Westview Press.

Ikenberry, Gerald, D. Lanke, and Michael Mastanduno. 1988. "Introduction: Approaches to Explaining American Foreign Economic Policy." *International Organization* 42: 1–14.

Inbar, Efraim. 1991. *War and Peace in Israeli Politics: Labor Party Positions on National Security.* Boulder, Colo: Lynne Rienner.

Jacobson, Harold K., William M. Reisinger, and Todd Mathers. 1986. "National Entanglements in International Governmental Organizations." *American Political Science Review* 80 (1): 141–159.

Janda, Kenneth. 1980. *Political Parties.* New York: Free Press.

Jentleson, Bruce W. 1986. *Pipeline Politics: The Complex Political Economy of East–West Energy Trade.* Ithaca, N.Y.: Cornell University Press.

______. 1984. "From Consensus to Conflict: The Domestic Political Economy of East–West Energy Trade Policy." *International Organization* 38 (4): 625–660.

Jervis, Robert. 1993. "Security Regimes." In *International Regimes*, edited by Stephen Krasner. Ithaca, N.Y.: Cornell University Press.

______. 1978. "Cooperation Under the Security Dilemma." *World Politics* 30: 167–214.

______. 1976. *Perception and Misperception in International Politics.* Princeton, N.J.: Princeton University Press.

Joffe, Josef. 1987. *The Limited Partnership: Europe, the United States, and the Burdens of Alliance.* Cambridge, Mass.: Ballinger.

Johnson, Richard Tanner. 1974. *Managing the White House.* New York: Harper and Row Publishers.

Kaack, Heino and Ursula, eds. 1974. *Parteien Jahrbuch.* Cologne: Opladen Westdeutscher Verlag.

Kaiser, Karl. 1982. "Nuclear Weapons and the Preservation of Peace: A German Response." *Foreign Affairs* 60 (5): 1157–1170.

Kaiser, Karl, and Markus Kreis, eds. 1977. *Sicherheitspolitik or neuen Aufgaben.* Frankfurt: Metzner Publishers.

Karl, Wolf-Dieter, Joachim Krause, and Lother Wilker, eds. 1980. *Verwaltete Außenpolitik: Sicherheits- und Entspannungspolitische Entscheidungsprozesse in Bonn.* Bonn: Nomos Verlagsgesellschaft.

Karns, Margaret P., and Karen Mingst. 1991. "Domestic Sources of International Cooperation: A Conceptual Framework." Paper presented at the annual meeting of the International Studies Association, Vancouver, B.C.

______. 1990. *The United States and Multilateral Institutions.* Boston: Unwin Hyman.

Katzenstein, Peter J. 1988. "The Third West German Republic: Continuity in Change." *Journal of International Affairs* 41 (2): 325–344.

______. 1980. "Problem of Model? West Germany in the 1980s." *World Politics,* July 32 (4).

______. 1976. "International Relations and Domestic Structures: Foreign Economic Policies of Advanced Industrial States." *International Organization* 30 (1): 1–45.

Katzenstein, Peter J., ed. 1989. *Industry and Politics in West Germany.* Ithaca, N.Y.: Cornell University Press.

______. 1978. *Between Power and Plenty: Foreign Economic Policies of Advanced Industrial States.* Madison: University of Wisconsin Press.

Keeble, David, P. Owens, and C. Thomson. 1982. *Centrality, Peripherality, and EEC Regional Development: The Influence of Peripheral and Cantral Locations on the Relative Development of Regions.* Cambridge, England: Cambridge University Press.

Kehr, Eckart. 1965. *Der Primat der Innenpolitik.* Veroffentlichungen der Historischen Kommission. Berlin: Walter de Gruyter Verlag.

Kelleher, Catherine McArdle. 1975. *Germany and the Politics of Nuclear Weapons.* New York: Columbia University Press.

Keohane, Robert O. 1989. "Reciprocity in International Relations." In *International Institutions and State Power*, edited by Robert O. Keohane. Boulder, Colo.: Westview Press.

______. 1988. "International Institutions: Two Approaches." *International Studies Quarterly* 32 (4): 379–396.

______. 1984. *After Hegemony: Cooperation and Discord in the World Political Economy.* Princeton, N.J.: Princeton University Press.

Keohane, Robert O., ed. 1986. *NeoRealism and Its Critics.* New York: Columbia University Press.

Keohane, Robert O., and Stanley Hoffman, eds. 1991. *The New European Community: Decision-Making and Institutional Change.* Boulder, Colo.: Westview Press.

Keohane, Robert O., and Joseph Nye. 1977. *Power and Interdependence.* Boston: Little, Brown.

Kiechle, Ignaz. 1985. *Und Grün Bleibt Unsere Zukunft.* Stuttgart: Stuttgart-Seewald Verlag.

Kingdon, John W. 1981. *Congressmen's Voting Decisions.* New York: Harper and Row.

Kirchner, Emil J. 1990. "Genscher and What Lies Behind Genscherism." *West European Politics* 13: 139–159.

Kirchner, Emil, and K. Schwaiger. 1981. *The Role of Interest Groups in the European Community.* Aldershot Hampshire: Gower Press.

Kitschelt, Herbert P. 1988. "Organization and Strategy of Belgian and West German Ecology Parties: A New Dynamic of Party Politics in Western Europe?" *Comparative Politics* 20: 127–154.

Knopf, Jeffrey W. 1993. "Beyond Two-Level Games: Domestic-International Interaction in the Intermediate Range Nuclear Forces Negotiations." *International Organization,* 47 (4): 599–628. Autumn.

Knorr, Klauss and Frank N. Trager, eds. 1977 *Economic Issues and National Security.* Manhattan, KS: Kansas State University Press.

Kohl, Helmut. 1973. *Zwischen Ideologie und Pragmatismus.* Bonn: Bonn Aktuell.

Krasner, Stephen D. 1978. *Defending the National Interest: Raw Materials Investments and U.S. Foreign Policy.* Princeton, N.J.: Princeton University Press.

______. 1977. "Domestic Constraints on International Economic Leverage." In *Economic Issues and National Security*, eds. Klaus Knorr and Frank Trager. Lawrence: University of Kansas Press.

Krasner, Stephen D., ed. 1982. *International Regimes.* Ithaca, N.Y.: Cornell University Press.

Kratochwil, Friedrich, and John Gerard Ruggie. 1986. "International Organization: A State of the Art on an Art of the State." *International Organization* 40 (2): 753–775.

Krell, Gert. 1976. *Rüstungsdynamik und Rüstungskontrolle: Die gesellschaftlichen Auseinandersetzungen um SALT in den USA 1969–1975.* Frankfurt am Main: Haag und Herchen.

Kruse, D. C. 1980. *Monetary Integration in Western Europe: EMU, EMS and Beyond.* London: Butterworth.

Lakatos, Imre, and Allen Musgrave, eds. 1965. *Criticism and the Growth of Knowledge.* London: Cambridge University Press.

Lantis, Jeffrey S. 1992. "A United Germany in the United Nations: Promise for the Future?" *German Politics and Society* 26: 75–89.

Laver, Michael, and Kenneth A. Shepsle. "Government Coalitions and Intraparty Politics." *British Journal of Political Science* 20: 489–507.

Layne, Christopher. 1994. "Kant or Cant: The Myth of Democratic Peace." *International Security* 19 (2): 5–49.

Leaman, Jeremy. 1988. *Political Economy of West Germany, 1945–1985.* New York: St. Martin's Press.

Lehmbruch, Gerhard, and Phillipe C. Schmitter, eds. 1979. *Patterns of Corporatist Policy Making.* London: Sage Publishers.

______. 1982. *Trends Toward Corporatist Intermediation.* London: Sage Publishers.

Lellouche, Pierre. 1984. "France and the Euromissiles." *Foreign Affairs* 62 (2): 318–334.

Levy, Jack S. 1988. "Domestic Politics and War." *Journal of Interdisciplinary History* 18: 653–673.

Lijphart, Arend. 1975. "The Comparable Cases Strategy in Comparative Research." *Comparative Political Studies* 8 (2): 159–177.

______. 1971. "Comparative Politics and the Comparative Method." *American Political Science Review* 65 (1): 682–694.

Lijphart, Arend, ed. 1992. *Parliamentary Versus Presidential Government.* Columbus: Ohio University Press.

Lodge, J. 1974. "The Role of E.E.C. Summit Conferences." *Journal of Common Market Studies* 12: 337–345.

Loewenberg, Gerhard, and Samuel Patterson. 1988. *Comparing Legislatures.* Washington, D.C.: American University Press.

Lorwin, Val. 1971. "Segmented Pluralism: Ideological Cleavages and Political Cohesion in Smaller European Democracies," *Comparative Politics* 3 (2): 141–177.

Lowi, Theodore J. 1967. "Making Democracy Safe for the World." In *Domestic Sources of Policy*, edited by James N. Rosenau. New York: Free Press.

———. 1964. "American Business, Public Policy, Case Studies, and Political Theory." *World Politics* 16: 677–715.

Ludlow, Peter. 1991. "The European Commission." In *The New European Community: Decision-Making and Institutional Change*, edited by Robert O. Keohane, and Stanley Hoffman. Boulder, Colo.: Westview Press.

———. 1989. *Beyond 1992, Europe and Its Western Partners.* Brussels: Brussels Center for European Policy Studies.

———. 1982. *The Making of the European Monetary System.* London: Butterworth.

Lutz, Dieter S. 1981. *Weltkrieg wider Willen?* Hamburg: Rowohlt Verlag.

Lützeler, Paul Michael. 1986. *Western Europe in Transition: West Germany's Role in the European Community.* Baden-Baden: Nomos Verlaggesellschaft.

Mahncke, Dieter. 1991. *Amerikaner in Deutschland: Grundlagen und Bedingungen der transatlantischen Sicherheit.* Bonn: Bouvier Verlag.

Mahnke, Hans-Juurgen. 1985. *Gefragt: Ignaz Kiechle.* Bonn: Dagmar Zirnibl-Verlag.

Manigart, Philippe, and Eric Marlier. 1993. "European Public Opinion on the Future of Its Security." *Armed Forces and Society* 19 (3): 335–352.

Maoz, Zeev, and Nasrin Abdolali. 1989. "Regime Types and International Conflict." *Journal of Conflict Resolution* 33: 3–35.

Markovits, Andrei S., ed. 1982. *The Political Economy of West Germany.* New York: Praeger Publishers.

Marsh, Ian. 1990. "Liberal Priorities, the Liberal-Labor Pact and the Requirements for Policy Influence." *Parliamentary Affairist* 43: 503–531.

Martin, J. J. 1979. "Nuclear Weapons in NATO's Deterrent Strategy." *Orbis* 22: 876.

Mastanduno, Michael. 1990. "CoCom and American Export Control Policy: The Experience of the Reagain Administration." In *East–West Trade Policy and the Atlantic Alliance*, edited by David A. Baldwin and Helen V. Milner. New York: St. Martin's Press.

———. 1985. "Strategies of Economic Containment: U.S. Trade Relations with the Soviet Union." *World Politics* 37 (4): 503–531.

Mastanduno, Michael, John Ikenberry, and David Lake. 1989. "Toward a Realist Theory of State Action." *International Studies Quarterly* 33 (4): 457–474.

McCormik, James M. 1980. "Intergovernmental Organizations and Cooperation Among Nations." *International Studies Quarterly* 24 (1): 75–98.

McFarland, Andrew S. 1991. "Interest Groups and Political Time: Cycles in America," *British Journal of Political Science.* 21: 257–284.

McGowan, Patrick J., and Howard Shapiro. 1973. *The Comparative Study of Foreign Policy.* Beverly Hills, Calif.: Sage Publishers.

McKee, Vincent. 1982. "Factionalism in the Social Democratic Party, 1981–1987." *Parliamentary Affairs* 42: 165–179.

Mearsheimer, John. 1982. "Maneuver, Mobile Defense, and the NATO Central Front." *International Security* 6 (3): 104–122.

Mechtersheimer, Alfred, ed. 1981. *Nachrüsten? Dokumente und Positionen zum Nato-Doppelbeschluß.* Reinbek bei Hamburg: Rowohlt Verlag.

Miller, Warren E., and Donald E. Stokes. 1963. "Constituency Influence in Congress." *American Political Science Review* 57 (1): 45–56.

Milner, Helen V. 1993. "Maintaining International Commitments in Trade Policy." In *Do Institutions Matter? Government Capabilities in the United States and Abroad*, edited by R. Kent Weaver and Bert A. Rockman. Washington, D.C.: Brookings.

______. 1992. "International Theories of Cooperation Among Nations: Strengths and Weaknesses." *World Politics* 44: 466–496.

______. 1988. *Resisting Protectionism: Global Industries and the Politics of International Trade.* Princeton, N.J.: Princeton University Press.

Mingst, Karen A. 1992. "Domestic Determinants of Franc Zone Cooperation." Presented at the Annual Meeting of the International Studies Association, Atlanta.

Mitrany, David. 1943. *A Working Peace System.* London: The Royal Institute of International Affairs.

Moore, Barrington Jr. 1966. *Social Origins of Dictatorship and Democracy.* Boston: Little, Brown.

Moravcsik, Andrew. 1991. "Negotiating the Single European Act." In *The New European Community: Decision-Making and Institutional Change*, edited by Robert O. Keohane and Stanley Hoffman. Boulder, Colo.: Westview Press.

Morgenthau, Hans J. 1978. *Politics Among Nations.* New York: Knopf.

Moyer, Homer E., and Linda A. Mabry. 1983. "Export Controls as Instruments of Foreign Policy: The History, Legal Issues and Policy Lessons of Three Recent Cases." *Law and Policy in International Business* 15 (1).

Mueller, Harald, and Thomas Risse-Kappen. 1987. "Origins of Estrangement: The Peace Movement and the Changed Image of America in West Germany." *International Security* 12: 52–88.

Mueller, John. 1973. *War, Presidents and Public Opinion.* New York: Wiley Books.

Neville, Rolfe. 1984. *The Politics of Agriculture in the European Community.* London: Oxford University Press.

Noelle-Neumann, Elisabeth, ed. 1981. *The Germans: Public Opinion Polls, 1967–1980.* Westport, Conn., Greenwood Press.

North, Douglas C. 1984. "Government and the Cost of Exchange in History." *The Journal of Economic History* 44 (2): 255–265.

Nugent, Neil. 1991. *The Government and Politics of the European Community.* London: Macmillan.

Nye, Joseph, and Robert Keohane. 1971. *Transnational Relations and World Politics.* Cambridge, Mass.: Harvard University Press.

Olson, Mancur, Jr., and Richard Zeckhauser. 1968. "An Economic Theory of Alliances." In *Economic Theories of International Politics*, edited by Bruce M. Russett. Chicago: Markham Publishers.

Olson, Mancur, Jr. 1965. *The Logic of Collective Action.* Cambridge, Mass.: Harvard University Press.

Ornstein, Norman J., and Shirley Elder. 1978. *Interest Groups, Lobbying, and Policymaking.* Washington, D.C.: Congressional Quarterly Press.

Oye, Kenneth A., ed. 1986. *Cooperation Under Anarchy.* Princeton, N.J.: Princeton University Press.

Padgett, Stephen, and Tony Burkett. 1986. *Political Parties and Elections in West Germany: The Search for a New Stability.* New York: St. Martin's Press.

Padoa-Schioppa, Tommaso. 1985. "Policy Coordination and the EMS Experience." In *International Policy Coordination*, edited by W. Butler and R. Marston. Cambridge, England: Cambridge University Press.

Page, Benjamin, and Robert Shapiro. 1983. "Effects of Public Opinion on Policy." *American Political Science Review* 77 (1): 175–190.

Parsons, D. W. 1977. "Notes on the Regional Development Fund," *The Political Quarterly* 48 (2): 163–181.

Pond, Elizabeth. 1992. "Germany in the New Europe." *Foreign Affairs* 71 (2): 127

Poquntke, Thomas. 1992. "Unconventional Participation in Party Politics: The Experience of the German Greens." *Political Studies* 40: 310–321.

Potter, William C. 1980. "Issue Area and Foreign Policy Analysis." *International Organization* 34: 411–421.

Pridham, Geoffrey. 1987. "Coalition Behavior and Party Systems in Western Europe: A Comparative Approach." *Parliamentary Affairs* 40(3): 374–388.

_______. 1977. *Christian Democracy in Western Germany.* London: Croom Helm Ltd.

Priebe, Harold. 1980. "GermanAgricultural Policy and the European Community." In Basevi, Giorgio, ed. *West Germany a European Global Power.* Lexington, Mass.: Lexington Books.

Pryce, Roy. 1973. *The Politics of the European Community.* Totowa: Rowman and Littlefield.

Puchala, Donald J. 1975. "Domestic Politics and Regional Harmonization in the European Communities." *World Politics* 27 (4): 496–520.

Putnam, Robert D. 1988. "Diplomacy and Domestic Politics: The Logic of Two-Level Games." *International Organization* 42 (3): 427–460.

Putnam, Robert D., and Nicholas Bayne. 1987. *Hanging Together: The Seven-Power Summits.* London: Sage.

Putnam, Robert D., and C. Randall Henning. 1986. "The Bonn Summit of 1978: A Case Study in Coordination." In *Can Nations Agree? Issues in International Economic Cooperation*, edited by Richard C. Cooper. Washington, D.C.: The Brookings Institution.

Quandt, William. 1986. "The Electoral Cycle and the Conduct of Foreign Policy," *Political Science Quarterly* 101 (5): 829.

Quirk, Paul J. 1989. "The Cooperative Resolution of Policy Conflict." *American Political Science Review* 83 (3): 905–921.

Rattinger, Hans. 1989. *Public Opinion and National Security in Western Europe: Consensus Lost?* London: Pinter Publishers.

______. 1987. "Change Versus Continuity in West German Public Attitudes on National Security and Nuclear Weapons in the Early 1980s." *Public Opinion Quarterly* 51 (4): 495–521.

Rattinger, Hans, and Gregory Flynn, eds. 1984. *The Public and Atlantic Defense.* Totowa, N.J.: Rowman and Allenheld.

Richardson, James L. 1966. *Germany and the Atlantic Alliance: The Interaction of Strategy and Politics.* Cambridge, Mass.: Harvard University Press.

Risse-Kappen, Thomas. 1994. "Masses and Leaders: Public Opinion, Domestic Structures, and Foreign Policy." In *The New Politics of American Foreign Policy*, edited by David A. Deese. New York: St. Martin's Press.

______. 1991. "Public Opinion, Domestic Structure, and Foreign Policy in Liberal Democracies." *World Politics* 43 (4): 479–512.

______. 1988. *Die Krise der Sicherheitspolitik: Neuorientierungen und Entscheidungsprozesse im politischen System der Bundesrepublik Deutschland, 1977–1984.* Mainz-Munich: Grünewald-Kaiser.

Ritter, Gerhard A., and Merith Niehuss. 1991. *Wahlen in Deutschland: 1946–1991.* Munich: C.H. Beck Publishers.

Root, William A. 1984. "Trade Controls That Work." *Foreign Policy* 56 (3): 61–80.

Rosenau, James N. 1990. *Turbulence in World Politics: A Theory of Continuity and Change.* Princeton, N.J.: Princeton University Press.

______. 1966. "Pre-Theories and Theories of Foreign Policy." In *Approaches to Comparative and International Politics*, edited by R. Barry Farrell. Evanston, Ill.: Northwestern University Press.

______. 1961. *Public Opinion and Foreign Policy.* New York: Random House.

Rosenau, James N., ed. 1969. *Linkage Politics: Essays on the Convergence of National and International Systems.* New York: Free Press.

Rotfeld, Adam Daniel, and Walther Stützle, eds. 1991. *Germany and Europe in Transition*. Oxford: Oxford University Press.

Russett, Bruce. 1993. *Grasping the Democratic Peace: Principles for a Post-Cold War World.* Princeton, N.J.: Princeton University Press.

______. 1990. *Controlling the Sword: The Democratic Governance of National Security*. Cambridge, Mass.: Harvard University Press.

Russett, Bruce, and Thomas W. Graham. 1989. "Public Opinion and National Security Policy: Relationships and Impacts." In *Handbook of War Studies*, edited by Manus I. Midlarshky. New York: Macmillan.

Sandholtz, Wayne, and John Zysman. 1989. "1992: Recasting the European Bargain." *World Politics* 42: 95–128.

Schelling, Thomas C. 1960. *The Strategy of Conflict.* Cambridge, Mass.: Harvard University Press.

Schmidt, Helmut. 1987. *Menschen und Mächte*. Berlin: Goldmann Verlag.

______. 1977. "The North Atlantic Summit Meeting, Remarks from Speech May 10, 1977." *Survival.* 19 (3): 177–179.

______. 1971. *The Balance of Power: Germany's Peace Policy and the Powers.* London: Kimber.

______. 1962. *Defense or Retaliation: A German View.* New York: Praeger Publishers.

Schmitter, Phillipe C. 1975. *Corporatism and Public Policy in Authoritarian Portugal.* London: Sage.

Schoppa, Leonard J. 1993. "Two-Level Games and Bargaining Outcomes: Why *Gaiatsu* Succeeds in Japan in Some Cases But Not Others." *International Organization* 47 (3): 353–386.

Schultze, Rainier-Olaf. 1990. "Föderalismus als Alternative? Überlegungen zur territorialen reorganization von Herrschaft." *Zeitschrift für Parlamentsfragen* 3.

Schüttmeyer, Suzanne. October 1990. "Die Ergebnisse der Landtagswahlen 1946–1990," *Zeitschrift für Parlamentsfragen* 21 (3): 464–472.

Schwartz, David. 1983. *NATO's Nuclear Dilemmas.* Washington, D.C.: The Brookings Institution.

Schweigler, Gerhard. 1985. *Grundlagen der Außenpolitischen Orientierung der Bundesrepublik Deutschland.* New York: Praeger Publishers.

______. 1984. *West German Foreign Policy, The Domestic Setting.* New York: Praeger Publishers.

Seers, David, and C. Vaitsos, eds. 1980. *Integration and Unequal Development: The Experience of the EEC.* London: Macmillan.

Shonfield, Andrew. 1976. *International Economic Relations of the Western World, 1959–1971.* New York: St. Martin's.

Small, Melvin, and J. David Singer. 1976. "The War-Proneness of Democratic Regimes, 1916–1965." *Jerusalem Journal of International Relations* 1: 50–69.

Smith, Roger K. 1987. "Explaining the Non-Proliferation Regime: Anomalies for Contemporary International Relations Theory." *International Organization* 41 (2): 253–271.

Snidal, Duncan. 1985. "The Game Theory of International Politics." *World Politics* 38: 25–57.

Snyder, Glenn H., and Paul Diesing. 1977. *Conflict Among Nations: Bargaining, Decisionmaking, and System Structure in International Crises.* Princeton, N.J.: Princeton University Press.

Snyder, Jack. 1991. *Myths of Empire: Domestic Politics and International Ambition.* Ithaca, N.Y.: Cornell University Press.

______. 1989. "International Leverage on Soviet Domestic Change." *World Politics* 42 (1): 1–30.

Snyder, Richard, H. W. Bruck, and Burton Sapin. 1954. "Decision-Making as an Approach to the Study of International Politics." *Foreign Policy Analysis Project Series,* no 3.

Statler, Jocelyn. 1979. "The European Monetary System: From Conception to Birth." *International Affairs* 55 (2): 206–225.

Stent, Angela. 1981. *From Embargo to Ostpolitik: The Political Economy of West German-Soviet Relations, 1955–1980.* Cambridge, England: Cambridge University Press.

Stern, Jonathan P. 1990. *Soviet Natural Gas Development to 1990: Implications for the CMEA and the West.* London: Heinemann.

______. 1984. *International Gas Trade in Europe: The Policies of Exporting and Importing Countries.* London: Heinemann.

______. 1982. "Specters and Pipe Dreams." *Foreign Policy* 48: 21–39.

Szabo, Stephen F. 1990. *The Changing Politics of German Security.* London: Pinter Publishers.

Talbot, Ronald B. 1977. *The European Community's Regional Fund.* Oxford: Pergamon Press.

Tanaka, Toyozo. 1987. "Breakup of the Tanaka Faction: End of an Era." *Japan Quarterly* 7: 114–129.

Thaysen, Uwe, Roger Davidson, and Robert Gerald Livingston. 1990. *The U.S. Congress and the German Bundestag: Comparisons of Democratic Processes*. Boulder, Colo.: Westview Press.

Thies, Jochen, and Wolfgang Wagner, eds. 1989. *Auf dem Wege zum Binnenmarkt: Eurpaische Integration und deutscher Föderalismus.* Bonn: Verlag für Internationale Politik.

Thomson, James A. 1984. "The LRTNF Decision: Evolution of US Theater Nuclear Policy, 1975–1979." *International Affairs* 60 (4): 601–615.

Tracy, Michael. 1982. *Agriculture in Western Europe.* New York: Praeger Publishers.

Treverton, Gregory F. 1979. "Nuclear Weapons and the 'Gray Area.'" *Foreign Affairs* 57: 995–1014.

Tsebelis, George. 1990. *Nested Games: Rational Choice in Comparative Politics.* Berkeley, CA: University of California Press.

Tsoukalis, Loukas. 1991. *The New European Economy: The Politics and Economics of Integration*. Oxford: Oxford University Press.

______. 1977. *The Politics and Economics of European Monetary Integration*. London: Allen and Unwin.

Van Ypersele, Jacques, and Jean-Claude Koeune. 1984. *The European Monetary System*. Brussels: Commission of the EC, European Perspectives Series.

Vogel, Bernhard, Dieter Nohlen, and Rainer Olaf-Schultze. 1971. *Wahlen in Deutschland: Theorie-Geschichte-Dokumente.* Berlin: Walter DeGruyter.

Voigt, Karsten. 1982. *Wege zur Abrüstung.* Frankfurt/Main: Eichborn.

Wallace, Helen. 1985. "Negotiations and Coalition Formation in the European Community." *Government and Opposition* 20 (4): 452–472.

______. 1973. *National Governments and the European Communities*. London: Chatham House.

Wallace, William, ed. 1991. *The Dynamics of European Integration*. London: Pinter, for the Royal Institute of International Affairs.

Walt, Stephen. 1987. *The Origins of Alliances.* Ithaca, N.Y.: Cornell University Press.

Waltz, Kenneth. 1979. *The Theory of International Politics.* Reading, Mass.: Addison-Wesley.

Wasserman, Sherri L. 1983. *The Neutron Bomb Controversy*. New York: Praeger Publishers.

Weaver, R. Kent, and Bert A. Rockman, eds. 1993. *Do Institutions Matter? Government Capabilities in the United States and Abroad.* Washington, D.C.: Brookings Institute.

Weede, Erich. 1984. "Democracy and War Involvement." *Journal of Conflict Resolution* 28: 649–664.

Weidenfeld, Werner. 1986. "Basic Questions of European Integration Seen From a German Point of View." In *Western Europe in Transition: West Germany's Role in the European Community*, edited by Paul Michael Lützeler. Baden-Baden: Nomos Verlaggesellschaft.

Wessels, Wolfgang. 1991. "The EC Council: The Community's Decision-Making Center." In *The New European Community: Decision-Making and Institutional Change*, edited by Robert O. Keohane, and Stanley Hoffman. Boulder, Colo.: Westview Press.

______. 1986. "Die Einheitliche Eurpäische Akte-Zementierung des Status Quo oder Einstieg in die Europäische Union?" *Integration* 2: 65–79.

Wettig, Gerhard. 1989. *High Road, Low Road: Diplomacy and Public Action in Soviet Foreign Policy.* Washington, D.C.: Pergamon-Brassey's.

Wilensky, Harold L. 1976. *The New Corporatism, Centralization, and the Welfare State.* London: Sage.

Wilker, Lothar. 1990. "Foreign Policy in the *Bundestag.*" In *The U.S. Congress and the German* Bundestag, edited by Uwe Thaysen, Roger Davidson, and Robert Gerald Livingston. Boulder, Colo.: Westview Press.

Wilson, Frank Lee. 1983. "French Interest Group Politics: Pluralist or Neo-Corporatist?" *The American Political Science Review* 77 (4): 895–910.

Wittkopf, Eugene. 1990. *Faces of Internationalism: Public Opinion and American Foreign Policy*. Durham, N.C.: Duke University Press.

Wogau, Karl von. 1989. *Binnenmarkt 1992—die Idealle Vision.* Bonn: Europa Union.

Wörner, Manfred. Fall 1977. "NATO Defense and Tactical Nuclear Weapons." *Strategic Review* 21: 11–18.

Yishai, Yael. 1992. "Three Faces of Associational Politics: Interest Groups in Israel." *Political Studies* 40 (3): 124–136.

Young, Oran R. 1991. "Political Leadership and Regime Formation: On the Development of Institutions in International Society." *International Organization* 45 (3): 281–308.

______. 1980. "International Regimes: Problems of Concept Formation." *World Politics* 32: 331–356.

______. 1979. *Compliance and Public Authority.* Baltimore: Johns Hopkins University Press.

Zimmerman, William. 1973. "Issue Area and Foreign Policy Process." *American Political Science Review* 67: 1204–1212.

INDEX

About the Author

JEFFREY S. LANTIS is Chair of the International Relations Program and Assistant Professor of Political Science at The College of Wooster. He was Associate Editor for *The Brassey's Mershon American Defense Annual, 1995–1996,* and he has written extensively on German and American foreign policy and the use of simulations in the international relations classroom.

www.ingramcontent.com/pod-product-compliance
Lightning Source LLC
LaVergne TN
LVHW102008210926
848483LV00010B/184
* 9 7 8 0 2 7 5 9 5 9 4 8 7 *